Data Analytics
for Internal Auditors

Internal Audit and IT Audit

Series Editor: Dan Swanson

Data Analytics for Internal Auditors

Richard E. Cascarino

CRC Press
Taylor & Francis Group
Boca Raton London New York

CRC Press is an imprint of the
Taylor & Francis Group, an **informa** business

AN AUERBACH BOOK

CRC Press
Taylor & Francis Group
6000 Broken Sound Parkway NW, Suite 300
Boca Raton, FL 33487-2742

Printed on acid-free paper
Version Date: 20161122

International Standard Book Number-13: 978-1-4987-3714-2 (Hardback)

Visit the Taylor & Francis Web site at
http://www.taylorandfrancis.com

and the CRC Press Web site at
http://www.crcpress.com

Contents

About the Author

Richard E. Cascarino, MBA, CIA, CISM, CFE, CRMA, well known in international auditing, is a principal of Richard Cascarino & Associates based in Colorado with more than 33 years of experience in audit training and consultancy.

He is a regular speaker at national and international conferences and has presented courses throughout Africa, Europe, the Middle East, and the United States.

Richard is a past president of the Institute of Internal Auditors in South Africa, was the founding regional director of the Southern African Region of the IIA-Inc, and is a member of ISACA and the Association of Certified Fraud Examiners, where he served as member of the Board of Regents for Higher Education.

Richard was chairman of the Audit Committee of Gauteng cluster 2 (Premier's office, Shared Services and Health) in Johannesburg and is currently the Chairman of the Audit and Risk Committee of the Department of Public Enterprises in South Africa.

He is also a visiting lecturer at the University of the Witwatersrand and author of the book *Internal Auditing—An Integrated Approach*, published by Juta Publishing and now in its third edition. This book is extensively used as a university textbook worldwide. In addition, he is the author of the *Auditor's Guide to IT*

Auditing published by Wiley Publishing, now in its second edition, and the book *Corporate Fraud and Internal Control: A Framework for Prevention*, also with Wiley Publishing. He is also a contributor to all four editions of QFINANCE, the UItimate Resource, published by Bloomsbury.

Introduction

Data Analytics for Internal Auditors

A Practitioner's Handbook

Including access to download the demo version of IDEA data analysis software.

The book is intended as a reference guide for IT and internal auditors as well as fraud examiners and students in all three disciplines.

Although there are many webinars and training courses on data analytics for internal auditors, there is no concise handbook written from the practitioner's viewpoint covering not only the need and the theory, but a practical hands-on approach to conducting data analytics. This has become a necessity since the spread of IT systems has made it a prerequisite that auditors as well as management have the ability to examine high volumes of data and transactions in order to determine patterns and trends. In addition, the increasing need to continuously monitor and audit IT systems has created an imperative for the effective use of appropriate data mining tools.

Although a variety of powerful tools are readily available today, the skills required to utilize such tools are not. Not only must the correct testing techniques be selected, but the effective interpretation of outcomes presented by the software is essential in the drawing of appropriate conclusions based on the data analysis.

This means that the users of such tools must gain skills not only in the technical implementation of the software, but also in the understanding of structures and meanings of corporate data, including the ability to determine the information requirements for the effective management of business.

Book Contents

Chapter 1: Introduction to Data Analysis

This chapter introduces the reader to the principles of information flow within organizations as well as data analytic methodologies and terminology.

The focus is on developing an understanding of where critical data exists for analysis, the obtaining of access, and the selection of the appropriate analytical techniques.

Chapter 2: Understanding Sampling

This chapter covers the fundamental assumptions underlying the use of sampling techniques, the nature of populations, and the use of variables. Distribution frequencies and central tendency measurement are covered as well as the impact on analysis of distribution characteristics.

Chapter 3: Judgmental versus Statistical Sampling

This chapter covers the differences between judgmental and statistical sampling, the applicability of both in audit practice, and the dangers inherent in confusing the two. The differences in selection methods are covered as well as their impact on the analysis and interpretation possible within the sampling methods.

Chapter 4: Probability Theory in Data Analysis

This chapter examines the fundamental principles of Bayesian probability theory. In general, this is a methodology used to try to clarify the relationship between theory and evidence. It attempts to demonstrate how the probability that the theory is true is affected by a new piece of evidence. This can be critical to auditors in drawing conclusions about large populations based upon small samples drawn.

Chapter 5: Types of Evidence

This chapter examines the various types of evidence available to the auditor in order to evaluate both the adequacy and effectiveness of the system of internal controls. This includes the identification of population types and the division into subpopulations for analytic purposes. Differing collection types and evidence sources are also identified.

Chapter 6: Population Analysis

This chapter examines the differences between a given set of data in the standard benchmark in terms of central tendency, variation, and shape of the curve.

Chapter 7: Correlations, Regressions, and Other Analyses

This chapter examines the differences between correlations and regressions as well as the auditor's usage of both. It focuses on determination of the type of situation in which correlations and linear regressions may be deemed appropriate.

Chapter 8: Conducting the Audit

This chapter examines how audit objectives are determined and how data analytics are selected in order to achieve those objectives. This includes the use of the appropriate risk analysis techniques in order to identify potential internal control failures. It also covers the definition of "exception" conditions.

Chapter 9: Obtaining Information from IT Systems for Analysis

This chapter covers the assessment of IT systems in order to determine the sources of evidentiary data appropriate for analysis as well as the techniques the auditor may use in order to obtain, extract, and, if necessary, transform such data to facilitate analysis.

Chapter 10: Use of Computer-Assisted Audit Techniques

This chapter examines typical CAATs in common use and the selection of the appropriate technique based upon the type of evidence and the audit objective. Included are the dangers to the auditor inherent in the prejudgment of expected results and the subsequent distortion of the analysis based upon these preconceptions.

Chapter 11: Analysis of Big Data

This chapter examines the audit advantages and methodologies for the analysis of Big Data. Big Data is a term given to large data sets containing a variety of data types. Big Data analysis allows the auditor to seek hidden patterns and identify concealed correlations, market trends, and other data interrelationships that can indicate areas for improved operational efficiencies within business processes.

Chapter 12: Results Analysis and Validation

This chapter examines how auditors may confirm the results of the analysis with business owners and, when necessary, revise the audit approach and re-perform selected analyses as appropriate.

Chapter 13: Fraud Detection Using Data Analysis

This chapter examines the techniques available to the auditor in order to identify the red flags and indicators that fraud may be occurring or may have occurred in the past as well as the obtaining of forensically acceptable data analytical evidence.

Chapter 14: Root Cause Analysis

This chapter examines the techniques available to the auditor in order to identify root causes of identified exceptions. This includes the selection of appropriate research techniques in order to identify known causes of common exception types.

Chapter 15: Data Analysis and Continuous Monitoring

This chapter examines the methods and processes facilitated by continuous monitoring to ensure that crucial policies, processes, and internal controls are both adequate and operating effectively. Although this is primarily a management role, the auditor may be required to express an opinion on the appropriateness and effectiveness of the continuous monitoring processes implemented by management. This can also provide the auditor with an assurance of the reliability of management's oversight of all internal controls and risks.

Chapter 16: Continuous Auditing

This chapter explores the difference between continuous monitoring and continuous auditing, which is a methodology resulting in audit results simultaneously with, or a short period of time after, the occurrence of relevant events. This facilitates continuous control assessment as well as continuous risk assessment based upon the ongoing examination of consistency of processes, thus providing support for individual audits as well as allowing the development of enterprise audit plans.

Chapter 17: Financial Analysis

This chapter examines the process of reviewing and analyzing an organization's financial information in order to evaluate risk, performance, and the overall financial health of the organization. Such analyses could include DuPont analysis and the use of ratios with horizontal and vertical analyses and facilitates the auditor in expressing an opinion on profitability, liquidity, stability, and solvency.

Chapter 18: Excel and Data Analysis

This chapter examines the use of Excel as a powerful data analysis tool. Properly used, data may be sorted, filtered, extracted to pivot tables, or utilized in what-if analysis in order to determine the probable effectiveness of the implementation of auditor recommendations. This may be coupled with financial, statistical, and engineering data analysis facilitating analysis using advanced techniques, such as analysis of variances (ANOVA), exponential smoothing, correlation, and regression analyses.

Chapter 19: ACL and Data Analysis

This chapter examines the use of ACL, which is one of the most commonly used generalized audit software applications presently in use. It is a powerful tool for a nontechnical auditor to examine data in detail from a variety of sources with a variety of standard audit tests and present the results in a range of high-impact presentation formats.

Chapter 20: IDEA and Data Analysis

This chapter examines the use of IDEA, which is the second most commonly used generalized audit software in use. Like ACL, it is a powerful tool for a nontechnical auditor to examine data in detail from a variety of sources with a variety of standard audit tests and present the results in a range of high-impact presentation formats. This chapter aligns with the downloadable software and covers practical uses to which this software can be put.

Chapter 21: SAS and Data Analysis

This chapter examines the use of SAS, which is perhaps one of the most commonly used large scale statistical analysis systems in use. SAS consists of a suite of software programs developed by SAS Software to provide the ability to access, analyze, and report on high volumes of data across a variety of business applications. Dating back to the 1970s, its primary use is for decision-making and business intelligence support. SAS is designed to access databases as well as flat, unformatted files.

Chapter 22: Analysis Reporting

This chapter examines the types of reports an auditor may produce depending on the nature of the findings as well as the audience for such reports. At the macro-analytic level, this could include business impact across the organization, and at the control and transaction levels, the report would be aimed at operational management in order to ensure the implementation of appropriate internal control structures.

Chapter 23: Data Visualization and Presentation

This chapter examines ways in which the results of data analysis are presented to management in a comprehensive manner. In many cases of audit data analysis, the analysis may be excellent, but the communication to the decision makers is frequently lacking. Data visualization and presentation tools and techniques allow the extraction of data from various formats and turning it into charts, tables, and pivot tables allowing audit presentations to have considerably higher impacts on decision makers.

Appendix 1: ACL Usage

This appendix is intended to cover all aspects of the use of ACL Version 9 in a hands-on environment. It is aimed primarily at auditors, both internal and external, who already have a working knowledge of generalized audit software and particularly in the use of ACL. It assumes that readers have access to the ACL software.

Appendix 2: IDEA Usage

This appendix is intended to cover all aspects of the use of IDEA Version 10 in a hands-on environment. It is aimed primarily at auditors, both internal and external, who already have a working knowledge of generalized audit software and particularly the use of IDEA. It assumes that readers have downloaded the software and data files of the demo version at http://ideasupport.caseware.com/public/downloadidea/.

Appendix 3: Risk Assessment: A Working Example

The Cascarino Cube

Appendix 3 is a generic approach to risk identification and prioritization. Its use requires tailoring to the requirements of an individual organization. It is referred to here as a "cube" although it is, in actuality, a cuboid with the numbers of layers dependent on the individual functions, threat sources, and risks to which the organization is exposed.

1

INTRODUCTION TO DATA ANALYSIS

Data analysis has been in use in auditing for many years, but with the advent of more advanced computer interrogation software, it has come to the fore and is a significant technique, allowing internal audits to leverage the enormous quantities of data existing within organizations to the extent that it has recently started to become standard practice.

Internal audit standards currently require consideration of the use of data analysis because these techniques allow auditors to drill down into the data in order to gain in-depth understanding of corporate business practices.

Data analysis may be most effective when implemented using data analysis technology to handle the high volumes and variety of data structures in use, and the Institute of Internal Auditors defines technology-based audit techniques as *"Any automated audit tool, such as generalized audit software, test data generators, computerized audit programs, specialized audit utilities, and CAATs."**

With the increase in national and international compliance regulations coupled with the growing sophistication of today's fraud schemes, the need for the ability to examine patterns within high-volume data systems has become an imperative. Data analytics facilitates such analyses.

According to a 2013 PwC study, which surveyed 1,700 internal audit leaders, CFOs, and CEOs, 85% said data analytics is important to strengthening audit coverage, and yet only 31% of respondents are

---

* http://www.theiia.org/guidance/standards-and-guidance/ippf/standards/full
-standards/?search=risk

using data analytics regularly. By 2015, the updated study* reported that

> While 82% of CAEs report they leverage data analytics in some specific audits, just 48% use analytics for scoping decisions, and only 43% leverage data to inform their risk assessment.

They also found that the internal audit's highest usage of data analytics was in the area of fraud management, but even at this level, less than 50% were currently utilizing data analytics as an effective audit tool. For the majority of audit operational areas, less than a third of respondents use data analytics as an essential component of their internal audit approach. In the same report, they noted,

> CAEs report that obtaining data skills is a top challenge. While 65% of CAEs report they have some data skills on their team either in-house or through third parties, our interviews revealed a lack of the combined business acumen and data skills.

Given the move of audit evidence from hard copy to digital, this shortage of skills and inability to effectively utilize data analytics is alarming from both the perspective of the organization as a whole and also the ongoing contribution to be made by internal audits as a function.

Benefits to Audit

The internal audit function can derive multiple benefits through effective data analysis including the following:

- *Improvements to general audit productivity*—By utilizing automated techniques, significant reductions in resource requirements to execute common audit procedures have been reported when audit data analysis has been implemented effectively. The ability to interrogate corporate information from a single location seeking direct evidence of internal control weaknesses

---

* http://www.pwc.co.za/en_ZA/za/assets/pdf/2015-state-of-internal-audit -profession.pdf

can obviate the costs associated with travel to remote locations across the organization.

- *Reduction in audit risk*—Audit risk may be defined as conducting the wrong tests on the right data or drawing erroneous conclusions from the correct analysis on the correct data. A common cause of such risk lies in a common practice of auditors conducting a single test and immediately drawing conclusions. With the appropriate analytical techniques backed by the use of effective audit tools, the auditor is in a position to repeat audit tests if required on the same data or on similar data independently obtained. Where conclusions have been derived, they can be tested by reanalysis of the data in a manner designed specifically to challenge the initial auditors' conclusions.

- *Improvement in audit independence*—By placing the tools directly into the hands of the auditor, the degree of dependence that the audit must place on the information technology function within the organization is significantly reduced. There will always be a certain degree of dependence in the locating of data sources within the corporate network as well as the gaining of access rights to data, but the conducting of the analysis itself as well as the reporting of results remains under the control of the individual auditor. It also facilitates the auditor refining the audit approach depending on the initial findings without having to revert to the IT department again to ask for subsequent analyses of the same data. Instead of having to specify exactly which analyses the auditor would like IT to perform or the specific view of the data required from IT, the auditor can take the data in an unamended form and slice it in as many ways as is required to achieve the degree of audit confidence required.

- *Improvements in audit assurance*—The ability to use advanced analytical procedures in substantive testing as well as the ability to operate at a significantly higher confidence level facilities the expression of an audit opinion with improved reliability.

- *Increased audit opportunities*—When data analysis is not used, time and resource constraints may limit audit approaches to the execution of audit procedures that are, themselves, "easy" to conduct within time and budget constraints. By opening up the opportunities to study high-volume data in an efficient manner using automation when appropriate, risk areas within the organization that previously were effectively unauditable may now be examined in depth at high degrees of confidence with much of the interpretation of results being carried out by software rather than relying on the individual auditor's degree of expertise.

Overall, data analysis is a judgmental process. One of the primary audit objectives is identification of anomalies in data presented or major changes in trends and relationships of data to facilitate the investigation of the reasons underlying those changes. The judgment process can be improved by experience and by use of appropriate audit analytical tools.

In essence, data analytics may be defined as the science of examining raw and unprocessed data with the intention of drawing conclusions from the information thus derived. It involves a series of processes and techniques designed to take the initial data and, having sanitized the data, removing any irregular or distorting elements, and transforming it into a form appropriate for analysis, to facilitate decision making. The IIA has defined such analysis techniques as the following:

> Analytical procedures involve studying and comparing relationships among both financial and nonfinancial information. The application of analytical procedures is based on the premise that, in the absence of known conditions to the contrary, relationships among information may reasonably be expected to exist and continue. Examples of contrary conditions include unusual or nonrecurring transactions or events; accounting, organizational, operational, environmental, and technological changes; inefficiencies; ineffectiveness; errors; fraud; or illegal act.[*]

Used effectively, such analysis can improve audit efficiency and effectiveness as well as increase the audit coverage achievable using the increased analytical capabilities. Overall audit quality can be enhanced with improvements in audit credibility and cost-effectiveness.

---

[*] IIA Practice Advisory 2320-1: Analytical Procedures.

All analyses draw data from a population that is a collection of items under review. With the power of today's computer systems, it is tempting to believe that data analysis will involve analyzing 100% of the data in order to ensure that the analysis is 100% accurate. In practice, this is neither desirable nor even possible.

Within this book, we shall be using the following definitions:

- *Data:* The body of facts and figures systematically gathered to achieve specific purposes
- *Information:* Data that has been processed into a form that is or is perceived to be valuable to a recipient and meaningful in the decision-making process

Data Classification

Classification of data has its foundation in the concept of *scale of measurement*, namely the following:

- *Nominal*—A qualitative, non-numerical, and nonranking scale that classifies features on intrinsic characteristics. For example, cars in a showroom may be classified by color, make, etc.
- *Ordinal*—This is a nominal scale with ranking that differentiates features according to a specific order. For example, in our car showroom, the make of car may be denoted by model type, such as sedan, hatchback, convertible, etc.
- *Interval*—This data follows an ordinal scale with ranking based on numerical values that are recorded with reference to an arbitrary datum, for example, the number of passengers in vehicles capable of holding a minimum capacity of two.
- *Ratio*—Such data follows an interval scale with ranking based on numerical values that are measured with reference to an absolute datum, for example, the engine capacity measured in cubic centimeters, liters, etc.

Data may be transformed into information by techniques such as organization, conversion, structuring, data mining, and modeling.

- *Organization* involves the arranging of data into a structured format so that access can be achieved in an efficient and effective manner.

- *Conversion* involves a transformation of data from one specific format into another to facilitate the analysis process.
- *Structuring* may be seen as a process whereby data can be placed in a form accessible to a specific information system or to an audit analysis software package.
- *Data mining* involves analysis of data in order to uncover useful, possibly unexpected patterns within data as well as the extraction of implicit, previously unknown, and potentially useful information from corporate data.
- *Modeling* involves the use of appropriate statistical analysis and interpretation of the data in order to assist its use in the identification of information that can be made use of in strategic decision making.

By utilizing these techniques, the auditor can facilitate the normal tasks associated with the audit analysis of data, including the following:

- Classification of data
- Clustering of information
- Discovery of data association rules
- Uncovering sequential patterns
- Regression analysis
- Deviation detection

In today's information technology environment, the use of advanced database management systems facilitates the sharing of data among diverse users or groups of users. In modern computer application systems, it is common to find a data-centric approach to the acquisition of software and hardware has been adopted such that the data itself drives the specification process. This is intended to ensure the hardware and software can meet the data requirements of the organization rather than the data needing to be transformed to make the hardware and software functional. Modern computer applications are therefore seen as enablers of business process improvements by facilitating the reengineering of the business process in order to make better use of information availability. The extraction of such information for audit purposes is covered in more detail in Chapter 9.

Audit Analytical Techniques

Audit analytical techniques may be applied on data both manually and using CAATs. These techniques facilitate the following:

- Computation of statistical factors, such as averages, standard deviations, high and low values, in order to determine the variability of the population as well as to seek abnormal items within the population
- Validation of transaction parameters, such as date of transaction, source of transaction, authorization of transaction, and the like, to find unauthorized or invalid transactions
- Identification of duplicate transactions where such duplication should not exist or may indicate authorized transaction patterns
- Identification of missing transactions where gaps in sequence numbers may be found to be inappropriate
- Identification of calculation or arithmetic errors in recorded values held on computer data master files
- Classification to find patterns and associations among data elements that do not correspond to expected or predicted patterns
- Identification of statistically unlikely occurrences of values using techniques such as Benford's law
- Analysis of multiple data relationships to identify suspicious transactions where, for example, data on the vendor file, such as bank details, names, or addresses, may be found to match similar data on the employee file

Data Modeling

Data modeling is the process of defining real-world phenomena or geographic features of interest in terms of their characteristics and their relationships with one another. It is concerned with different phases of work carried out to implement information organization and data structure.

There are three steps in the data-modeling process, resulting in a series of progressively formalized data models as the form of the database becomes more and more rigorously defined:

- *Conceptual data modeling*—Defining in broad and generic terms the scope and requirements of a database
- *Logical data modeling*—Specifying the user's view of the database with a clear definition of attributes and relationships
- *Physical data modeling*—Specifying the internal storage structure and file organization of the database

Data Input Validation

Data validation is the process of evaluating collected analytical data against established acceptance criteria to determine data quality and usability in the analysis process prior to conducting the analysis itself. Data validation procedures are selected in accordance with the audit objectives and with the data needs of the analysis.

Data quality for analytic purposes may be defined by such characteristics as the following:

- *Fit for purpose*—Data retrieved is appropriate for its intended analysis.
- *Accuracy*—Data is correct and reflects exactly the transaction or process under review. There are no errors in the data in comparison to data in an original data source or to what actually happened.
- *Availability or accessibility*—Data enables identifying transactions or events correctly and can be retrieved relatively rapidly when needed.
- *Completeness*—All the elements of information needed for analysis are present in the data, and no elements of required information are missing.
- *Relevance*—Supports audit findings and recommendations and is consistent with the objectives for the audit.
- *Reliability*—Data extracted for analysis is the best attainable through the use of appropriate audit techniques.

- *Timely*—Original data is recorded at the time of transaction or service delivery and is available in time for the analysis to provide meaningful management information.
- *Valid*—Data meaningfully represents exactly what it is believed to represent.

Overall, data analysis has been defined as the following:

[P]rocedures for analyzing data, techniques for interpreting the results of such procedures, ways of planning the gathering of data to make its analysis easier, more precise or more accurate, and all the machinery and results of (mathematical) statistics which apply to analyzing data.*

Organizations use a variety of techniques to identify and map the flow of information within the organization where it can then be graphically shown using data flow diagram, which, themselves, may take a variety of forms, such as bubble charts, process models, and workflow diagrams.

Getting the Right Data for Analysis

In general, the purpose of an internal audit using data analysis is to seek evidence in order to determine that the control objectives of the area under review have been met, are being met, and will continue to be met.

Even after the introduction of computerized systems, the over-all control objectives for information processing have not changed, although the control points may vary. In any business area, the auditor will normally seek to identify the controls used by management and relied upon for normal operations. In many cases, the auditor will find that the majority of controls relied upon by management to achieve its control objectives will be preventative controls, which may not, by themselves, leave behind appropriate evidence. The auditor must therefore seek sources of such evidence from other data sources. Such evidence would normally indicate that the activity is being conducted as intended by top management, prescribed

---

* Tukey, John W. "The Future of Data Analysis," *Ann. Math. Statist.* Volume 33, Number 1 (1962), 1–6.

policies are being followed, and administrative and financial controls are effective and the cost of controls is in line with the function's effectiveness and risk.

Data is available in raw form from a variety of sources, such as printouts, computer data files, spreadsheets, text files, and PDFs. To make the most effective use of such data, *generalized audit software* (GAS) may be incorporated into audit assurance plans. Such software comes with prefabricated audit tests built in, giving the auditor direct control of interrogations that are fast to implement and at a lower development cost than other forms of interrogation.

Such software may be used for general audit analyses, such as the following:

- Detective examination of files
- Verification of processing controls
- File interrogations
- Fraud investigation

All such software has common capabilities, including file access to multiple types of data sources, arithmetic and logic operations, file comparisons, and statistical sampling with outputs in the form of reports, graphics, or data files for ongoing processes.

The selection of the appropriate audit technique will depend upon the audit objective, whether it is desired to verify the processing operation or to verify the results of processing, and only after the appropriate technique is selected can the appropriate tool be chosen. The auditor may be in the process of conducting

- Compliance audits
- Operational audits
- Financial audits
- Application system audits
- System development audits
- Forensic audits
- Governance, risk, and compliance audits

In each case, the controls, sources of evidence, audit techniques, and analysis utilized will differ. For example, in financial auditing, extensive use is normally made of generalized audit software and various forms of statistical analysis, and in IT audits, specialized audit software and general utilities are prevalent.

In some cases, the audit analysis required may exceed the capabilities of generalized audit software, and the auditor may be required to utilize specialized audit software specifically designed to operate in unique circumstances, for example, handling of abnormal data file structures or processing of Big Data. In these situations, the development of unique tests is normally expensive, requires a high level of IT skills in the auditor, and may not result in the answer the auditor thought he or she was looking for, but depending on the circumstances, it may be the only viable solution.

In situations such as these, the auditor may fall back on the use of data analyzers and query languages that were not written specifically as audit tools but which may, nevertheless, be highly effective in audit data analysis.

Statistics

When auditors talk of statistics, they usually refer to a set of individual numbers or numerical facts or to the audit use of specific statistical techniques. It is important to differentiate between describing the characteristics of a set of data and making generalizations, estimates, forecasts, or other judgments based on the analysis of the data. The former is referred to as *descriptive statistics*, and the latter is called *inferential statistics*. Both approaches are common in audit usage but for different purposes.

Descriptive statistics are used by auditors to summarize and describe the data they have collected. For example, upon examination of payment records, the auditor may find that 25% of payments have been made using a credit card. If so, the figure "25%" is a descriptive statistic.

In more common audit use are inferential statistics, sometimes referred to as *inductive statistics*. Here, the auditor will go beyond mere description of the data and draw inferences regarding the criteria for which *sample* data was obtained. For example, based on the examination of a sample of inventory records, the auditor may draw conclusions about the overall error rate. In so doing, the auditor is assuming that an acceptable proportion of all inventory records (the *population* or *universe*) will display the same characteristics as the sample.

A common problem for the auditor is the acquisition of data in large quantities with no clear audit objective in mind. As a result, statistical analysis may be carried out in great depth by the auditor with no clear result because the auditor had no starting point or audit question requiring the need for identification of an evidence source to be analyzed.

As with any audit, the first stage is the identification of the business objectives of the area under review. Once these have been agreed upon with the auditee and management, the overall control objectives specific to that business area may be identified in conjunction with management and the auditee so that the controls relied upon by management to achieve the control objectives may also be identified. It is at this stage that many auditors go wrong in seeking to prove that individual controls are functioning. The critical element is the achievement of the control objectives. Many specific controls are preventative in nature and leave behind no evidence as to their previous effectiveness or future effectiveness, and auditing becomes a test of the control as at a point in time. Rather, the auditor should seek the source of evidence from which satisfaction can be derived regarding whether the individual control objectives

- Have been achieved
- Are being achieved
- Will continue to be achieved

Only after the sources of such evidence have been identified is the auditor in a position to choose the appropriate technique and, subsequently, the appropriate tool to derive the evidence required. If the evidence cannot be found, this is commonly an indicator of errors in the data or, more significantly, the existence of fraud. Because the auditor is clear on the evidence sought and why it is sought, the interpretation is considerably simplified, and audit opinions and recommendations are demonstrably supported by the evidence obtained. In all cases, the confidentiality and integrity of data extracted for analysis becomes the responsibility of the auditor. At its most fundamental, the auditor now has available corporate information that is of a highly confidential nature, and any breach of confidentiality attributable to the auditors can significantly damage the organization and, at the same time, destroy the credibility of the internal audit function. Even without direct disclosure, the auditor must ensure that the data itself cannot be accessed or tampered with, resulting in the drawing of invalid conclusions. This corruption need not necessarily be deliberate. Another auditor may accidentally corrupt the data in the course of normal audit operations. Overall, the integrity of the audit analytical procedures is of paramount importance, and the responsibility to ensure the reliability of the audit processes rests with both the audit function and the individual auditor.

Statistical analysis is covered in more depth in Chapters 2 and 3.

Overall, data analysis has become indispensable for achieving audit objectives. Given that paper trails are fast disappearing, auditors themselves must be computer-literate in order to handle the volumes and variety of data forms. From a practical perspective, an efficient and effective audit data analytic procedure will follow a predefined program consisting of the following:

- Defining the audit evidence requirements
- Identifying the source of the evidence
- Identifying and acquiring the appropriate skill mix to conduct the analysis
- Selecting a data analytics strategy
- Acquiring data access rights
- Selecting the appropriate analytical architecture

By implementing a standardized methodology, the internal audit function can ensure the consistent application of high-quality data analytics to support the overall audit, the objectives, and the program on an ongoing basis, resulting in significant improvements in audit quality and auditor productivity and delivering an enhanced level of service to management, the audit committee, and legal and compliance authorities as well as to the organization as a whole, including all stakeholders.

2

UNDERSTANDING SAMPLING

This chapter covers the fundamental assumptions underlying the use of sampling techniques, the nature of populations, and the use of variables. Distribution frequencies and central tendency measurement will be covered as well as the impact on analysis of distribution characteristics.

Generically, audit use of statistical sampling within a business can be described as the collection, summarization, analysis, audit, and reporting of numerical findings relevant to a business decision or situation. An audit uses the records of past business transactions in order to analyze internal control structures and to predict future weaknesses and deviations so that remedial action can be taken in an early time scale.

Population Sampling

Statistics has been defined as providing a basis for decision making on the basis of imperfect or incomplete data. Statistics as we know them today trace their origins to the work carried out by Carl Friedrich Gauss who, in the early 1800s, developed various principles that became an integral part of statistics as well as probability theory. Although many of his findings were only published after his death in 1855, his earlier work on the *classical theory of errors* formed the basis of probability theory into the 1930s. It is commonly recognized that there are three basic types of errors, namely:

- *Systematic*—These errors will either overestimate or underestimate the results of measurements and typically arise from the effect of the environment or incorrect usage of measuring equipment.
- *Gross*—This class of error typically arises from miscalculations or incorrect reading of measurements.
- *Random*—These errors arise from a variety of reasons with an unforeseen effect on measurements, resulting in both underestimating and overestimating results.

The theory of errors focuses on the study of gross and random errors with the intention of studying distribution laws of random errors to seek estimates of unknown parameters using the results of measurements.

In many audits, conducting audit tests on the entire population under examination may be impossible due to the volume of the population or the cost of such testing. Where large numbers of items are involved and less than 100% certainty is acceptable, considerable time-savings can be gained if a reduction in the number of items are examined could be achieved. Statistical sampling is a technique used to permit the auditor to reduce the amount of testing whereby, instead of examining every item within the overall population against specified audit criteria, the testing may be done on a significantly lower number selected on a statistically valid basis. A sample is drawn from the selected population in such a way that it can be expected to be representative of the population. The intention is that, following examination of the sample, the characteristics of the sample will be representative of the population as a whole. The sample results may then be used to extrapolate to the population the results of audit tests in order to estimate the specific values for the population as a whole. The more representative the sample is, the more accurate the extrapolation will be.

In its Practice Advisory 2100–10 on Audit Sampling, the Institute of Internal Auditors classifies audit sampling as the following:

> When using statistical or non-statistical sampling methods, the auditors should design and select an audit sample, perform audit procedures and evaluate sample results to obtain sufficient, reliable, relevant and useful audit evidence. In forming an audit opinion auditors frequently do not examine all of the information available as it may be impractical and valid conclusions can be reached using audit sampling.
>
> Audit sampling is defined as the application of audit procedures to less than 100% of the population to enable the auditor to evaluate audit evidence about some characteristic of the items selected to form or assist in forming a conclusion concerning the population.*

---

* Institute of Internal Auditors. *Practice Advisory Audit Sampling 2100-10*, April 2005, IIA, Altamonte Springs, FL.

Obviously, the results of the testing will not be as reliable as carrying out a 100% examination of the population. The auditor must work to a specified degree of certainty and express an opinion within an acceptable tolerance.

In conducting data analysis, it is critical that auditors use statistical jargon accurately. In doing this, auditors must differentiate between qualitative concepts and quantitative measures. Qualitative concepts include *accuracy, precision, trueness, reproducibility*, and the like, and quantitative measures must be specified in statistical terms, such as *standard deviation, bias, mean*, etc. It is, unfortunately, common for the auditor to refer to results in terms of qualitative concepts instead of quantitative measures. The International Standards Organization (ISO) has created definitions for the qualitative concepts such that

- *Accuracy:* The closeness of agreement between the test result (i.e., an observed calculated or estimated value) and the accepted reference value or "true value"
- *Precision:* The closeness of agreement between independent test results obtained under stipulated conditions in that their results are repeatable (the precision under similar conditions) and reproducible (the precision under different conditions)
- *Trueness:* The closeness of agreement between the average value obtained from a large series of tests and the accepted reference value

Overall accuracy can be defined as being the sum of precision and trueness.

Population sampling involves taking a representative selection of the population, conducting the audit tests, and extrapolating the results to the population as a whole. In order for these conclusions to be valid, the auditor will normally use a variety of statistical techniques in order to ensure that the selected sample is as representative as possible. Failure to do so will normally result in the drawing of invalid conclusions regarding the population.

Sampling Risk

All auditing, whether internal, external, operational, forensic, or IT, involves a degree of risk or uncertainty. The auditor is constantly faced with the risk that errors or material regularly will not be detected despite use of the appropriate auditing procedures. This uncertainty is termed *audit risk*. When statistical sampling is used as an audit technique, the auditor faces increased risk because, working at less than 100% certainty, the conclusions drawn about the population may contain some material error. This element of audit risk can be divided into two components:

- *Sampling risk* is the risk that the sample chosen by the auditor may not appropriately reflect the characteristics of the population as a whole.
- *Non-sampling risk* is the risk that, having obtained a sample that is appropriately representative of the population, the audit tests still miss detecting a significant error.

Use of statistically valid techniques permits the auditor to control the sampling risk and reduce it to an acceptable level. By operating at, for example, a 95% certainty level, the auditor has accepted a 5% chance that the sample drawn will not reflect the population accurately or completely. In a normal population (see below), operating at 95% certainty indicates that, should the auditor draw a sample of a given size 100 times, 95 of those times the complete sample would be derived from a representative part of the population. In five of those times, the sample would include one or more items that would not fully represent the population. This is commonly referred to as the *risk of sampling error*. No matter how the sample is selected, this risk will always exist because of the 95% certainty specified by the auditor. The acceptance of this risk involves the auditor making a judgment call regarding the level of assurance desired. This judgment is normally arrived at following consultation with auditee management in order to minimize the risk of sampling error while, at the same time, ensuring a sample size that is both sufficient and efficient. Sampling error can also be minimized by the choice of the appropriate statistical model and by following the correct sample selection methodology.

Regardless of whether statistical sampling, judgmental sampling, or full population surveys are conducted, the risk of non-sampling error remains. Typical causes of this type of error include the following:

- Lack of understanding of the nature and characteristics of the population
- Mistakes in application of the techniques for selecting a sample

- Use of inappropriate audit techniques on the items examined
- Failure to recognize irregularities or errors in the items examined
- Other misjudgments or errors by the auditor in carrying out tests or interpreting the results

From the sampling risk perspective, the two main aspects to be considered in analyzing data for a compliance test of internal controls are the following:

- The risk of overreliance on control. This typically occurs when testing of the sample leads the auditor to place reliance on the controls when, in fact, it is not justified. This is known as a β (beta) risk.
- The risk of under-reliance on controls. This would occur when the testing of the sample leads the auditor to wrongly evaluate the population as falling below the level of tolerance. This is known as an α (alpha) risk.

Some things must also be taken into consideration in the performance of substantive tests:

- Once again, the risk of incorrect acceptance, a β (beta) risk, occurs when the sample appears to support the auditor's conclusion that an amount or quantity in the full population is not materially misstated when, in fact, it is so misstated.
- In addition, the risk of incorrect rejection, an α (alpha) risk, is a risk that the sample leads the auditor to believe that an amount or quantity in the full population is materially misstated when in fact it is not.

Alpha characteristics of the population impact the efficiency of the audit in the detection of material errors because they typically result in the increasing of substantive testing unnecessarily because of the doubt that has been cast on the accuracy of the figures or the unacceptability of the quality of control.

Beta characteristics relate to the effectiveness of the audit because the auditor may draw erroneous conclusions regarding the population based on the results from the sampling.

With the advent of computer technology, many auditors doubt the requirement for sampling since the computer can, theoretically, examine every item in the population against preset audit criteria.

Even when such examination is possible, it may not be desirable due to the time and cost of such examination particularly when the risk level is deemed to be low. When the audit tests involve human intervention, the ability of the computer to select every item in a population will not reduce the time, cost, and effort required to conduct the tests themselves. For example, in a large population of purchase orders, the ability of the computer to select all orders will not reduce the audit time required to check signatures on the purchase orders themselves.

As such, the auditor must determine whether 100% assurance is required. If so, no sampling will be done and a *survey* of the full population will be needed. When less than 100% confidence is acceptable to the auditor, sampling may be an appropriate technique. It must be reemphasized, however, that when a sample is to be drawn and examined in order to draw conclusions about the population as a whole, the sampling must be done on a statistically valid basis. The differences between statistical sampling and judgmental sampling are covered in more detail in Chapter 3.

General Advantages

The obvious advantage to sampling is that audit tests can be conducted on a smaller number of subjects, reducing the overall cost in terms of both auditors' time and money. In some cases, data analysis of samples may be more instructive than studying the full population because general correlations may be more obvious in a sample while being concealed in the sheer volume of a survey. When the results of audit testing and analysis will be re-input to the computer, human error is more difficult to avoid when handling larger data sets.

Planning the Audit

Once the auditor has made the decision that risk levels indicate that 100% confidence is not required, he or she must take into consideration the audit objectives of conducting the data analysis as a whole as well as the characteristics of the population.

Data Analysis Objectives

The first stage of any data analysis involves the consideration by the auditor of the control objectives of the area under review. Only after these control objectives have been determined can the auditor establish the source of the evidence and the nature of the analysis required to evaluate the evidence. When sampling will be utilized, the appropriate technique chosen will reflect the nature of the opinion to be expressed. If the opinion required is on the error rates within the population, the use of *attribute sampling* techniques would normally be employed. When the analysis is intended to facilitate the auditor expressing an opinion on the accuracy of values demonstrated within the population, *variable sampling* or *monetary unit sampling* may be more appropriate.

These techniques are covered in more depth in Chapter 3.

Characteristics of Populations

Auditors will typically evaluate populations based on *random variables*— that is to say, a variable that assumes a numerical value when one and only one value is assigned. Random variables may be categorized into *discrete random variables* and *continuous random variables*, both of which may be used in audit practice. A *discrete random variable* is one in which the possible values may be counted or listed. For example, the number of errors in a population may be 0, 1, 2, and so on. In such a case, the values of the random variables are countable and potentially infinite. When a random variable may assume any numerical value in one or more intervals, the random variable is designated a *continuous random variable*. For example, in assessing the value within a population, the numerical count may not necessarily be 1 or 2. Between these two finite points, there is a multiplicity of possibilities, such as 1.1, 1.2, 1.25, 1.255, etc.

When the auditor is attempting to establish the probabilities associated with the different values, it is often critical that the auditor know the *probability distribution* associated with each possible value that the variable can assume.

Population Variability and Probability Distributions

Binomial Distributions

Binomial distributions are discrete random variables used in the evaluation of processes in which a fixed probability prevails for each possible outcome. One single occurrence of the process, commonly known as a *trial*, will end in one of two results generally classified as either *success* or *failure* (hence the term *binomial*). The probability of a success will remain constant from trial to trial, and repeated trials are independent.

The probability distribution of the number of successes (the *binomial distribution*) follows the following formula:

$$P(X) = C_x^n p^x q^{n-x}$$

where
  n = the number of trials
  x = 0, 1, 2, 3, ... n
  p = the probability of success in a single trial
  q = the probability of failure and a single trial ($q = 1 - p$)
  C_x^n is a combination
  $P(X)$ gives the probability of successes in n binomial trials.

Binomial distributions are important in auditing when, for example, the auditor may be required to express an opinion on success rates in an operation.

For example, in a manufacturing process, the records indicate a rejection rate of 12%. The auditor wishes to determine what the probability is that of 10 randomly selected products, not more than 2 will fail?

This is a binomial distribution because there are only two outcomes (the product produced will fail or not).

Let X equal the rejected products.

Here n = 10, p = 0.12 (number of failures), and q = 0.88 (number of successful products).

The probability of no rejects ($x = 0$) is

$$P(X) = C_x^n p^x q^{n-x} = c_0^{10} (0.12)^0 (0.88)^{10} = 0.2785$$

The probability of one reject ($x = 1$) is

$$P(X) = C_x^n p^x q^{n-x} = c_1^{10}(0.12)^1(0.88)^9 = 0.37977$$

The probability of two rejects ($x = 2$) is

$$P(X) = C_x^n p^x q^{n-x} = c_2^{10}(0.12)^2(0.88)^8 = 0.23304$$

Thus, the probability of getting no more than two rejects is

$$= P(X \leq 2)$$
$$= 0.2785 + 0.37977 + 0.23304$$
$$= 0.89131$$

When testing a process with such objectives, it is critical that the audit opinion be expressed in terms of probabilities.

Poisson Distribution

This is a discrete probability distribution expressing the probability of a given number of events occurring in a fixed time frame at a known average rate. It generally applies when it is meaningless to count how many events have not occurred. It is the equivalent of the binomial distribution without q = the probability of failure and a single trial ($q = 1 - p$). It is more commonly used with rare events.

The Poisson distribution may be applied when

- It is possible to count how many events have occurred
- Occurrences are independent
- The event is something that can be counted in whole numbers
- Average frequency of occurrence for the time period in question is known

As an example, the number of customers arriving at a depot per hour may exhibit a Poisson distribution but, in that case, a normal distribution would be used because Poisson is most often utilized with rare events that can successfully be mimicked.

Continuous Probability Distributions

Continuous probability distributions are used to find probabilities concerning continuous random variables. Of these distributions, the most critical to the auditor of the normal distribution are the uniform distribution and exponential distributions.

When using sampling methods, it is critical that the variability of the population be determined in order to validate the sample selection.

Auditors operate using confidence levels—that is to say, how confident the auditor requires it to be that the sample selected adequately represents the population as a whole.

Normal Distribution

An assumption that is commonly made is that the population distribution is "normal." When such an assumption is valid, the degree of representativeness of the sample can be measured as seen below.

As may be seen from Diagram 2.1, the mean average plus or minus one standard deviation will include 68.2% of the population. When that variability is pushed out to two standard deviations, the area under the curve contains 95.4% of the population. Auditors commonly work with a 95% confidence level, which would mean, in a normal distribution, an area under the curve equivalent to the mean plus or minus 1.96 standard deviations.

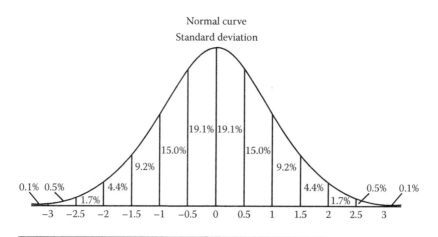

Diagram 2.1   Normal population.

A 95% confidence level would mean that, given a normal distribution of the population, if the same size of sample was drawn over and over again, 95% of the time it would be a fair reflection of the population. The auditor is therefore accepting that 5% of the time there would be items included in the sample that would not be representative of the population as a whole.

In determining the confidence coefficient, the auditor will take into consideration the risk of incorrect rejection, for example,

CONFIDENCE LEVEL	RISK OF INCORRECT REJECTION	CONFIDENCE COEFFICIENT
80%	20%	1.28
90%	10%	1.64
95%	5%	1.96
99%	1%	2.58

Uniform Distributions

A uniform distribution is one in which every possible result is equally likely—that is, the probability of each outcome is the same. The uniform distribution is commonly taken as the null or initial hypothesis in testing the accuracy of mathematical models. The common example used for such a distribution is the distribution of values when tossing a die, which is equally likely to land on any number from one to six.

In an audit context, the auditor may, over a period of time, have determined that the time to service customers in a queue may range from zero to four minutes. When all of the waiting times were arranged into a histogram, the auditor observed that the bars had approximately equal heights, giving the histogram a regular appearance, which implies that the frequencies of waiting times are approximately the same.

Given that the corporate requirement is that waiting in the queue for more than 2.5 minutes would be unacceptable, the auditor wishes to determine the probability that a given customer will spend at least 2.5 minutes waiting.

This probability would be indicated by the area in a triangle having a base equal to $4 - 2.5 = 1.5$ and a height equal to ¼—that is, 0.375. The probability is therefore that 37.5% of all customers will spend at least 2.5 minutes in the queue. Because this would, in all probability, be an unacceptable probability to management, the auditor may recommend additional till points be manned in order to reduce customer wait time to levels of corporate acceptability.

Exponential Distribution

The *exponential distribution* (or *negative exponential distribution*) is a probability distribution describing the time between events in a process that occurs continuously and independently at a constant average rate (a Poisson process). If, for example, we wish to study the time lapse between manufacturing errors rather than an error rate, the lapsing time would be a continuous random variable described by an *exponential distribution*. If the rejections per workshop error rate averaged 41.6 errors per year, the workshop is averaging a mean of 41.6/52 denoted by lamda (λ) errors per week = 0.8 errors per week, giving a mean of 52/41.6 = 1.25 weeks between successive errors.

In general, if the number of occurrences of errors per week has a Poisson distribution with mean λ, then the time between errors would have an exponential distribution with a mean $1/\lambda$.

Central Tendency and Skewed Distributions

In any population, a common evaluation technique is to determine the average value of the population. Three averages are possible: the *mean*, the *median*, and the *mode*. The mean or *arithmetic average* value of the data set may be calculated as a sum of all values divided by the number of data points. The median represents the *middle value in a population* range, and the mode represents the *most frequently occurring value* in a population.

The amount of deviation overall defines the spread of values. A common way of determining the variability of the population is to determine its variability from the mean. The *standard deviation* (σ) measures the dispersion of values around the mean. This may be calculated as a square root of the average of squared deviations of each member of the population from the mean.

In statistics, skewness is a measurement of the asymmetry of the probability distribution around the mean. The example shown above as a "normal" distribution is classed as unimodal because there is one

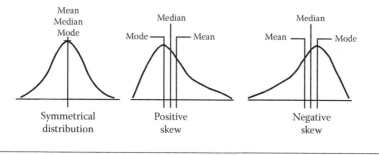

Diagram 2.2   Skewed distributions.

value that is frequently occurring. Deviations with only one peak are referred to as unimodal distributions.

A negative skew would indicate that the *tail* on the left side of the graph is longer or fatter than the right side. Conversely, positive skew indicates that the tail on the right side is longer or fatter (Diagram 2.2).

Skewness computation is a process involving taking the deviations from the mean, dividing the deviations by the standard deviation, and raising them to the third power. These figures are then added together and divided by the number of data points.

Population Characteristics

Perhaps the most critical element of data analysis is the determination of the characteristics of the population to be examined. The analysis of the sample is made in terms of the population from which the sample was drawn.

Should the objective of the analysis be to determine which customers exceeded their credit limit, the appropriate population would be customer records and not the financial transactions themselves. Similarly, if the intention of the auditor is to select records for further testing, it is essential that the population from which the sample will be drawn is itself complete and accurate.

If the auditor seeks to express an opinion based upon a sample drawn from transactions over the previous three months, any opinion expressed can only be valid in terms of the three months. Any conclusions drawn or inferences made beyond this time span would be invalid.

Similarly, the auditor may choose to express an opinion regarding only high-value items. Any opinion expressed based on a sample specifically biased toward high-value items would only be valid in terms of the population of high-value items.

It is also important that the auditor is clear regarding the manner of testing to be conducted. If the auditor wishes to examine customer orders to ensure that all items ordered were dispatched, the sample must be drawn from the orders themselves and checked forward to dispatch notes. If the intention is to express an opinion regarding proof that all dispatches were for legitimate customers, the population to be drawn from would be the dispatch notes, and the auditor would then check backward against the customer orders.

3

JUDGMENTAL VERSUS STATISTICAL SAMPLING

This chapter covers the differences between judgmental and statistical sampling, the applicability of both in audit practice, and the dangers inherent in confusing the two. The differences in selection methods are covered as well as their impact on the analysis and interpretation possible within the sampling methods. The Institute of Internal Auditors has differentiated these as the following:

> Statistical sampling involves the use of techniques from which mathematically constructed conclusions regarding the population can be drawn.
>
> Non-statistical sampling is not statistically based on results and should not be extrapolated over the population as a sample is unlikely to be representative of the population.*

Judgmental Sampling

Judgmental sampling is a nonprobability sampling technique with which the auditor selects the units to be sampled based on his or her professional judgment and experience. The sample to be chosen is not intended to be representative of the whole population, and it is commonly used when the auditor has a specific and limited reason for biasing the sample, and no attempt will be made to extrapolate results to the general population. If an auditor is aware that the known section of the population may be subject to a higher risk, then the auditor may exercise his or her professional judgment in selecting the population

---

* Institute of Internal Auditors. *Practice Advisory Audit Sampling 2100-10*, April 2005, IIA, Altamonte Springs, FL.

to be reviewed, and any conclusions drawn from such reviews must be carefully judged to ensure the validity of the conclusion.

This form of sampling, based as it is on the auditors' judgment, should not be used as the primary audit procedure when the auditor has no special knowledge on which to base such a judgment and no indication of which items in a population are more likely to contain significant misstatements. It is, however, a common technique in examining a limited number of items with no intention of extrapolating results to the population. Judgmental samples may be useful in, for example, corroboration of the outcome of other analyses for which the selection of a few detailed transactions may facilitate the validity of forecasts derived from other audit techniques.

As an example, the auditor may wish to examine purchase orders around the boundary of authorization limits. If a certain level of staff has the authority to place purchase orders up to a specific limit, the auditor may deliberately choose to examine purchase orders just below the authority limit, at the authority limit, and just above the authority limit. In doing this, the auditor is using professional judgment to determine that the risk to be examined is the unauthorized placement of orders beyond the individual's authority level.

In a similar way, the auditor, based on previous experience in the business area, may be aware that specific transactions are at greater risk of duplication and may choose to draw a sample of transactions from that area to confirm or refute that hypothesis. Once again, based upon the results found, no extrapolation will be made to the general condition of the population as a whole.

The major drawback to judgmental sampling is that there is no ready mechanism for evaluating the *reliability* of the auditor's selection and the extent to which *bias* has influenced the sample examined. As such, sampling error, the extent to which the sample is not representative of the population as a whole, cannot be readily determined. The number of items to be examined and audited is based purely upon the degree of expertise of the auditor with the potential for substantial under- or over-auditing.

At a minimum, bias will occur in the selection process because no randomization was used in the drawing of the sample such that, across the population, individual items did not have an equal chance of being selected. As a result, the demographics of the population may be misrepresented and no general conclusions can be drawn.

Nevertheless, this technique can be effective within audit practice in determining specific risk when, as previously stated, no requirement exists to express an opinion on the population as a whole.

The Statistical Approach

The statistical sampling approach is intended to produce a sample that can be expected to be representative of the population. This means that the auditor believes the relative characteristics of the sample, such as error rates or sizes, will be mathematically proportional to those contained within the full population. For this belief to be valid, an appropriate selection technique, such as random selection, and an adequate sample size must be chosen to be representative of the auditors' selected degree of confidence.

Before sample sizes can be calculated, the auditor must be clear as to the type of sampling required based on the nature of the population.

Sampling Methods

Differing methods of sampling are appropriate for use in different circumstances, and the auditor must be aware of the types and their advantages and disadvantages in order to ensure the selection of the appropriate sampling method.

- *Attribute sampling* is used to assess how frequently the particular event or attribute occurs within the population as a whole. An attribute is dichotomous in that there are only two possible values: true or false. It can therefore be used to, for example, ascertain whether probable error rates within the population are within acceptable limits or not but not the values of the errors. This is most commonly used to ensure the population deviation rate is below the level of acceptance previously agreed upon with management.

    Within attribute sampling, the auditor may choose variations, such as the following:
    - *Discovery sampling:* This is a specific form of attribute sampling, which is used when a single deviation would be

classed as a critical finding. It is assumed that the expected deviation rate is 0% or close to it. The sample size is then calculated so that the sample includes at least one error if it occurs within the population. Obviously, this is once again at a specific confidence level.

- *Acceptance sampling:* This technique, commonly used in quality control, is appropriate when the population consists of lots that are to be inspected and classified as acceptable or unacceptable. Use of this technique involves the selection of appropriate lot sizes, determining the acceptable quality level, and calculating the number of samples required and the level of testing or inspection required on each item selected. This technique may also be used in classic variable sampling (see below).

- *Stop-or-go sampling:* Again, this is an attribute sampling technique with which the objective is, in this case, to minimize the sample size required to be drawn. In this case, items are selected and subjected to audit tests as sampling proceeds. If the testing indicates that the deviation rate exceeds or equals the maximum tolerable error, the auditor can cease sampling because the objective of the audit testing has been achieved.

- *Classic variable sampling* is a technique commonly applied to monetary amounts although other measures can also be handled. It is commonly used to obtain evidence regarding the probability of material misstatement within the stated amount, for example, a value of inventory held. It is used to predict a total error in the population based on the errors found in a sample. Once again, this prediction will be at a specific confidence level and to a specified degree of *precision* (also known as *confidence interval*) and will not represent the true balance. This technique is appropriate when several errors are expected in the overall population and is commonly used to estimate the total account balance based upon an audited sample. *Acceptance sampling for variables* may be used when the characteristic to be tested can be calculated on a continuous scale. Once again, as with acceptance sampling for attributes, the population would generally be split into lots that may be accepted or rejected depending on whether the mean value of the sample items falls within the acceptable tolerance levels.

- *Probability proportional to size (PPS) sampling:* Unlike other sampling methods in which members of the population form the sampling unit (invoices, delivery notes, checks, etc.), PPS sampling utilizes the monetary unit as a sampling unit. The monetary unit may be the dollar or any other currency appropriate to the audit. The sampled item is then the invoice, delivery note, or other member of the population that contains the sampled monetary unit. This approach requires a cumulative total of the monetary values under review with a systematic selection method so that every nth monetary unit is selected. In this way, an automatic bias is introduced so that the larger values or amounts in the population will have a proportionately larger probability of selection. Although this sampling technique is highly appropriate when seeking overstated values, conversely the probability of selecting negative items is reduced because of the cumulative nature of the values examined. When large numbers of over- or understatements are anticipated, classic variables sampling is normally selected rather than PPS.

Once the sample is chosen, closely following the requirements of the technique selected, the appropriate tests may be conducted and the results of the tests on the sample extrapolated to the full population in order to determine the error rate or to estimate a specific value for the population as a whole. Obviously, the more representative a sample is, the more accurate the extrapolation will be. Under normal circumstances, this may be taken to mean that the larger the sample size, the more accurate the extrapolation. The overall approach for the use of statistical sampling is the following:

- *Define the objectives of the audit tests:* Based upon the objectives, the auditor will decide the type of testing that will be required. To estimate the error rate in a population, one of the varieties of attribute sampling will typically be used. To estimate the recorded amount of a value in a population, the auditor may choose classic variable testing. If overvaluation is suspected, the auditor may select probability proportional to size (PPS) testing.

- *Decide on the level of confidence required:* This is normally done by the auditor in conjunction with the auditee and management and is an attempt to reduce the level of uncertainty to a known and acceptable level. Auditors commonly work at a 95% confidence level. When a risk level is known to be high, this may be increased to 98% or 99%. Conversely, in a lower risk or lower value area, the auditor may agree with management on a confidence level of 90%.

- *Establish the expected error rate:* In attributes sampling, the auditor must establish the error rate that is anticipated within the population with the assistance of management and the auditee. This may be based on the past history of the area under review or on a small judgmental sample selected to give a first impression of an error rate within the sample. When values are involved, the auditor may be attempting to determine the estimated range of the value anticipated. Again, past history or use of the judgmental sample may give a preliminary indication.

- *Establish a maximum tolerable error rate or value range:* Again, in attributes sampling, this is normally established by management in order to indicate beyond what level the overall risk must be reevaluated and the nature of the audit in terms of confidence levels, expected error rates, or even the validity of using sampling may have to be reconsidered.

- *Establish the dispersion of the population:* In classic variable sampling, a critical element is the determination of how much dispersion occurs within the population. In general, the more dispersed the data, the larger the sample size will need to be. This is normally determined by calculating the *standard deviation* of the population (see Chapter 2).

- *Calculate the sample size required:* Using the information already derived, the minimum sample size required to conduct testing at an acceptable confidence level must be calculated. This will involve a variety of formulas based upon the type of statistical sampling to be carried out.

- *Choose the sample selection method:* With the sample size known, the auditor must then choose the appropriate selection method.

The ideal would be a *simple random selection* process in which each item of the population has an equal chance of being selected every time. In practice, sampling with replacement (i.e., each item selected is returned to the population and may be selected again) is seldom used. More commonly, sampling without replacement is used, and the population number is reduced by one each time a sample item is extracted. This is commonly referred to as a *degree of freedom* of one. Obviously, this changes the probability of a given member of the population being selected. In a population of 50,000 items, the probability of one item being selected is one in 50,000. After selection, the probability of another item being selected is one in 49,999. In large populations, this degree of freedom has very little impact on the probability of selection. In small populations, generally taken to be under 5,000 items in the population, a more significant impact can be seen as multiple items are selected. As a result, the sample size may require adjustment for known population size in small populations. As previously mentioned, simple random selection would seem to be an ideal method that may not always be possible or practical. It does have the advantage of being able to produce defensible estimates of the population non-sampling error, but for it to be used effectively, it requires a complete and accurate population listing, which may not be possible in an unnumbered population. Additionally, it may not be practical if remote items are selected for sampling.

- An alternative selection method may be *systematic selection* in which, after randomly selecting a starting point in the population between one and n, if the nth unit is selected, then n equals the population size divided by the sample size. In many cases, this way can be easier to extract the sample than with simple random selection. It also has the added advantage that this method ensures cases are spread across the population. From a disadvantage perspective, it is unwise to use this when there's a pattern to the population distribution and it can result in costly and time-consuming selection if the sample is not conveniently located.

- When the population deviation is high, it may be more effective to subdivide it into mutually exclusive layers prior to selection. These strata may have equal sizes, or the auditor may choose to ensure a higher population in specific strata in order to emphasize areas of higher risk. This has the advantage of ensuring that the units from each main group included in the sample selected may therefore be more reliably representative within a particular strata. *Stratified sampling* in this manner typically results in a lower sample size but the selection process is more complex and requires reliable population information.
- When units in the population can be found in naturally occurring groups or clusters, such as geographical location, by depot, etc., *cluster sampling* may prove to be a more effective alternative. A random sample of such clusters is taken, then all units within those clusters are examined. It can be quicker, easier, and cheaper than other forms of random sampling and does not require complete population information. This type of sampling is useful for selecting a sample to be used, for example, for face-to-face interviews. It does, however, have certain disadvantages. If clusters are not small, a larger sample size may be needed to compensate for a greater sampling error, and the process can become expensive. In addition, it works best when each cluster can be regarded as a microcosm of the whole population.

Calculation of Sample Sizes

Sample sizes may be determined using sample tables, formulas, or computer software.

Attribute Sampling Formula

In calculating the sample size for attributes sampling, the following formula is commonly used:

$$n = \frac{C^2 pq}{P^2}$$

where:

C = confident coefficient (1.96 for a 95% confidence level)

p = expected error rate (.05 if the expected error rate is 5%)

q = 100% − p (.95 in the example above)

P = precision per item (the gap between the maximum tolerable error and the expected error)

In auditing a large population, this sample size may be adequate; however, in a smaller population, the sample size may require correction for a finite population. This can be achieved using the following formula:

$$new \ n = \sqrt{1 - \left(\frac{n}{N}\right)}$$

where:

$new \ n$ = the sample size adjusted for the finite population

n = original sample size

N = number of units in the population

For example, in a population of 10,000 invoices, the auditor wishes to determine if the number of erroneous invoices exceeds management's tolerance of a 3% error rate. The expected error rate is 1%, and the auditor wishes to express an opinion to a 95% confidence level. The sample size would then be the following:

$$n = \frac{1.96^2 \times 0.03 \times 0.97}{.02^2}$$

$$n = \frac{3.8416 \times .0291}{.0004}$$

This gives a sample size of 279.4, which must be rounded up to 280. Sample size is always rounded up to give the smallest sample size that will adequately represent the population at the specified confidence level and precision.

Classic Variable Sampling Formula

In calculating the sample size for classic variable sampling, the following formula is commonly used:

$$n = \frac{C^2 \sigma^2}{P^2}$$

where:

  n = sample size

  C = confidence coefficient (1.96 for a 95% confidence level; see Chapter 2)

  σ = standard deviation of the population (may be directly calculated or an estimate based on a non-statistical sample)

  P = precision per item

For example, the number of items in the population is 10,000 invoices. Based upon the invoice values, a population mean of $1,700 and a standard deviation of $125 have been determined. The auditor wishes to operate at a 95% confidence level, and at a desired precision of $15, the sample size would then be the following:

$$n = \frac{1.96^2 \times \$125}{\$15^2}$$

$$n = \frac{3.84 \times 15625}{225}$$

This gives a sample size of 266.67, which must be rounded up to 267. Once again, the sample size is always rounded up to give the smallest sample size that will adequately represent the population at the specified confidence level and precision.

PPS Sampling Formula

In calculating the sample size for PPS unit sampling, the following formula is commonly used when the anticipated misstatement is zero:

$$n = \frac{BV}{\dfrac{[TM - (EM \times EF)]}{RF}}$$

where:

    n = sample size

    BV = book value

    TM = tolerable misstatement

    EM = expected misstatement

    EF = expansion factor (adjusting the expected misstatement for the risk of incorrect acceptance)

    RF = reliability factor based upon the Poisson distribution (see Chapter 2) combined with the internal auditor's specified risk of incorrect acceptance

For example, the auditor is examining accounts receivable with a total of $3,500,000. Following discussions with management, the maximum tolerable misstatement is $150,000 with an expected misstatement of $30,000. This would give a tolerable misstatement of 4% ($150,000/$3,500,000) and an expected misstatement of 1% ($30,000/$3,500,000). If the auditor is working to a confidence level of 95% given the reliability factor of 3.0 (see Table 3.1), the risk of incorrect acceptance would be 5%, which would give an expansion factor of 1.6 (see Table 3.2)

$$n = \frac{\dfrac{\$3,500,000}{[\$150,000 - (\$30,000 \times 1.6)]}}{3.0}$$

Table 3.1 Reliability Factors for Overstatement and Understatement Errors

NUMBER OF OVER- OR UNDERSTATEMENT ERRORS	5% RISK OF INCORRECT ACCEPTANCE		10% RISK OF INCORRECT ACCEPTANCE	
	RELIABILITY FACTOR	INCREMENTAL FACTOR	RELIABILITY FACTOR	INCREMENTAL FACTOR
0	3.00	0.00	2.31	0.00
1	4.75	1.75	3.89	1.58
2	6.30	1.55	5.33	1.44
3	7.76	1.46	6.69	1.36
4	9.16	1.40	8.00	1.31
5	10.52	1.36	9.28	1.29
6	11.85	1.35	10.54	1.26

Table 3.2   Expansion Factors for Expected Errors

RISK OF INCORRECT ACCEPTANCE	EXPANSION FACTOR
1.00	1.90
5.00	1.60
10.00	1.50

The sample size would therefore be 102.94 rounded up once again to give 103. In the population of $3,500,000, this would give a sampling interval of $33,980.58.

The incremental change indicated above reflects the difference between the reliability factor for the current number of errors and reliability factor for the previous number of errors.

Selecting the Sample

Extracting the list of invoices and accumulating their values would give us Table 3.3.

The auditor then selects a random number between one and a sampling interval of $33,980.58, for example, 5,000, as the random start position, and the customer account containing the 5,000th dollar is selected for testing. In this case, Alpha Inc. with a balance of $5,320.00 would be selected. The next customer to be selected would be the customer account containing the 38,980.58th dollar (5,000 plus 33,980.58)—in this case, Smith and Co. The next customer account would be that containing the 72,961.16th dollar (38,980.58 plus

Table 3.3   Example of Probability Proportional to Size Sample Selection

CUSTOMER NUMBER	CUSTOMER	ACCOUNT VALUE ($)	CUMULATIVE VALUE
1	Alpha Inc.	5,320.00	5,320.00
2	Beta Corp.	16,394.00	21,714.00
3	Smith and Co.	25,222.00	46,936.00
4	Jones Inc.	8,967.00	55,903.00
5	Amer Ink Inc.	29,234.00	85,137.00
6	UK Ltd.	12,189.00	97,326.00
7	Anglo Alpha	13,314.00	110,640.00
8	Betta Brand	21,299.00	131,939.00
9	Even Betta Inc.	32,000.00	163,939.00
10	Not So Good Int.	15,167.00	179,106.00
3,421	Last One Inc.	15,281.00	3,500,000.00

33,980.58), which is Amer Ink Inc., and so on until all 103 accounts have been selected for testing. As can be seen from this example, the advantage of this approach is that, while each dollar in the population as a whole has an equal chance of being selected, larger accounts have a higher chance of falling into the sample selected. Effectively, Jones Inc. has 8,967 chances of being selected, and Even Betta Inc. has 32,000 chances. From an audit perspective, this means that large value accounts have a greater chance of being selected for examination. Obviously, this selection method is ideal for seeking overstatements of accounts but will be biased against understatements. As such, variables sampling would be a more appropriate sampling method when seeking under-valuations. Accounts with a value greater than the sampling interval are guaranteed to be selected with this method. As can be seen, there is then the possibility that high-value accounts may be selected more than once. If this occurs, the account is selected once only, and the number of accounts to be examined may be less than the computed sample size.

Interpreting the Results

Any errors detected in the sample must then be projected to the population as a whole. This is referred to as the *projected misstatement*. The auditor then will calculate an allowance for sampling risk and add it to the projected misstatement, giving an *upper limit on misstatement* (ULM). If no misstatements were detected in the sample, the projection would be $0 plus an allowance for sampling risk, which would be taken as the *basic precision*. In the example above, given that no errors were found, the auditor would calculate the upper limit on misstatement by multiplying the reliability factor for the risk of incorrect acceptance by the sampling interval. The *basic precision* would therefore be 3.0 × $33,980.58 or $101,941.74. That is to say, at a 95% confidence level, having found no errors, the upper limit on misstatement (ULM) for the population as a whole could be as high as $101,941.74.

If a misstatement was found, for example, Smith and Co. was found to be overstated by $2,165, a *tainting factor* would be calculated, which is the book value minus the audit value divided by the book value or (25,222 − 23,057)/25,222, which would come to a tainting factor of 9%. The projected misstatement for the account would then be the sampling interval ($33,980.58) multiplied by the tainting factor (9%) or $3,058.25. In this case, the allowance for sampling risk is calculated by multiplying the projected misstatement by the incremental change in the reliability factor for a single error at 1.75 (see Table 3.1 above) giving a projected misstatement plus the allowance for sampling risk of $5,351.94. Adding the basic precision (3.0 × $33,980.58) would give a ULM of $107,293.68. In this case, because the ULM is lower than the maximum tolerable error, the auditor should conclude that, at the 95% confidence level, the error in the population as a whole does not exceed $150,000.

In the event that there is more than one error, the errors would be listed in descending order of the tainting factor, and the appropriate incremental changes for the individual errors would be applied.

Nonparametric Testing

Nonparametric statistics are used for the auditor who is required to evaluate data of "low quality," such as from small samples or on variables regarding which the auditor has no information, such as its distribution. Nonparametric sampling does not rely on the estimation of parameters, such as the standard deviation or the mean.

When the auditor seeks to determine differences between *independent groups*, tests such as the *Mann–Whitney U test*, the *Kolmogorov–Smirnov two-sample test*, or the *Wald–Wolfowitz runs test* would typically be used. When multiple groups are involved, the auditor may choose to use *analysis of variance* or *ANOVA*. The Kruskal-Wallis analysis of ranks would be a nonparametric equivalent. When the groups are *dependent*, for example, in order to compare two variables measured in the same sample, the auditor would usually use the *t test for dependent samples*. The nonparametric alternative would normally be the *Wilcoxon's matched pairs test* or *McNemar's chi-square test*.

Relationships between variables are normally computed using the correlation coefficient (see Chapter 4). Nonparametric versions of such testing could include the *Kendall tau* or *Spearman R* as well as the *Gamma coefficients*.

Each of these testing procedures has its own unique requirements but also its own drawbacks. Because nonparametric tests are primarily geared toward small sample sizes and the auditor is normally working on large data sets, nonparametric testing is not included in detail within this book.

Confusing Judgmental and Statistical Sampling

One of the more common mistakes made in use of sampling is the confusion of the two approaches. When the auditor is using a judgmental approach and then attempting to express an opinion on a full population based on the results of the tests in the sample, the conclusions normally cannot be substantiated.

Judgmental sampling is, by its nature, non-statistical. Unfortunately, many auditors use their judgment in deciding the sample size and assume that by utilizing a random selection technique the whole sample will become statistically valid. This is incorrect. Regardless of the selection technique, the audit tests cannot be extrapolated to the population. Common non-statistical selection techniques include *judgmental selection* in which the auditor uses his or her judgment to place a bias on the sample based on their previous experience. For example, the auditor may choose to regard only items over a certain value or only areas in which there have been problems in the past. *Haphazard selection* is a technique in which the auditor samples avoid the introduction of a conscious bias but without following a structured selection methodology. Once again, due to its non-statistical nature, extrapolation of results to the population is unreliable and should be avoided.

Common Statistical Errors

A major form of statistical error comes from threats to the internal validity of the sampling. This may result from a selection bias or even auditor bias when the auditor transfers his or her expectation to the population in a manner that affects the performance for dependent variables.

The external validity of the population is commonly assumed, permitting findings to be generalized across populations, settings, and time. This may not be objectively valid and can lead to a non-representative sample.

Possibly the most common error in the conclusion phase of statistical sampling is the identification of the number of errors in the sample and using this as a straight extrapolation to the population. For example, assume that two errors found in a sample of 50 would mean a 4% error rate in the sample but NOT necessarily in the population as a whole. The meaning of the number of errors found in the sample will depend on the assumptions the auditor made in calculating the sample size. As in the PPS example above, the error rate in the population is dependent upon the number of errors found in the sample as well as the degree of confidence and the maximum tolerable error rate. In attributes sampling, when error rates are examined, the only valid conclusion the auditor can draw is that, at a given confidence level, based upon the number of errors found in the sample, the error rate in the population does or does not exceed the maximum tolerable error rate.

In variables sampling, once again, at a given confidence level, the auditor can only conclude that variable is within the desired precision interval or not.

4
PROBABILITY THEORY
IN DATA ANALYSIS

This chapter examines the fundamental principles of Bayesian probability theory. In general, this is a methodology used to try to clarify the relationship between theory and evidence. It attempts to demonstrate how the probability that the theory is true is affected by a new piece of evidence. This can be critical to auditors in drawing conclusions about large populations based upon small samples drawn.

Probability Definitions

Statistical analysis draws its origins from probability theory.

Generally, data may be divided into two main categories: observational/historic data and experimental data. These two classes are differentiated by the principle that experimental data results from processes that may be repeated and observational or historical data results from events that have already occurred and are by their nature non-repeatable. A third class of information is based on a combination of observation and information supplied by theory and is generally classed as hypothetical–observational data. From an audit perspective, data analysis will generally focus on observational/historical data. With the advent of computers, the ability to gather data has escalated to the extent at which our ability to examine data and draw conclusions based on the data entirety has become limited.

For many auditors, the terminology of probability theory appears to be a major barrier to understanding the subject. The jargon must be learned before the techniques can be put into full effect in implementing data analytics. This is particularly true given the multiplicity of ways it is possible to use statistical analysis badly. Although probability theory is critical for effective data analysis, deductive logic seeks to move from a cause to determine probable effects or outcomes.

Inductive logic or plausible reason seeks to move from observation of effects to determine possible causes.

Risk and uncertainty are factors that must be taken into account in all business decisions. These can commonly be expressed in terms of probability. Probability may be defined in its simplest terms as a chance of an event occurring. From a business perspective, the probability is a basic concept on which inferential statistics are based. Business predictions are based upon probability, and hypotheses are tested by using probability. Critical to the use of probability are five definitions:

- An *experiment* may be defined as an activity or a measurement resulting in an outcome.
- *Sample space* consists of all possible outcomes of a given experiment.
- An *event* consists of one or more outcomes of an experiment and may be taken to be a subset of the sample space.
- A *complementary event* is a set of outcomes in the sample space that are not included in the outcomes of the original event. For example, if a die is rolled, the sample space will contain the outcomes 1, 2, 3, 4, 5, and 6. The event E of getting even numbers consists of the outcomes 2, 4, and 6. The event of not getting an even number consists of outcomes 1, 3, and 5 and is known as the complement of the event E and is denoted by $\bar{E}$ (E bar).
- The *probability* itself is indicated by a number between zero and one expressing the likelihood that a given event will occur.

Classical Probability

The classical approach to probability theory describes the probability of an event occurring in terms of the proportion of times than an event can theoretically be expected to occur in terms of the total possible numbers of outcomes. Thus, the probability of a specific number coming up when a six-sided die is rolled would be one in six, given that there are six possible and equally likely outcomes.

This gives a classical probability formula:

$$P(E) = \frac{n(E)}{n(S)}$$

where

$P(E)$ = the probability of an outcome
$n(E)$ = the number of outcome events
$n(S)$ = the total number of outcomes in the sample space

Empirical Probability

This view of probabilities is common in evaluating probabilities in games of chance, but it has less applicability when the possible outcomes are not equally likely, and so the auditor will typically use the variation known as the *relative frequency* or *empirical probability* approach. The concept is fairly straightforward in that, with a sufficiently large population, the frequency that an event will occur over a large number of trials will come close to the probability of its occurrence in a single trial. If a coin is tossed once (a *probability experiment*), the *outcome* may be either heads or tails, and the relative frequency for either outcome could be either zero or one. If the coin is tossed a large number of times, the relative frequency of either occurrence within the *sample space* will approach 0.5. When multiple results are possible, the auditor would typically observe the frequency of the outcomes and use these to determine the probability of an outcome.

For example, customers may opt to pay for a given item by cash, check, or card. Within a file of payments, the auditor may analyze frequencies and determine that, in a population of 50,000 payments,

- 15,281 customers pay with cash
- 19,322 pay by check
- 15,397 pay by card

This gives the probabilities of payment by cash 31%, check 39%, and card 30%.

Subjective Probability

Subjective probability is a technique whereby the auditor will arrive at a probability value based upon his or her expertise to determine a probability value. As with non-statistical sampling, discussed in previous chapters, there is a place in audit work for the use of subjective probability. Its most common use is in applications when the auditor is dealing with inexact information, such as attempting to determine gross probabilities of future events without placing direct reliance on the results.

Probability Multiplication

When calculating the probability that at least one of several events will occur, probabilities are added together. In the case of the auditor sampling invoices from a population whose error rate is believed to be 0.02%, the probability that an individual invoice will be an error will also be 0.02%. When 10 invoices are selected, the probability that a single invoice would be in error would be 10 times 0.02 or 2%. This is referred to as *marginal probability.*

With the same error rate and sampling the same 10 items, the auditor would like to determine the likelihood of two errors in the sample. This would be an example of *joint probability* and is determined by multiplying the probability of the two events together thus, 0.02 × 0.02, giving a joint probability of 0.0004 that both will be in error.

Conditional Probability

There is a third potential and that is the *conditional probability* that an event will occur given that another event has already happened. In the example above, this could be seen as the probability of a second invoice being in error given that the first invoice has already been found to be in error. As can be seen in Diagram 4.1, when the events are independent, that is, one event will have no probability that another will occur, straight multiplication rules apply.

Events are classed as *dependent events* when the occurrence of one event changes the probability that the second will occur. In the above

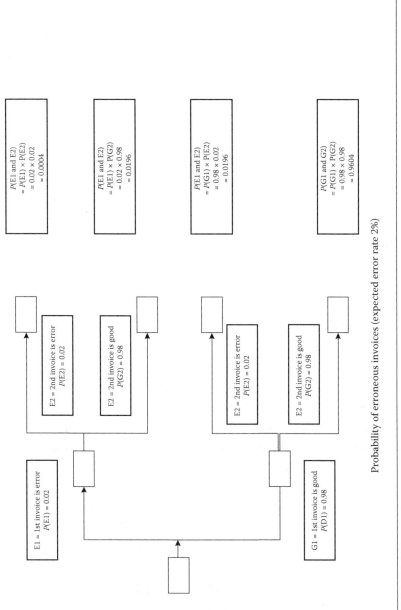

Diagram 4.1   Conditional probability example.

example, the invoices were selected and replaced into the population, giving each invoice an equal chance of being selected every time. In reality, the auditor normally samples without replacement, and therefore, the probability of a second erroneous invoice being selected is impacted by the fact that the population is shrinking by a factor of one after each selection. In large populations, the probabilistic impact of selecting without replacement is so low as to have a negligible impact on probability. When population sizes are low, however, the probability of a second selection being an error may increase significantly. For example, in a total population of 100 invoices, for example, in which the suspected error rate is also 2%, the likelihood of the first invoice selected being erroneous would be 2 in 100 (0.02%), but subsequent selections will be working with the probability of 2 in 99, 2 in 98 down, to 2 in 90 (0.0222) by the 10th selection, and this *degree of freedom* has to be taken into account in calculating overall probabilities.

Bayes' Theorem

In the 1700s, the Reverend Thomas Bayes postulated a theory that it was possible, given the outcome of the second event in a sequence of two events, to determine the probability of various possibilities for the first event. An example of this is that there exist two files, each containing both correct invoices and incorrect invoices. Each file contains 100 invoices. A file was chosen, and an invoice was selected. File A contains one erroneous invoice, and File B contains two erroneous invoices. In normal circumstances, the auditor would be seeking to discover whether the invoice selected was erroneous or not. In this case, an erroneous invoice was uncovered, and the auditor was tasked with discovering the probability that it came from File B.

- It is known that the probability of selecting file A is ½, and the probability of selecting file B is ½.
- It is further known that there are 100 invoices contained in File A with an anticipated error rate of 1% with a probability of selecting an erroneous invoice being 1 in 100.
- In File B, with its error rate of 2%, there is a probability of 2 in 100.

- The probability that the erroneous invoice was drawn from File A can be calculated as follows:

$$= \frac{\frac{1}{2} \times .02}{\left(\frac{1}{2} \times .01\right) + \left(\frac{1}{2} \times .02\right)} = \frac{.01}{.015} = 67\%$$

Use in Audit Risk Evaluation

The auditor's level of confidence in an audited account balance would therefore be represented by the probability that the balance is correct, conditional on the following:

- First being subject to internal controls
- Second being subject to substantive testing

Audit risk (AR) itself may be defined as the risk that the conclusions drawn from the audit process may themselves be invalid. This can arise from the conjunction of three separate risks:

- *Inherent risk* (IR) refers to the risks that occur in the nature of the business process. Such risks are typically evaluated without consideration of the mitigating factors introduced by appropriate internal controls. This is normally stated as $p(e)$.
- *Control risk* (CR) is generally accepted as being the risk that the auditee's internal control systems may *not* effectively detect and correct an error occurring because of an inherent risk. This is normally stated as $p(i\,|e)$.
- *Detection risk* (DR) is the risk that the auditor's test procedure may *not* reveal an uncorrected error. This is normally stated as $p(a|e,i)$.

Only when all three of these events occur in conjunction can audit risk be said to have occurred. Thus,

$$AR = IR \times CR \times DR$$

The Canadian Institute of Chartered Accountants defined "the overall audit risk"* as being the joint risk divided by the joint risk plus

---

* Canadian Institute of Chartered Accountants. 1980. *Extent of Audit Testing: A Research Study.*

the inherent confidence. That is to say that "joint risk" refers to joint probability $p(e, i, a)$ and inherent confidence is the probability of no inherent risk in the balance tested $\sim e = 1 - p(e)$. This is an example of a Bayesian model.

Other Uses

Bayes' theorem has also been used effectively in evaluating the overall effectiveness of control structures, particularly within computer systems. In a given system, for example, online purchase ordering, a single control, such as the use of purchase order numbers, may exist but only provide an 80% degree of assurance that missing purchase orders would be detected. Additional controls, such as confirmation of receipt by the vendor and end-of-week reconciliation, may provide additional controls to increase the overall confidence level that missing purchase orders would be detected in a timely manner to acceptable levels. The overall effectiveness using Bayes' theorem would therefore be derived as $E = 1 - ((1 - E1)^*(1 - E2)^*(1 - E3)...)$, where E equals the effectiveness of a single control.

Financial Auditing

In 2007, in a paper called "Data Mining Techniques for the Detection of Fraudulent Financial Statements,"* the authors evaluated three data mining techniques for their applicability in managing fraud detection in terms of their predictive accuracy:

- Decision trees
- Neural networks
- Bayesian belief networks

The input data is utilized in the form of financial ratios derived from financial statements taken from a variety of manufacturing companies. The study was carried out against the background of the

---

* Kirkos, E., Spathis, C., and Manolopoulos, Y. 2007. Data Mining Techniques for the Detection of Fraudulent Financial Statements. http://140.118.5.28/MIS_Notes/Lit_Data.Mining.Applc/2007-Data%20Mining%20techniques%20for%20the%20detection%20of%20fraudulent%20financial%20statements.pdf.

1997 Statement on Auditing Standards (SAS) 82 on Consideration of Fraud in a Financial Statement Audit.* The standard requires the assessment of fraud risk during every audit.

The study concluded that, used appropriately and coupled with the appropriate data mining algorithms, a Bayesian belief network could reveal dependencies between falsification and the ratios of debt to equity, net profit to total assets, sales to total assets, working capital to total assets, and z scores with over 90% accuracy.

Overstatement of Assets

A common problem for auditors is establishing an upper bound for total amount of overstatement of assets within a set of accounts. Confidence bounds are critical because audit interest naturally focuses on whether assets declared materially exceed the organization's actual assets. Monetary unit sampling as detailed in Chapter 3 and the assumption that the actual value never exceeds the book value lead to a problem of setting nonparametric upper confidence bounds on the meaning of the population using values between zero and one on the basis of a sample from the population. The traditional approach has been to use the Stringer bound nonparametric upper confidence bound for the total error amount in an accounting population when using monetary unit sampling.

Probability Distributions

A probability distribution may be taken to be a list of all possible outcomes and the associated probability of occurrence.

Probability distributions may be classified as *discrete* or *continuous*.

- *Discrete* probability distributions relate each value of a discrete random variable with its probability of occurrence. For example, if a coin is flipped twice, there are four possible outcomes:
  - Heads/heads
  - Heads/tails

---

* American Institute of Certified Public Accountants. *Consideration of Fraud in a Financial Statement Audit*: 1997 SAS 82. http://www.aicpa.org/Research/Standards /AuditAttest/DownloadableDocuments/AU-00316.pdf.

- Tails/heads
- Tails/tails

The probability of occurrence of heads would therefore be the following:

Zero heads   0.25
One head   0.50
Two heads   0.25

Because the above probabilities relate to the probability of occurrence of a discrete random variable, this represents a *discrete* probability distribution.

Two of the more common discreet probability functions, binomial and Poisson, as well as continuous probability distributions are discussed in depth in Chapter 2.

5

TYPES OF EVIDENCE

This chapter examines the various types of evidence available to the auditor in order to evaluate both the adequacy and effectiveness of the system of internal controls. This includes the identification of population types and the division into subpopulations for analytic purposes. Differing collection types and evidence sources are also identified.

Influencing Factors

Audit evidence may be broadly defined as all of the evidence required by the auditor in order to arrive at conclusions that then form the basis for the audit opinion. It is not necessary for auditors to examine every piece of information, but audit evidence itself is cumulative in nature and will include evidence obtained from multiple sources, such as results of previous audits as well as discussions with auditees and management. In addition, this includes evidence drawn from minutes of meetings, confirmations from third parties, benchmarking results, and evidence as well as information derived from audit procedures, such as observation, inspection, and inquiry.

The types of audit evidence are normally classified as evidence derived from the following:

- Inspection

    This involves the physical examination of the tangible asset, such as inventory, as well as the inspection of records and documents in paper or electronic form. Certain of these documents may represent direct audit evidence of the existence of an asset but not necessarily the ownership or value. Again, the auditor may know of the existence of the asset but have insufficient skill personally to determine the appropriateness, condition, and value of that asset. Should this occur, the auditor may be obliged to seek additional expertise.

- Observation

   This may include observation of activities within the client's business, such as work or procedures being carried out. Although this is commonly used as audit evidence, it should always be borne in mind that the evidence provided is at a point in time and may be influenced by the fact that the observation is taking place.

- Documentation

   This includes both internal and external documents and records.

- Confirmation

   Confirmation is normally related to the existence and value of assets, such as accounts receivable, cash in bank, or liabilities declared, such as accounts payable, mortgages payable, etc. In addition, confirmation of declared information, such as contingent liabilities, existence of collaterals, or even insurance coverage may be included.

- Inquiry

   This involves the seeking of information from knowledgeable persons within the organization or external to it. Evidence in this case may come in the form of oral responses to direct questions or written responses either to questions or questionnaires. Inquiry continues throughout the course of the audit and a critical component is the evaluation of responses.

- Analytical procedures

   Choice of the appropriate analytical procedures involves an understanding of the client's industry as well as their position within that industry. The auditor will seek to determine the presence or extent of any possible misstatements in the financial records of the organization as well as to assess the organization's ability to continue as a going concern. The analytical procedures may be conducted for a variety of purposes, including *risk assessment*, allowing the auditor to focus on areas of higher corporate risk in order to determine the extent, timing, and nature of the appropriate audit procedures to be carried out. Analysis may form a significant part of substantive testing, seeking evidence of errors or misstatements, and may also be used in evaluating the overall conclusion reached by the auditor.

- Recalculation

    This involves the use of the appropriate analytical procedures to ensure the calculations made by the client are accurate and complete.

- Re-performance

    Once again, analytical procedures will be involved in order to ensure the accuracy and completeness of the client's own accounting procedures and record keeping. Recalculation can provide a high level of assurance regarding arithmetic accuracy within the client's record keeping. Such a performance may be conducted manually or more commonly using computer-assisted audit techniques (CAATs).

These last three classifications involve the types of evidence most commonly subjected to analytical procedures although all may be subject to some form of analysis.

Overall, the auditor will plan and perform appropriate procedures in order to obtain evidence that is sufficient to provide a reasonable basis for his or her conclusions and appropriate to achieve the audit objectives.

Quantity Required

The actual quantity of evidence required is largely determined by the risk of material misstatement. The larger that risk, the greater the quantity of evidence the auditor would require to maintain an appropriate degree of confidence.

The quantity of evidence required is also impacted by the quality of evidence obtained. When the quality of evidence is high—that is, it can be readily relied upon—the need for additional corroboration will decrease. Unfortunately, when the quality of evidence is low, obtaining more evidence of a similar quality will not lead to evidence sufficiency.

Reliability of Evidence

The reliability of the evidence derived will depend, to a large extent, on the source of the evidence as well as the circumstances under which it is derived. Auditors will generally give greater credence to evidence that is derived independently of the organization rather than evidence solely derived internally. When evidence is available only from within the organization, the reliability will obviously be affected by the quality of the organization's internal controls. The reliability of internally produced evidence is also affected by the auditor's belief in the effectiveness of internal controls—whether this comes from the auditor's own direct knowledge or from the results of previous audit examination. Reliability of evidence may also be influenced by the timeliness with which the evidence is obtained.

When audit evidence obtained from a particular source appears inconsistent with other evidence obtained or the auditor has reason to doubt the authenticity of reliability of such evidence, additional audit procedures may be required to resolve the differences in order to ensure sufficiency of evidence for the conclusions reached.

Taking into consideration the intent to produce sufficient evidence, the auditor must also take into consideration the overall cost of obtaining such evidence. The cost of deriving evidence should not be used as an excuse for omitting a procedure when there is no alternative available at a lower cost.

Relevance of Evidence

Evidence obtained by the auditor, in whichever form, should be deliberately sought with the use of the appropriate audit procedures in order to specifically test a given control or assertion made by the client. Occasionally, the auditor will come across such evidence by accident, but this should be the exception rather than the rule. It will fall upon the auditor's professional judgment to ensure the evidence sought and obtained is appropriate, and a degree of professional skepticism is always required in evaluating the relevance, sufficiency, and appropriateness of the evidence upon which the audit opinion will be based.

Management Assertions

The responsibility rests with management to ensure fair presentation of all financial statements and other records, reflecting the operations of the organization. As such, management makes assertions regarding the accuracy, completeness, presentation, and disclosure of such information. Such assertions may be used by the auditor to form a preliminary judgment regarding entity risk and the potential for misstatements that may occur. This judgment may direct the initial analyses to be carried out for each class of transaction or record balance. The auditor must therefore evaluate the nature and reliability of assertions made, volumes of data, or transactions related to the assertion as well as the use of information technology controlling the information supporting management's assertions.

Audit Procedures

Generally, the auditor will start with an initial risk assessment procedure to determine the risks of material misstatement within assertions and records. This assessment is not intended to provide a basis for the audit opinion, but forms the basis on which further audit procedures will be required to test the operating effectiveness of the system of internal control and substantive audit testing procedures. When the initial risk assessment indicates a potential for poor operational effectiveness of controls, the auditor will design the audit procedures in order to seek evidence regarding the past, current, and anticipated future effectiveness of the controls. Should the evidence indicate that, indeed, the controls being relied upon are operating at poor levels of effectiveness, the auditor may seek other sources of evidence to indicate the actual level of effectiveness of the system of internal controls.

The nature of the audit procedures may, to a certain extent, be impacted by the nature of the records to be examined. In a modern corporate environment, original source documents, such as invoices, checks, purchase orders, and the like, may no longer be available in hard copy form. Transactional evidence may exist only in electronic form and will require scrutiny using the appropriate CAATs. Even when original source documents existed at some point in hard copy, use of image processing systems facilitates the scanning of such documents into electronic images for storage and reference. This form of evidence may only exist temporarily, and the auditor must examine the retention policies to ensure adequate information is available for review.

Chapter 10 covers the use of computer-assisted audit tools in more detail.

Documenting the Audit Evidence

In line with the *Standards for the Professional Practice of Internal Auditing* (Institute of Internal Auditors or IIA) and *Generally Accepted Auditing Standards*, "working papers" is the generic name given to the documents that are prepared throughout the auditing process. Working papers should reflect clearly the extent of the auditor's examination and the methods of verification used and contain sufficient evidence to support the conclusions reached.

Working Papers

Working papers should promote efficiency in the planning and performing of individual assignments throughout the current audit as well as for subsequent audits or reviews. They serve as a reference guide for information, notations, quantitative data, etc., and support all material contained in the report during and subsequent to the completion of the audit.

Working papers evidence the scope and depth of coverage of the examination, and supervisory and external auditors use working papers to help them assess and/or review the adequacy and quality of the work performed.

Working papers evidence the auditor's adherence to generally accepted auditing and IIA standards by documenting the planning and supervising of the audit, the procedures followed, the evidence obtained, and the conclusions reached.

The findings, recommendations, and statistics contained in the audit report must be supported in the working papers. They must stand on their own to the extent that a reviewer should be able to understand clearly the objective for each test as well as the conclusion reached without an oral explanation from the auditor.

Working Paper Types   Working papers for an audit are made up of two general types of files. The first type of file is the permanent file, which contains all the relevant information that may be of interest during future audits. The second type of file is the current file, which contains various schedules and documents prepared as the compliance and substantive audit procedures are completed. These current files contain a record of all of the audit work completed and any conclusions reached.

The term *working papers* thus refers to both the current year's audit documentation and the permanent file. The working papers represent a clear, self-contained record of the audit and should not require any supplemental oral explanation.

A good working paper technique is an essential element to the successful completion of any audit. Remember that all work will be reviewed by a number of people, some of whom will not be part of your organization (i.e., regulators and independent auditors). A reviewer should be able to easily understand all of the audit work performed and the conclusions drawn from this work.

These papers are used for a number of important functions:

- They demonstrate whether professional standards were adhered to during the audit.
- They aid in the organization, control, administration, and review of the audit work.
- They evidence the audit work performed and the conclusions drawn from that work.
- They show whether the reported data are in agreement or have been reconciled with the actual records.
- They provide the principal evidentiary support for the report issued about the audit performed.
- They record conclusions reached during the audit.

A high degree of consistency must be maintained when preparing the working papers in order to ensure their clarity and functionality.

Although all audit testing and audit findings must be adequately documented and supported in the working papers, the amount of actual supporting data requires judgment.

The factors that will affect the necessity for inclusion of specific data include the following:

- The type of audit being performed: A larger amount of detailed information should be included if the examination involves a potential fraud as opposed to a lesser amount of data for a routine audit.

- The type of findings encountered: A larger amount of detailed information should be included if the examination includes a million dollar receivable error as opposed to a lesser amount of data for a minor error in petty cash.
- The strength of the internal control system in place: A larger amount of detailed information should be included if the internal controls are found to be very weak and the auditor is unsure whether the system can catch all errors of omission and commission.
- The amount of supervision and review of the assistant's work necessary: If the auditor performing the audit is new or inexperienced, the lead auditor may ask for a greater amount of detailed data to ensure that the area has been covered adequately.
- The condition of the auditee's records: If the auditee's records are found to be unreliable, the auditor must gather and document more detailed information to support the audit findings.

There is no definitive guideline for the inclusion or exclusion of data; however, the above list may aid in the decision-making process and in preparing your working papers.

Contents of Permanent File

There is no standard organizational rule for the permanent files; however, the following types of documents should normally be included:

- Organization charts
- Description of business activities, systems, procedures, and business plan
- Key ratios, loss norms, etc.
- Latest corrective action plan
- Legal and regulatory issues impacting the business
- Risk assessment
- Deviations
- Other correspondence
- Updated audit program

Contents of Current File

Current working paper files should have a consistent organization and documentation irrespective of the type of audit.

The front of the file should display the business or department name, the nature of the audit (or the name of the audit), the names of the staff that participated, the as-of audit date, and the audit number. The number of files varies depending on the quantity of working papers prepared and the number of locations audited.

The current file contains a number of sections that will change from audit to audit:

1. Selection
2. Client background
3. Internal control descriptions
4. Audit program
5. Results of audit tests
6. Audit comment worksheets
7. Report planning worksheets
8. Copy of the audit report
9. Follow-up program
10. Follow-up of prior audit findings
11. Audit evaluation
12. Ongoing concerns
13. Administrative/correspondence

Selection

This section is used for documenting the audit selection planning. This is where the results of any risk assessment are recorded. All of the planning efforts and documents should be recorded in this section.

Client Background

This section contains the overall statement of the audit area's business and control objectives together with the principal control structures relied upon, the auditor's first impression of overall control, and the sources of information to be used in the audit.

Internal Control Descriptions

This section details, for each of the control objectives outlined in Section 2, the preventative, corrective, detective, and directive controls that management believe they have in place and rely upon.

Audit Program

This section contains the tailored and updated audit program. This is a schedule of the detailed testing to be carried out, which will document the work performed. These schedules should start from the control objectives in the internal control description, detail the steps to be carried out, and demonstrate logical support of audit conclusions.

This audit program is essential to all levels of corporate audit. It allows the audit manager an advance view of the planned scope of work and, at completion, a record of work performed. In fact, the audit program, together with the budget and the work schedule, documents corporate audit's accountability for the upcoming audit.

For the audit manager or in-charge auditor, it provides a means of communicating the necessary instructions to the audit staff and furnishes a sound basis for determining staffing requirements and budgeting man hours. It also serves as a checklist in reviewing the working papers and controlling the audit.

Finally, for the auditor, it serves as a means of becoming familiar with the assignment and furnishes the detailed plan of action for guiding and controlling the audit work.

Results of Audit Tests

This section contains a record of the actual audit work performed and the detailed results. Each procedure point in the audit program should be referenced to the appropriate working paper. By the time an audit is completed, you may have hundreds of sheets of paper containing the various data collected during the audit process. Proper cross-referencing is essential for the reviewer to find the details of the work performed for each audit procedure without having to go through all the working papers.

Audit Comment Worksheets

Detailed comments are written for each audit exception, finding, or control weakness encountered during the audit. Each finding must clearly and concisely enumerate the *condition* found, the *criteria* or standard that is supposed to be complied with, the *cause* expressed in terms of the absence of or failure of the appropriate control, and the *effect* expressed in terms of the impact on the business. In addition, the auditor records his or her opinion and recommendations.

By completing these as the audit progresses, the auditor will save valuable time when preparing to write the audit report.

Report Planning Worksheets

This section contains the worksheets used to plan the final audit report. The audit comment worksheets are collated to group together findings with common causes. These are then used to complete the report planning worksheets, allowing the auditor to produce, in outline format, the sections of the audit report. Sorting these planning worksheets into order of business priority will put the structure to the final audit report.

Copy of the Audit Report

This section contains the final report issued to the business being audited. This report is prepared according to the corporate audit report guidelines. It contains a brief description and/or background of the business, the scope of the audit, and the summary of the evaluation.

Follow-Up Program

This section contains the follow-up audit program. This is a schedule of the detailed testing to be carried out that will examine the results of any changes carried out as a result of the original audit. Care should be taken not to simply repeat the original audit.

Follow-Up of Prior Audit Findings

This is the section in which the auditor follows up on all prior audit exceptions. It includes a copy of the previous audit report and its exceptions. The file should note whether or not the exceptions found in previous audits have been cleared.

Audit Evaluation

This section is used to evaluate the audit process recording the positive features, the failures, and lessons to be carried forward into subsequent audits in this or other areas.

Ongoing Concerns

This section is used to record items of ongoing concern for future audits in this area, such as depreciation tables, long-term plans, or issues with ongoing impacts.

Administrative/Correspondence

This section contains all minutes of meetings together with administrative and/or correspondence memos and documents. It contains the following:

- Engagement memo
- Closing meeting memo/minutes

The audit engagement memo should be addressed to the business manager that you will be working with during the audit. This memo should be sent by the audit manager in order to explain your plans and reasons for conducting the audit. It includes the agreed upon scope and objectives of the audit together with the time scales.

This section also includes minutes summarizing the closing meeting where the audit report is discussed as well as the tick mark schedule.

General Standards of Completion

Cross-Referencing

Cross-referencing serves two useful purposes. First, it promotes accuracy in the preparation of working papers because it means that a member of the audit team has compared two findings and found them to be the same. Of more importance, however, is the second purpose. Many of the elements of operational and financial information that are considered during the audit are interrelated. Cross-referencing demonstrates that the audit team understands and has considered such interrelationships.

Tick Marks

Tick marks are numbers and letters that are marked on the schedules. These are used

- To tie a particular explanation to a specific item
- To tie a series of items to one explanation

Tick marks should always be letters or numbers and be written on the right of the item.

A useful standard is to ensure that numbers are used for remarks, notes, or where no errors are detected. Lettered explanations are used when errors are detected while performing the audit work or when the audit work cannot be completed as planned.

The typical tick marks (i.e., checkmarks, crosses) are not used to allow for consistency between manually prepared working papers and automated working papers generated using MS Word. Each tick mark should have a clear and precise explanation of what it represents. This explanation should include a verb describing what was done, an object on which the work was done, and when appropriate, a description of the results of the work.

Ticking an item means that the indicated work was completed. Thus, an item on a working paper should not be ticked until the work has been completed exactly as indicated in the tick mark explanation.

Tick mark explanations should be placed on the schedule. When the same tick marks will be used throughout a file, a standard tick mark sheet can be very helpful. The standard tick mark sheet should be placed in the administrative/correspondence section of the file and can be referred to whenever standard tick marks are used on a working paper.

Tick mark use can greatly reduce the need for lengthy explanations, thus saving time in doing and reviewing the audit work.

Notes

Notes are commonly used to describe the purpose, source, and scope of a test when the reason for the test is not obvious and/or not described by the audit program. They may also be used to describe work done relating to most or all the items on a schedule as described in the audit program or to describe work done on items not appearing on a schedule but relating to that schedule.

Notes should be placed in a conspicuous location so that the reviewer will read the notes when starting the review. As with all documentation, the information presented in the notes should be complete yet concise. You should be careful not to put too much or too little information in the notes. In the case of under-documentation, you would have to go back later and add information. This could lead to inefficiencies or possibly a duplication of efforts. In the case of over-documentation, time is spent on unnecessary information. Thus, you should not include details that are irrelevant or redundant.

Working Paper Review

Working paper review is part of the overall quality control process because it falls into the category of supervision. Just as business management must review the work performed by its department, the internal audit must internally review its own work.

The working papers generated from the audit will be subject to review.

Everything an auditor does in an audit must be properly substantiated. It is the audit supervisor's responsibility to thoroughly review all working papers in order to ensure that all of the audit team's work is verified and proven. When reviewing the working papers, the audit supervisor strives to ensure that audit program coverage is adequate to meet the audit objectives, the audit was expedited efficiently and utilizing the minimum resources, and that the working papers are in accordance with departmental and professional standards. If the audit work performed cannot be adequately supported by documentation, the work has been worthless because any opinion expressed is a personal opinion without substantiation.

When either an internal or external quality assurance review takes place, a selection of the working papers are used to verify that the overall effort of the audit team was effective.

General Review Considerations

The following is a list of questions an audit supervisor would consider while reviewing working papers:

- Does each working paper properly show the following:
  - Descriptive title?
  - The name of the business and area audited?
  - Appropriately descriptive column headings?
  - The date the working papers were prepared in the bottom center?
  - The auditor's initials in the bottom left-hand corner?
  - The appropriate and necessary indexing symbols?
  - A conclusion if necessary?
- Are all tick marks properly explained?
- Were all of the important calculations tested and checked by the auditors?
- Are all of the necessary cross-references included?
- Are all of the data sources included and thoroughly described in a manner that exactly represents the tests from start to finish?
- Are the data and the testing valid? Do they support all of the actions of the auditors? Do they support the conclusions reached by the auditor(s)?
- Is the method of selection indicated?
- Were computer-prepared retrievals and/or photocopies used (when practical) rather than handwritten copies? When used, did the auditor adequately support the reason for including the retrievals or copies? Was the schedule prepared in such a way that will prevent unnecessary repetition in future audits?
- When a schedule was prepared by an auditee, is it clearly indicated in the working papers?
- Were all unnecessary items removed from the working papers?
- Were all findings discussed with the appropriate individuals?

- Are the papers arranged in a logical sequence that follows the program?
- Are all of the program steps individually signed off and referenced to their respective points of origin? If an audit step was not performed, is it appropriately referenced to an explanation for the omission?
- Are the papers neatly prepared and in a logical format?

As a part of ongoing professional development as well as for quality purposes, it is critical that each auditor perform a self-review of all working papers produced. A thorough self-review enables other reviewers to concentrate on the true meaning of the audit findings rather than poor working paper technique.

A thorough working paper review is one of the most valuable tools available to auditors and helps to improve and strengthen their audit skills.

Working Paper Retention/Security

Working papers contain confidential information and should be accessed only by authorized personnel. Working papers must be secured during all phases of an audit and subsequent to an audit's completion.

Working papers must also be retained for specified periods of time so that they can assist with any subsequent audits or investigations. The length of retention should be determined in consultation with the appropriate corporate legal advisors and should be in line with other corporate vital record retention policies.

6

POPULATION ANALYSIS

This chapter examines the differences between the types of data and a given set of data as the standard benchmark in terms of central tendency, variation, and shape of a curve.

Types of Data

Data falls into different categories, such as *nominal, ordinal, interval,* and *ratio.*

- *Nominal data* refers to data of the discrete nature, such as the name of the country, a person's name, the name of a product, or similar information.
- *Ordinal data* refers to information that has a natural sequence of ordering, such as the finishing order in a race or items that have been evaluated on a rating scale of one to 10 (a Likert scale). Although ordinal data tends to be numeric and the temptation is to use it for arithmetic purposes, this is problematic because it is not possible to state with certainty that the interval values are equal. For example, runners in a race who come in first, second, and third will not normally come in at equal intervals. Similarly, when rating scales are used, the difference between two and three is not necessarily the same as the difference between eight and nine. In the same way, if the scale reads "hate, dislike, neither hate nor like, like, love," the difference between hate and dislike is not necessarily the same as the difference between like and love. Auditors in particular must take care when attempting to use ordinal data for arithmetic purposes. It is possible to convert ordinal data into interval data using a technique known as *correspondence analysis.*

- *Interval data* is similar to ordinal data with the difference that the intervals between each value are equal. The difference between $5 and $6 is the same as the difference between $120 and $121.
- *Ratio data* is a form of interval data with a natural zero. Elapsed time is an example of ratio data. In a race, all the athletes finish in a time measurable from the start, which is the zero base. Once again, the interval between each time will have the same degree of magnitude.

Correspondence Analysis

This technique is used to analyze tabular information when there is some measure of correspondence between the elements of two data sets, such as between rows and columns. This technique is well documented by Greenacre.* As an example, a population survey consisting of eight yes-or-no customer satisfaction questions is given to a sample of customers in a supermarket. The instructions on the survey allow the customers to answer only those questions that they want to. The results of the survey are tabulated as in Table 6.1.

As can be seen, many customers did not answer all the questions, making the response patterns difficult to analyze. The solution to the problem of differential response rates is to create a table of row percentages or *row profiles* as seen in Table 6.2.

Using Table 6.2, the patterns within the table become clear; for example, on Question 5, it can be seen that 96% of customers responded "yes," and on Question 1, only 32% answered "yes." This can then go on to be represented in graphical form as in Diagram 6.1.

Factor Analysis

With such survey questionnaires, the traditional statistical methods for analysis include frequency analysis, *t* tests, and measures of central tendency; however, an alternative designed to increase the number of insights gained is factor analysis. This procedure extracts a small

---

* Greenacre, M. J. (1993). *Correspondence Analysis in Practice*. San Diego, CA: Academic Press.

Table 6.1 Customer Satisfaction Survey Results—Counts

QUESTION	YES	NO	TOTAL
Q1	155	322	477
Q2	119	23	142
Q3	256	137	393
Q4	261	34	295
Q5	402	17	419
Q6	231	176	407
Q7	332	82	414
Q8	125	235	360

Table 6.2 Customer Satisfaction Survey Results—Percent

QUESTION	YES	NO	TOTAL
Q1	32.49	67.51	100
Q2	83.8	16.2	100
Q3	65.14	34.86	100
Q4	88.47	11.53	100
Q5	95.94	4.06	100
Q6	56.76	43.24	100
Q7	80.19	19.81	100
Q8	34.72	65.28	100

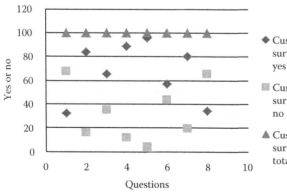

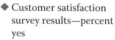

◆ Customer satisfaction survey results—percent yes

▧ Customer satisfaction survey results—percent no

▲ Customer satisfaction survey results—percent total

Diagram 6.1 Graphical representation: customer satisfaction.

number of latent variables or *constructs* from among a larger set of observed variables. The overall objective is to identify underlying relationships in variables so that appropriate management decisions may be made. Factor analysis encompasses a book in its own right, and Kim and Mueller's* work in this area may be seen as definitive.

Populations

In conducting data analysis, the auditor must be in a position to clearly define the population he or she is dealing with. The population distribution will be made up of all of the individual classes or values of variables upon which the auditor will express an opinion, and the distribution is a statement regarding the frequency with which the units may be observed within each of those classes. Generally, the auditor will be concerned with three different types of distribution, namely, the *population* distribution, the *sample* distribution, and the *sampling* distribution.

- *Population distribution:* The population distribution consists of all the classes or values of the variables under examination contained within the population.
- *Sample distribution:* Given that the sample is a subset of all the individual units in the population, the sample distribution indicates a frequency with which the classes or values of the variables occur within the sample itself.
- *Sampling distribution:* This is made up of values of statistics calculated from a number of sample distributions. It differs from the sample distribution in that the sampling distribution refers to the scores or values within the population of the sample, and the sampling distribution can be derived after repeated samples are taken.

   The auditor's sample taken is just one of an infinite number of samples that we could have taken. Taking into account the sampling distribution, the auditor may expect that, although the statistic we got from our sample is probably near the center of the sampling distribution, he or she could have gotten a

---

* Kim, J. O., and Mueller, C. W. (1978). *Factor Analysis: Statistical Methods and Practical Issues*. Beverly Hills, CA: Sage Publications.

sample including one or more of the extreme values by chance. If this were assessed as the average of the sampling distribution, that is, the average over an infinite number of samples, the sample average would be much closer to the true population average. Sampling distributions are commonly used to construct sampling distributions of means.

As discussed in Chapter 2, measurements of central tendency and dispersion can be derived in order to characterize the distribution of the entire population using measures, such as the mean, medium, mode, standard deviation, and variance. Based upon these, a sample may be drawn in a manner designed to adequately represent the whole population at a given confidence level.

Sampling distributions of means allow auditors to draw conclusions about sampling errors as well as giving insights into probability and facilitating the testing of hypotheses.

Sampling Error

Obviously, when working on a sample, there are no guarantees that the sample itself will be 100% representative of the population. Characteristics of the population as a whole and characteristics of the sample may differ, and this is known as *sampling error*. When multiple samples are taken, the sampling distribution that results is also the distribution of the amounts of sampling error encountered by the auditor.

The difference between the sampling distributions for the mean and for variance illustrate two things: first, all sampling distributions are not identical; second, we have to know the "shape" (actually, the mathematical formula) of the sampling distribution so that we can see if it is biased and to correct for any bias that is present. The sampling variance and the standard error are measurements of the dispersion around the mean of the sampling distribution. In the case in which sampling error amounts are small, the sampling statistics would be similar to each other although not identical. In essence, they would be similar to the population parameter. As this sampling error increases, the differences between the individual sample statistics and the overall population will increase with the sampling variance and standard error also increasing.

In general, the larger the variance in the population, the larger the sampling error will be. When the population distribution shows a small variance, the majority of the population will cluster around the population mean. Samples selected randomly from this population will favor items close to the population mean, and there will be little sampling error. Where the population is more dispersed, sampling error will increase.

One of the major factors influencing sampling error is the size of the sample to be drawn from the overall population. The greater the sample size, the smaller the sampling error because the greater the sample size, the closer the sample is to the actual population itself.

Central Tendency

As discussed in Chapter 2, the central tendency involves the derivation of the "middle" value of the population and is normally calculated using the *mean*, *median*, and *mode*.

- *Mean* is the auditors' most commonly used measurement of central tendency. The mean is the arithmetic sum of the values divided by the total number of items in the population. It is frequently referred to as the *arithmetic mean*. In statistical terms, this is frequently referred to as μ. Because the calculation of the arithmetic mean utilizes all values in the population, it can be influenced by values that are at the extreme ends of the data set. For example, in a population consisting of 10, 15, 17, 28, and 80, the mean would be the sum of those numbers divided by the quantity of numbers, $150/5 = 30$.

  The mean is, perhaps, the most popular measure in business. It has the advantage of being unique, that is, there's only one answer. Its disadvantage lies in the fact that it can be affected by extreme values of the high or low end of the distribution (outliers).
- *Median* is arrived at by sorting the population into values from lowest to highest and taking the value that is in the middle of the sequence. With the same population consisting of 10, 15, 17, 28, and 80, the median would be 17. If there are an even number of items in the population, there is no single point in

the middle, and the median is calculated by taking the mean average of the middle two points in the distribution.

The median is commonly used when there are believed to be extreme values that could significantly impact the mean and distort the "typical" distribution because the median is not influenced by outliers at the extremes of the data set.

As with the mean, there is only one answer.

- *Mode* represents the most frequently occurring value in a data set. Depending on the nature of the data set, it is possible to have multiple modes. Modes can also be useful when dealing with nominal data. For example, if analysis were done on individuals' names, the mode would represent the most popular name. The mode may also be used with interval and ratio data.

  The mode is most commonly used from data that is non-numeric. Again it is unaffected by outliers. When no values repeat within the population, the mode equals every value and is useless for audit purposes.

These measurements of central tendency are not the only such measurement indicators. Measurements such as the *geometric mean, truncated mean*, and *Windsorized mean* may also be used as indicators of central tendency although they are less useful in an audit situation.

Variation

Standard notation and calculation population variability include the following:

- σ^2: Variance of the population
- σ: Standard deviation of the population
- s^2: Variance of the sample
- s: Standard deviation of the sample
- μ: Population mean
- $\ddot{x}$: Sample mean
- N: Number of observations in the population
- n: Number of observations in the sample
- P: Proportion of elements in the population that has a particular attribute

- p: Proportion of elements in the sample that has a particular attribute
- Q: Proportion of elements in the population that does not have a specified attribute—note that $Q = 1 - P$
- q: Proportion of elements in the sample that does not have a specified attribute—note that $q = 1 - p$

Within the population of any data set, three popular measures that are used to quantify the degree of variation include the *range*, the *variance*, and the *standard deviation*.

- *Range* is determined by the difference between the biggest and the smallest random variable, thus range = maximum value − minimum value. For example, the range of five variables (2, 6, 7, 7, and 8) would be $8 - 2 = 6$.
- *Variance of the mean* is determined by calculating the average squared deviation from the mean. In this case, it is important to differentiate between the variance of the population mean and the variance of the sample mean.

  These are calculated using slightly different formulas. The variance of the population mean uses the formula

$$\sigma^2 = \Sigma(X_i - \mu)^2 / N$$

  where σ^2 is the population variance, μ is the population mean, X_i is the ith element from the population, and N is the number of elements in the population.

  Variance of the sample mean uses a different formula:

$$s^2 = \Sigma(x_i - \ddot{x})^2 / (n - 1)$$

  where s^2 is the sample variance, $\ddot{x}$ is the sample mean, x_i is the ith element from the sample, and n is the number of elements in the sample.

  When the auditor is using a simple random sample, the sample variance can be assumed to be an unbiased estimate of the true population variance.

For example, when the population consists of four data elements—1, 3, 6, and 8—and the auditor wishes to determine the variance, the first objective would be to determine the population mean, which, in this case, would be $(2 + 4 + 6 + 8)/4 = 5$. Once the population mean is known, it is simply a question of plugging the values into the formula:

$$\sigma^2 = \Sigma(X_i - \mu)^2/N$$

$$\sigma^2 = [(2-4)^2 + (4-4)^2 + (6-4)^2 + (8-4)^2]/4$$

$$\sigma^2 = [(-2)^2 + (0)^2 + (2)^2 + (4)^2]/4$$

$$\sigma^2 = [4+0+4+16]/4 = 24/4 = 6$$

If the items were a random sample rather than the full population, the same formula would be used.

- *Standard deviation* is a measurement that summarizes the amount by which every value within the data set, either population or sample, varies from the mean. It allows the auditor to determine how tightly the values are grouped around the mean value taking into consideration every variable in the data set. Where the values deviate from the mean due to chance, the distribution is classed as a *normal distribution*. This is commonly used to determine which proportion of values within the population lie within a particular range of the mean value as noted in Chapter 2.

  The standard deviation is taken as a square root of the variance. For audit purposes, it is commonly the population standard deviation that is used, although by using a different formula the standard deviation of the sample may also be determined. To determine the standard deviation population, the auditor would use the following formula:

$$\sigma = \sqrt{\sigma^2} = \sqrt{\frac{\sum(X_i - \mu)^2}{N}}$$

where σ is the population standard deviation, μ is the population mean, X_i is the ith element from the population, and N is the number of elements in the population.

Shape of Curve

For audit purposes, the shape of the curve indicates the shape of the probability distribution and may be classified as *bell-shaped* or *multimodal*. The shape is also affected by quantitative factors, such as skewness and kurtotis.

- *Bell-shaped* is also known as a *normal distribution* or a *Gaussian distribution*. The highest point in the curve represents the mean value in the population or sample. Values above and below the mean create the downward-sloping sides of the curve.
- *Rectangular distribution* is also known as a *continuous uniform distribution* and indicates a distribution that has constant probability.
- The shape is also affected by quantitative factors, such as skewness and kurtotis. Skewness is a measure of the degree of asymmetry of the population or sample distribution. If the distribution is skewed to the left as in Diagram 6.2, the distribution is said to have *negative skewness*. If the tail is to the right, the distribution is said to have a *positive skewness*. By knowing the way the data set is skewed, the auditors are in a better position to estimate whether future data points will be greater or less than the mean. Skewness is not restricted to normal distributions but may also be seen in a variety of

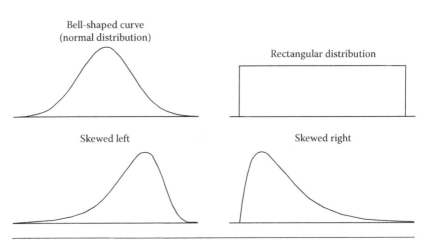

Diagram 6.2   Curve shapes.

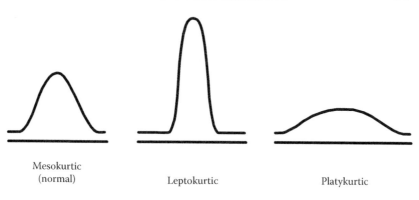

Mesokurtic
(normal)
                          Leptokurtic   Platykurtic

Diagram 6.3   Distribution kurtosis examples.

other distributions, such as Poisson distributions, Bernoulli distributions, and the like.*

• *Kurtosis* is generally used to describe trends in charts in terms of degrees of peakedness of distributions. A high kurtosis typically portrays a chart with a fat table and a low, even distribution, and a low Kurtosis would indicate a chart with skinny tables that are close to the mean. A normal distribution is seen as a *mesokurtic* distribution. A pure *leptokurtic* distribution has a higher peakedness than normal and typically has heavier tails, and a *platykurtic* distribution has a lower peak than normal and lighter tails. Examples of these may be seen in Diagram 6.3.

---

* Stuart, A., and Ord, J. K. (1998). *Kendall's Advanced Theory of Statistics, Vol. 1: Distribution Theory,* 6th ed. New York: Oxford University Press.

7

CORRELATIONS, REGRESSIONS, AND OTHER ANALYSES

This chapter examines the differences between correlations and regressions as well as the auditor's usage of both. It focuses on determination of the type of situation in which correlations and linear regressions may be deemed appropriate.

Quantitative Methods

In addition to statistical analysis, a variety of quantitative methods are also available to be selected by the internal auditor. These mathematical tools are commonly used to obtain an understanding of operations and permit the drawing of conclusions in a variety of circumstances through analyzing the complexities of situations. Of the many quantitative methods available to the auditor, the following sections examine the most commonly used.

Trend Analysis

Trend analysis is used to measure whether the data in a selected numeric field is showing an upward or downward trend over time and then to fit the best-fitting straight line to the data to forecast values into the future on the assumption that the trending pattern will continue.

Such analyses can serve as evaluation criteria to determine the reasonableness of fluctuations over an extended period. Comparisons of this year's turnover to last year's turnover or, alternatively, this month's turnover to the same month last year are popular.

Trend analysis helps management and audit understand how the business has performed and predict where current business operations and practices will take an operation. Overall, it can give the auditor indications about how recommendations might change things to move the organization in the right direction.

Trend analysis can be used to help improve the organization by

- Identifying areas where operations are performing well so the success may be duplicated
- Identifying areas where operations are underperforming and remedial action should be undertaken
- Providing evidence to inform and substantiate audit recommendations

In choosing data on which to conduct trend analysis, it is often useful for the auditor to examine the organization's key performance indicators (KPIs) in order to determine the factors that drive the achievement of organizational objectives. Financial as well as operational trends will typically have a direct impact on organizational performance.

Effective trend analysis is a three-stage process involving the following:

- *Analysis preparation*—This involves the auditor determining which data will give the greatest confidence regarding operational performance.
- *Deciding the threshold*—The auditor, in conjunction with management, must decide the level at which a variation becomes significant. For example, over a period of time, an increase in sales that exceeds industry trends or alternatively a decrease in profitability over the same period may indicate the need for further investigation.
- *Root cause analysis*—This would then be required to determine why the variations occurred to provide a direction for future improvements.

Analyzing trends in specific key performance areas and at times of peak activity may be appropriate using the appropriate CAATs. At all times, the auditor must keep in mind the limitations of trend analysis. For example, if the business environment changes significantly, historical data may not give the best indicator of future trends.

Additionally, not all influencing factors may be recognized during conventional trend analysis. Analyzing a single trend rarely yields conclusive results, but when combined with other business observations and analytical techniques, it can be a powerful audit tool.

Chi-Squared Tests

Chi-squared analyses are *nonparametric tests* capable of analyzing relationships between qualitative data. For example, do operating units in the South have particular patterns of operation different from those in the North?

Chi-squared tests can check for the independence of normal classifications and ordinal data and require no particular distributional pattern for the data. To perform a chi-squared test (or any other statistical test), the auditor must first establish his or her *null hypothesis*. For a simple coin toss example, the null hypothesis is that the coin is equally likely to land heads up or tails up every time. The null hypothesis allows the auditor to state expected frequencies. In reality, this is unlikely to be the case. If the auditor examines actual occurrences, it will be seen that the observed occurrences will differ from the expected occurrences, based on our null hypothesis.

The chi-squared test is a way to determine if a frequency distribution differs from the expected distribution. To use this chi-squared test, the auditor must first calculate chi squared:

$$\text{chi squared} = (\text{observed} - \text{expected})^2 / (\text{expected})$$

The auditor will then consult a table of critical values of the chi-squared distribution in order to determine whether the deviations are normal or indicate an abnormality in the distribution.

Multiple versions of the chi-squared test exist with *Pearson's chi-squared test* perhaps being the most commonly used. This test is also known as the chi-squared goodness-of-fit test or chi-squared test for independence. When the chi-squared test is mentioned without any modifiers or without other precluding context, this test is often meant.

The *chi-squared test for independence* is applied when the auditor has two categorical variables from a single population. It is used to determine whether there is a significant association between the two variables.

Correspondence Analysis

Correspondence analysis is a technique for graphically displaying a two-way table by calculating coordinates representing its rows and columns.* These coordinates are analogous to factors in a principal components analysis (used for continuous data) except that they partition the chi-squared value used in testing independence instead of the total variance.

Oppenheim (p. 120)† defines attitude scales as consisting of "half-a-dozen to two dozen or more attitude statements, with which the respondent is asked to agree or disagree."

This is commonly used when a Likert scale has been used (see Chapter 6) with evaluations of strongly agree, agree, neither agree nor disagree, disagree and strongly disagree. These evaluations are normally arbitrarily allocated the numerical values of one to five. Because these scales do not behave in a linear fashion and "the scale offers no metric or interval measures" (Oppenheim), the data would need to be rescaled using *correspondence analysis* to determine both the *Eigenvalue* and the *Euclidean distance* in order to convert the scale from ordinal to interval data ranging from one to five. This technique enables subsequent statistical manipulation and statistically valid interpretation of inherently ordinal data. Diagram 7.1 indicates the results of conducting correspondence analysis on a Likert scale within a questionnaire. It is interesting to note that the interval scale derived from this process varied so strongly across the industry sectors while the "other" sector saw no apparent difference between "strongly agree" and "neutral."

Cluster Analysis

Data can also be subjected to hierarchical cluster analysis techniques using dendograms in order to determine the significant groupings of factors.

In addition, nonhierarchical cluster analysis using k-means cluster analysis on the data can be carried out as a confirmation.

---

* Greenacre, M. J. (1993). *Correspondence Analysis in Practice*. San Diego, CA: Academic Press.
† Oppenheim, A. N. (1966). *Questionnaire Design and Attitude Measurement*. London: Heinemann.

Rescaling of a five-point Likert scale to interval data by industry sector

Likert Scale	Notional	Finance	Mining	Insur.	Retail	Manuf.	Service	Other	Ext prv	Mgmt.	Mean
Strongly agree	1	1	1	1	1	1	1	1	1	1	1
Agree	2	2.15	1.22	1.56	1.22	1.68	2.53	1	1.25	1.97	2.38
Neutral	3	3.11	2.01	2.11	1.85	3.08	3.61	1	1.57	2.56	3.32
Disagree	4	3.73	2.77	3.46	2.36	4.05	4.71	3	2.44	4.17	4.82
Stongly disagree	5	5	5	5	5	5	5	5	5	5	5

Diagram 7.1 Likert rescaling.

This double check is normally carried out due to the known disadvantages of hierarchical methods, namely the substantial impact of outliers. The number of clusters would be determined and matched to that of the correspondence analysis.

Graphical Analysis

Graphical analysis can be useful to the internal auditor in identifying interrelationships in data, anomalies, and simple data errors.

A common form of graphical representation used by the auditor is a *scatter diagram*, which refers to any graph of data points. The more discernible a pattern appears in the graph, the more likely one variable is related to another and therefore can be used to predict the other's value. Where no pattern can be noted, there would appear to be little, if any, correlation between the two variables.

Where a strong correlation exists, either positive or negative, the correlation value will approach one. Where little correlation exists, the correlation value will approach zero. Unfortunately, correlation values only measure linear patterns. Where there is a nonlinear relationship, correlation statistics will not disclose this.

Correlation Analysis

The measurement of the extent of association of one variable with another is known as a correlation analysis. Two variables are said to be correlated when they move together in a detectable pattern. A direct correlation is said to exist when both variables increase or decrease at the same time although not necessarily by the same amount. For example, one would expect inventory to decrease as sales increased.

The direction of the relationship may be seen to be positive when high scores on one variable tend to be associated with high scores on the other variable. For example, it may be seen that an increase in student studying time may result in an increase in exam results. Conversely, a negative relationship can be seen when high scores on one variable may be associated with low scores on the other variable. For example, it may be seen that age-related diseases are lower in younger patients. There is also the possibility of a zero relationship in which the two variables can be seen to have no direct connection. An example in this area may be seen when increases in production costs may have no impact on sales in the marketplace.

Correlation analysis is used by internal auditors to identify those factors that appear to be related. An operational auditor, for example, may use correlation analysis to determine whether corporate performance is in line with industry standards by comparing the correlation of company costs of imported parts with the exchange rate fluctuations. Problems with how these statistics are computed, shortcomings in the internal auditor's understanding of the auditees' operations, or real inefficiencies or misstatements can be pinpointed through correlation analysis.

As previously noted, correlation is positive when there is a positive association between the variables. As an example, human height and weight have a positive association because people who are above average in height tend also to be above average in weight, although the reverse is not necessarily true. In this case, both the standardized height and the standardized weight are positive. At the same time, people who are below average in height also tend to have below-average weight. In this case, both standardized height and standardized weight are negative although, again, the correlation between weight and height will be different because people who are above and below average weight may or may not be above or below average height. In the same way, there may be a correlation between sunshine and the amount of ice cream consumed. In this case, there may be a causal relationship, that is, the more sunshine there is, the more ice cream may be consumed. There may also exist a reverse relationship in which eating more ice cream may indicate that there is more sunshine, although the eating will not cause the sunshine.

The variable that causes the change in this case is sunshine, and it is called the *independent variable*. The variable that changes, in this case ice cream consumption, is called the *dependent variable*. Variables other than the independent variable may also have an effect on the dependent variable, and these are referred to as *relevant variables*. In using correlation analysis, the auditor must be aware of the danger that two or more variables may seem to be connected to another variable called a *spurious variable*. A spurious relationship is an apparently true yet actually false or misleading relationship that is caused by a third variable that is related to both the independent and dependent

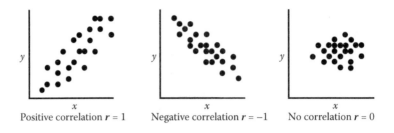

Diagram 7.2   Correlation examples.

variables. That third variable causes the independent and dependent variables to vary together so that the independent variable only seems to cause the dependent variable to change. Introducing control variables that are related to both the independent and dependent variables may be used to investigate possible confounding relationships; in essence, it would mean that the control variable changes what we originally thought to be true.

The Pearson correlation (r) is a parametric measure of the correlation coefficient and is always between 1 and –1. The strength of the linear relationship increases as r moves away from 0 toward either 1 or –1 while values near 0 indicate a very weak linear relationship.

Values of close to 1 or –1 indicate that the points in a scatterplot lie close to a straight line. The extreme values 1 and –1 occur only in the case of a perfect linear relationship, when the points lie exactly along a straight line. Occasionally, the correlation value can be distorted by a single data point not conforming to the general pattern. Although this may be readily seen on a graph, it may be less obvious in examining the correlation value (see Diagram 7.2).

Correlation may be used to measure the strength of only a linear relationship between two variables. Correlation does not describe curved relationships between variables, no matter how strong they are.

Audit Use of Correlation Analysis

A common area for audit use of correlations may be found in performance auditing. Measuring production efficiency may be a critical business metric used by management or audit to gauge overall production trends and monitor the business performance relative to the resources invested in production. Production efficiency may be regarded as an expression of the relationship between resources used and the respective result. In auditing, this is where identifying how production processes in a business currently operate can also lead to identifying efficiencies that save money and improve productivity. When patterns show that use of a particular material drives up costs of production, the correlation can lead auditors to recommend that managers attempt to identify substitute supplies that could potentially lower manufacturing costs. In the same way, using correlation analysis to model employee behavior may indicate that the implementation of a bonus-pay-for-improvement system could improve overall production. The correlation could allow the quantification of the production improvement required to make such an additional payment cost-effective.

Problems with correlation lie principally in that the correlation coefficient does not imply causality—that is, although it may show that two variables are strongly correlated, it need not mean that they are responsible for each other. In addition, if the relationship is not linear, then the result is inaccurate.

Learning Curves

In conducting operational audits of performance levels of the implementation of new procedures for the quality of training of new staff, a learning curve would normally be expected to be observed. As employees gain experience with the new procedures or as the new employee becomes more experienced, the length of time taken to accomplish a task should decrease.

Learning curves are evaluated by computing the time required per unit of production each time that the cumulative output is doubled. A decrease in production time per unit of 25% would result in a 75% curve. A 60% curve would result if the production time was reduced by 40% (see Diagram 7.3).

By measuring this curve, the auditor can determine how quickly a new procedure or employee becomes productive. When a new procedure is recommended, calculating the initial time per unit under the old system and comparing it to a series of observations over time using the new procedures can objectively determine the impact of the revision to the procedures.

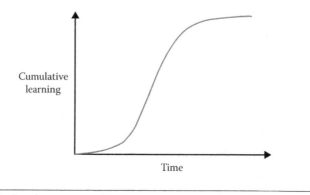

Diagram 7.3   Learning curve example.

Ratio and Regression Analysis

We have seen that correlation analysis can determine the strength of a relationship. From an audit perspective, the question then becomes, "If *x* changes, how much will *y* change?" Unlike correlation, regression analysis infers a causal relationship between the two sets of data so that not only is the data related, but a change in one will cause a change in the other. A simple correlation analysis may indicate a strong positive relationship between sunshine and the sale of ice cream, but it does not indicate how much ice cream we may expect to sell if tomorrow's sunshine is twice as many hours as today's. Ratio analysis assumes a given proportional relationship between two numbers and is normally used for comparisons over time. A more advanced form of ratio analysis attempts to quantify the interrelationship in order to facilitate predictions in a *regression analysis*. As we have seen, correlation measures the direction and strength of the straight-line (linear) relationship between two quantitative variables. If a scatterplot shows a linear relationship, we would like to summarize this overall pattern by drawing a line on the scatterplot. A *regression line* summarizes the relationship between two variables but only in a specific setting—that is to say, one of the variables helps explain or predict the other. Thus, regression describes a relationship between an *explanatory or indepen-dent variable* and a *response or dependent variable*.

Regression analysis is used to estimate the effect that a movement in one variable (the independent variable) causes a movement in the other variable (dependent variable); for example, if the sun shines, more ice cream will be sold, but how much more? By performing a regression analysis, the relationship, if any, can be identified and quantified and sales levels predicted.

Regression analysis can thus assist the auditor in understanding and quantifying data interrelationships. Unusual variations between expectations and recorded values may be noted for further investigation.

Using software, the auditor can additionally conduct a multiple discriminant regression analysis relating the independent variable to a number of dependent variables simultaneously. By determining the comparative strength of the relationships, the auditor can choose the focus area to the achieve greatest impact in performance improvement. Such analysis has also been used to attempt to predict bankruptcy. Regression is also referred to as the *least squares method*.

The Least Squares Regression Line

Working by eye, different people might draw different lines on a scatterplot. This is particularly true when the points are more widely scattered than those in Diagram 7.2. The auditor needs a method of drawing a regression line that doesn't depend on a guess as to where the line should go. No single line will pass exactly through all the points on the scatterplot. Overall, the line passes above some of the points and below others. In order to determine the "best fit," the auditor needs a line where the distance between the lines and the points is minimized. The most common method is the least squares method, which uses the least squares regression line. The least squares line is calculated by examining the means and standard deviations of the two variables and their correlation. The auditor finds the vertical distance of each point on the scatterplot from a regression line (see Diagram 7.4). The least squares regression line makes the sum of the squares of these distances as small as possible; that is, the sum of the squares above the line minus the sum of the squares below the line are closest to zero.

As with most statistical tools, regression analysis is based on a set of underlying assumptions that must be met for its use and interpretations to be valid.

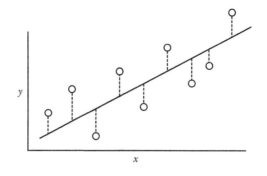

Diagram 7.4 Least square regression line.

Audit Use of Regression Analysis

Regression analysis helps auditors, managers, and business owners forecast future conditions; lends quantitative support to auditors' judgments and recommendations; points out flaws in management thinking; and provides new insights that can help company decision makers move their businesses toward a more profitable future.

Because of the extensive audit use of data on finances, operations, and customer purchases, auditors who once relied on their experience and intuition must now look to data and analysis to inform business decisions. Regression techniques lend a scientific angle to managing data, reducing large amounts of raw data to actionable information. In some instances, the analysis will support an auditor's gut feeling. For example, an auditor who examines a manager's belief that expanding into a new facility will increase customer traffic and sales may find support in a regression model that finds a correlation between facility size and company revenues. Alternately, he or she may find the manager's belief unfounded.

Linear Programming

Linear programming may be defined as the problem of maximizing or minimizing a linear function subject to linear constraints.

Linear programming is an operations research tool used for the allocation of scarce resources or to determine optimal blends of raw materials. The subject is also referred to as *linear optimization*.

It involves the process of taking various linear inequalities relating to some situation and seeks the "best" value obtainable under those conditions. An example would be seeking the "best" production levels for maximal profit making given specific limitations of materials and labor. The constraints applicable are reduced to algebraic formulas, which are then solved by simultaneous equations.

For example, in a production environment, limitations on production capacity mean that no more than 200 basic ATMs and 170 advanced ATMs with check depositaries can be made daily. To satisfy a shipping contract, a total of at least 200 ATMs must be shipped each day.

If each basic ATM sold results in a $220 loss but each advanced ATM produces an $1,100 profit, how many of each type should be made daily to maximize net profits?

The question of how many of each machine should be used for optimum production can be solved using linear programming.

Production is seeking the optimal number of ATMs, so the variables will be the following:

x: number of basic ATMs produced
y: number of advanced ATMs produced

Because they can't produce negative numbers of ATMs, there are constraints that $x \geq 0$ and $y \geq 0$. The planning also gives maximums: $x \leq 200$ and $y \leq 170$. The minimum shipping requirement results in $x + y \geq 200$; in other words, $y \geq -x + 200$. The profit relationship will be the optimization equation: $P = -220x + 1100y$. So the entire system is the following:

$$P = -220x + 1100\,y, \text{ subject to:}$$
$$100 \leq x \leq 200$$
$$80 \leq y \leq 170$$
$$y \geq -x + 200$$

This can be mapped graphically or calculated.

Parametric Assumptions

In using these types of analyses, audit assumptions normally include that data will be the following:

- Independent
- Normally distributed
- Of equal variance
- With a reasonable sample size available
- Using at least an interval scale

When such assumptions cannot be validly drawn, the auditor may revert to the use of nonparametric measurement.

Nonparametric Measurement

Nonparametric tests are typically used by auditors when no solutions can be made regarding the data, and the auditor may be unwilling to rely on the results of parametric tests.

A nonparametric test, as such, is appropriate "when the assumptions required of other popular techniques, usually called parametric tests, are not met, when it is necessary to use a small sample size and it is not possible to verify that certain key assumptions are met, when it is necessary to convert qualitative data (nominal or ordinal data) into useful decision-making information."[*]

Spearman's rho (r_s) is a nonparametric measure of correlation coefficient and would be used by the auditor when the data does not conform to the general assumption that is required of a parametric test but there is still a *monotonic relationship* between your variables.

A monotonic relationship is a relationship whereby as the value of one variable increases, so does the value of the other variable or, conversely, as the value of one variable increases, the other variable value decreases.

Kruskal-Wallis Analysis of Variance (ANOVA) Testing

Kruskal-Wallis tests are used to ascertain whether the replies to questionnaires are statistically the same across the various industries.

---

[*] Hanke, J. E., and Reitch, A. G. (1994). *Understanding Business Statistics*, 2nd ed. Burr Ridge, IL: Irwin.

In this case it is essential that no assumptions are made about the underlying form of the population data. It is a generalized version of the Mann-Whitney test, which is used to determine whether two samples come from symmetrical populations that have equal means or medians.

The assumptions of the Kruskal-Wallis test are the following:

- The variable of interest is continuous (not discrete). The measurement scale is at least ordinal.
- The probability distributions of the populations are identical except for location. Hence, the auditor still requires that the population variances are equal.
- The groups are independent.
- All groups are simple random samples from their respective populations.
- Each individual in the population has an equal probability of being selected in the sample.

8

CONDUCTING THE AUDIT

This chapter examines how audit objectives are determined and how data analytics are selected in order to achieve those objectives. This includes the use of the appropriate risk analysis techniques in order to identify potential internal control failures. It also covers the definition of "exception" conditions.

Audit Planning

Planning is fundamental to successful auditing. Bad planning commonly results in a failure to achieve the audit objectives as well as the conducting of audits that are either insufficient in scope with unidentified risks, resulting in incomplete audits, or alternatively over-audited and making inefficient use of resources.

It must always be recognized that, in any analysis, poor data quality can result in erroneous audit conclusions, which can potentially undermine the credibility of the internal audit itself. When auditors compile reports by automatically consolidating and integrating information across many different departments and disparate source systems, they need to be confident that the information is completely accurate. In many companies, inconsistent data values and formats are prevalent.

Analytics software offers auditors the opportunity to verify that the data utilized in the organization's financial and operational reports has been integrated effectively. Auditors can use analytics software to run tests on the data relied upon by management, using different rules, to check data quality. Tests such as parallel simulations are covered in more detail in Chapter 10.

Risk Analysis

In 1992, the American Institute of Certified Public Accountants, the Institute of Internal Auditors, the American Accounting Association, the Institute of Management Accountants, and the Financial Executives Institute issued a jointly prepared study titled *Internal Control—An Integrated Framework*. This document identifies the fundamental objectives of any business or government entity. These included economy and efficiency of operations, safeguarding of assets, achievement of desired outcomes, reliability of financial and management reports, and compliance with laws and regulations.

Internal control was defined by the Committee of Sponsoring Organizations (COSO) as a broadly defined process, effected by people, designed to provide reasonable assurance regarding the achievement of the three objectives that all businesses strive for:

1. Economy and efficiency of operations, including achievement of performance goals and safeguarding of assets against loss
2. Reliable financial and operational data and reports
3. Compliance with laws and regulations

In order to achieve these objectives, COSO defined five components that would assist management in achieving these objectives. These consisted of the following:

- Sound control environment
- Sound risk assessment process
- Sound operational control activities
- Sound information and communications systems
- Effective monitoring

In general, business risks may affect a company's ability to successfully compete, its ability to maintain financial strength and its positive public image, and, ultimately, its ability to survive. Risks will impact the overall quality of an organization's products, people, and/or services. Risks cannot be eliminated—only managed.

Auditors have traditionally been tasked with gaining and confirming an understanding of the system of internal control as fundamental to evaluating the adequacy and effectiveness of management's internal controls. Internal control has been presumed to be a response to business risk. In order to evaluate the effectiveness of risk control measures, the auditor must have a comprehensive understanding of the underlying business risks.

Within a heavily computerized organization, such an understanding requires, initially, a thorough understanding of the business process in order to identify critical processes where less than optimum performance could have severe consequences. In addition, an understanding of the risks inherent within a computerized environment is essential in order to assess the appropriateness and mitigating effects of the control environment.

With the high volumes of information flowing within an organization, it is critical that auditors focus their attention in the areas of highest corporate impact. An effective risk assessment process requires the communication of an awareness of the risks and obstacles to successful achievement of business objectives and the development of an ability to deal with them. As such, organizations must establish a set of objectives that integrate all the organization's resources so that the organization operates in unison. The risk assessment itself involves the identification, analysis, and management of the risks and obstacles to successful achievement of the three primary business objectives.

Risk assessment is a critical element in the governance of any organization. In a public company, it falls under the legal duty of care to shareholders. In many jurisdictions, it comes under the heading of regulatory compliance.

Three types of risk normally are considered when evaluating corporate risk:

- *Inherent risk:* Inherent risk is the likelihood of a significant loss occurring before any risk-reducing factors are taken into account. In evaluating inherent risk, the evaluator must consider the types and nature of the risks as well as the factors indicating that a risk actually exists. To achieve this, a high degree of familiarity with the operational environment of the organization is required.
- *Control structure risk:* Control structure risk measures the likelihood that the control processes established to limit or manage inherent risk are ineffective. In order to ensure that the controls are evaluated appropriately, the risk evaluator

must understand how to measure the effectiveness of individual controls. Doing this involves identifying those controls that provide the most assurance that specific risks are being minimized within the organization. Control effectiveness is strongly affected by the quality of work and the degree of supervisory control.

• *Residual risk:* Residual risk is the degree of risk remaining after control structure risk has reduced the likelihood and impact of inherent risk. The objective of the exercise is not to eliminate residual risk but to reduce it to a level that management can accept.

To evaluate the effectiveness of risk control measures, a thorough understanding of the business process addressed by those controls is required. This understanding allows the auditor to prioritize the processes in terms of which of them are delivering less-than-optimum performance that could have serious consequences. Based on this assessment, a risk model or risk framework can be structured to describe and quantify the effects and likelihood of possible negative consequences.

Risks themselves are commonly categorized based on the organization's response, thus

• *Controllable risks* are risks that exist within the processes of an organization and are wholly in the hands of the organization to mitigate.
• *Uncontrollable risks* are risks that can arise externally to the organization and cannot be directly controlled or influenced but nevertheless call for a risk position to be taken by the organization.
• *Influenceable risks* are risks that arise externally to the organization but can be influenced by the organization.

Specific threats can be grouped into common causative groups; for example, one group might contain multiple individual types of fraud risk that are all caused by a lack of supervisory control, and another group of risks may all be caused by inadequate physical access controls.

Grouping risks based on causation makes it possible to identify those control elements that, if properly designed and implemented, can be most effective in reducing the likelihood that a risk will occur or in reducing the impact if it does occur. Such groupings also allow control structures to be designed to ensure that all causative factors are considered when evaluating the relative strength or weakness of the control environment. This evaluation is normally carried out on the assumption that all controls will function as intended on an ongoing basis.

Risk analysis is an iterative process that must be carried out continuously as the business environment changes.

Techniques to identify risk usually involve both quantitative and qualitative prioritization. Quantitative information, such as value at risk, may be comparatively easy to determine. The probability of risk may be more subjective and based on perceptions of previous negative experiences. *Process analysis* is a technique that permits the identification of key dependencies and control nodes within a business entity where, for example, fraud occur. The risk analysis then involves estimating the significance of the risk in that particular process and assessing the likelihood of frequency of such a risk occurring.

Risk analysis is far from a foolproof technique.

Inherent limitations include an auditor's poor judgment in assessing the probability of occurrence and lack of adequate or accurate information on the potential cost of occurrence. In addition, the effectiveness of the internal control structure in offsetting the risk may fail to consider the probabilities of collusion between insiders and outsiders to bypass the internal controls or the ability of management to override the internal control structures with no independent scrutiny. Nonetheless, meaningful risk analysis can guide the auditor to the areas where audit intervention may have the biggest impact.

The initial phase of the risk assessment process involves a clear definition of the intended deliverables as well as the extent and depth of the assessment. One effective model uses a five-stage process:

- Identify participants in the process by business unit and establish the key risks from their perspective.
- Conduct a high-level assessment with each of the participants to clarify their corporate risk concerns.
- Conduct a workshop with participants drawn from a common business unit in order to elicit their prioritization of the risks and their identification of the key control elements.

- Consolidate individual business unit results and accumulate them toward the overall corporate risk assessment.
- Based on identified shortcomings, develop a risk response strategy and implementation plan.

Identifying the participants includes educating them so that all participants are clear as to what risk is and the definition of risk within their own particular business area. They must also be up to date on the control environment currently relied on to detail and detect risk occurrences. This phase of the exercise may come as a shock to some of the participants who have never had to consider their business operations in terms of potential risk.

A high-level individual assessment can be a useful exercise because participants in an open workshop may be reluctant to admit concerns regarding risk and lack of control in public. In an operation where a strong manager dominates, it may be difficult to get participants to go up against the boss without the assistance of a strong facilitator.

In all such cases, the auditor must be clear that the purpose of conducting such a risk assessment is to assist in determining the overall audit objectives. An example of such an assessment may be found in Appendix 3.

Determining Audit Objectives

Using the power of computers, the auditor can inspect large quantities of data from a variety of sources in the course of an audit. Data may come from external sources as well as internal ones and may take the form of computerized records or printouts that can be scanned into digital form for analysis. Digital data for subsequent interrogation and data mining may also include the following:

- Transaction logs
- Access control records
- E-mail records
- Mobile phone records
- Corporate phone records

Care must be taken to ensure that all documentary and digital data is legally gathered and securely maintained and that the chain of custody remains unbroken and fully documented.

Data analysis tools have become considerably more sophisticated over the last few years and can be used to scan databases for specific events.

The overall objectives of the audit are, to a large extent, dictated by the nature and type of internal audit requested by management, including the following:

- Compliance audits
- Environmental audits
- Financial audits
- Performance and operational audits
- Fraud audits
- Forensic audits
- Quality audits
- Program results audits
- IT audits
- Audits of significant balances and classes of transaction

Compliance Audits

These audits are typically carried out in order to ensure that the organization is compliant with specific policies, plans, procedures, laws, regulations, or contracts impacting upon the successful attainment of organizational objectives. The overall audit objective is thus to seek assurance by examining the appropriate audit evidence that the compliance has been achieved in the past, is being achieved at present, and is likely to continue being achieved in the future. This evidence may be obtained via interviews with management and staff responsible for carrying out the business activity requiring compliance. In addition the auditor may use examination of records and contracts, examination of computer records to ensure controls are functioning as intended, and examination of the policies and procedures of the organization to determine the likelihood of ongoing compliance.

Environmental Audits

Environmental auditing may be seen as a derivation of compliance auditing given the rapid growth of international environmental regulations. This type of auditing may be defined as a systematic, documented, periodic, and objective review by regulated organizations of both operations and practices related to meeting environmental legislation. In the course of such an audit, a team of qualified inspectors will conduct an extensive examination of a facility in order to ensure that records are kept indicating compliance with environmental laws and regulations and that the records appear to match the reality seen by the investigators. Information analysis in this type of audit will normally involve the analysis of records retained and checking anomalies against standard operating procedures and prior records.

Financial Audits

In the course of a financial audit, an auditor, whether internal or external, is seeking evidence relating to the degree of reliability and the integrity of financial information. This commonly involves the examination of historical records, either clerical or computerized, against standards laid down in recognized financial reporting frameworks, such as the IFRS. From an internal audit perspective, the evidence examined would normally be utilized by management as part of their normal decision-making process. As such, the evidence may take the form of financial records as well as operational process tracking records.

The audit objective of financial examination from an internal perspective may include an evaluation of controls intended to ensure that the organization receives all payments to which it is entitled, makes no payments that are not authorized, and utilizes funds earned in an approved and authorized manner.

When the internal auditor is involved in the analysis of financial statements, the audit objective is typically to ensure the accuracy and completeness of such records. This is commonly done by comparing the financial records with operational and transactional records on an analytical basis.

Performance and Operational Audits

This type of audit involves an initial determination of management's performance and operational objectives. Once these have been established, the auditor must identify which key performance indicators (KPIs) management is using on an ongoing basis to determine whether these objectives have been achieved, are being achieved, and will continue to be achieved. Once the KPIs are identified, the auditor must evaluate their appropriateness in measuring the attainment of both the performance and operation objectives. Once it has been established that the KPIs are appropriate, the auditor will typically seek evidence of management's ongoing review of these indicators and that they show proof of ongoing achievement of objectives. Once again, such evidence may be subject to appropriate analytical procedures, such as trend analysis, correlation analysis, and regression analysis.

Fraud Audits

Fraud is a legal concept existing within the criminal laws of countries with slight variations based upon local situations. In general, fraud is deemed to have occurred if specific elements exist:

- An untrue representation regarding a material issue is intentionally made by an individual or organization.
- Such representation may or may not be believed by the person or organization to which the representation was made.
- The person or organization may suffer the possibility of harm or prejudice as a result of such misrepresentation.

Fraud auditing, as opposed to forensic auditing, is a proactive function that involves the auditor in assisting management to establish a system of internal controls in which fraud is unlikely to occur or, should it occur, early detection is likely. In order for such a system of internal control to be established, a full fraud risk assessment is required in order to identify those opportunities attainable within a given set of operations. The internal auditor may assist in the conducting of such a risk analysis as well as in evaluating the adequacy of the design system of internal controls.

One critical element of fraud prevention is the use of a well-trained and attentive staff. Even when the system of internal controls is deemed adequate, its effectiveness may be negatively impacted if staff members are unaware of potential fraud opportunities, their responsibility in preventing and detecting fraud, those indicators that they should be aware of, and how potential frauds may be reported. The primary use of data analytics would rather be in the realm of forensic auditing.

Forensic Auditing

Forensic auditing is a reactive activity with the auditor responding to allegations, red flags, tip-offs, or even rumor. The forensic auditor's role is to determine whether fraud, theft, or embezzlement has occurred and, if so, whether there is a criminal law dealing with the matter and whether an apparent breach of that law has occurred. If the answer to these questions is yes, the auditor will then seek to determine who the perpetrator was, who the victim was, and how it can be proven. When conducting a fraud investigation, the auditor will typically be involved in the following:

- Taking statements
- Conducting investigations
- Obtaining evidence
- Writing reports
- Testifying in court as to findings

A critical element within a fraud investigation is *predication*, which involves the auditor examining the totality of circumstances that would lead a reasonable, professionally trained, and prudent individual to believe that a fraud *has occurred, is occurring*, and/or *will occur*. This is critical in that, should a layperson suspect a fraud, all evidence discovered will appear to underline that belief regardless of whether a fraud has in fact taken place.

Evidence typically sought will include four primary factors:

- *Motivation*, which, in most frauds, will involve some form of economic motivation, that is, financial gain. It should be noted, however, that the financial gain is not necessarily directly for the perpetrator and may involve raising funds for some third party.

Some fraud is motivated out of the need to retaliate when the perpetrator believes that he or she has been badly wronged by perhaps having been passed over for promotion or having been denied the raise to which he or she feels entitled. Some fraud is committed for egocentric reasons with the individual wishing to show off to peers how clever he or she is in being able to bypass antifraud measures. This is particularly common in computer fraud.

- *Opportunity* to commit fraud may come in a variety of forms, such as inadequacies in access controls permitting unauthorized individuals to carry out fraudulent activities. Opportunities may also come in the form of a perpetrator who has legitimate access to process transactions but, with a lack of management oversight, may also process the transactions for fraudulent reasons.
- *Means* to carry out fraud with a reasonable chance of success and the ability to remain undetected are fundamental requirements to the fraudster.
- *Method* by which the fraud was committed is a critical piece of evidence for a fraud auditor to seek. This may also involve seeking evidence of the duration of the fraud through analysis of previous transactions.

Depending on the nature of the fraudulent activity, the auditor may have to draw upon a variety of techniques, such as document analysis, interviewing, use of polygraph, and data analysis.

Data analysis may involve the auditor interrogating high volumes of data from a variety of sources, including noncomputerized records as well as digital data. This may take form of

- Transaction records
- Accounting records
- Access control logs
- E-mail logs
- Corporate phone records
- Mobile phone records

For audit purposes, a common tool will be the use of generalized audit software (GAS), which is covered in depth in Chapter 10.

Quality Audits

Quality auditing may be defined as *a systematic and independent examination to determine whether quality-related activities are implemented effectively and comply with quality systems and/or quality standards.* Overall, quality assurance (QA) involves a set of aspirations that place quality as a cardinal objective of an organization. QA is a management function involving the deployment of quality enhancing strategies to create a corporate culture centered on quality. This is a development from the old quality control processes, which were typically reactive processes occurring after the event and which commonly involved the rejection of substandard products and services.

Quality auditing is an audit focus on systems and processes rather than outcomes, following the overall corporate governance concept that systems and processes form the basis of a properly constituted organization if implemented effectively.

Program Results Audits

These audits involve the determination of the accomplishment of established goals and objectives for operations and programs. In order to effectively conduct such examinations, the auditor must ascertain whether a particular function has clearly defined objectives or goals as well as whether such objectives and goals are relevant and consistent with management's intent. Once this has been determined, the auditor will seek evidence of any deviations between the actual results and the original goals and objectives. As a by-product, the cost-effectiveness of a given organizational program may be evaluated.

Within the public sector, effectiveness and efficiency are commonly measured in terms of service delivery and the quantification of the benefits received both to the beneficiaries of a given program as well as the community at large. Auditors operating in this area will typically make extensive use of statistical analysis over a period of time in order to draw inferences on program effectiveness based on the results of the statistical analysis.

Within the private sector, efficiency and effectiveness are commonly measured in terms of profitability. Once again, the statistical analysis of key performance indicators enables the auditor to evaluate the impacts of a given corporate program such as a cost-reduction program.

IT Audits

IT audits have evolved as the size, capacity, and complexity of systems implemented within organizations have grown. Net-based technologies, such as cloud computing, electronic data interchange (EDI), e-commerce, and mobile computing, have had a fundamental impact on the nature of business and society in today's world. In order for organizations to survive in this complex and rapidly changing environment, it is critical that the systems deployed are controlled and dependable.

From an analytical perspective, the bulk of the information and evidence utilized by auditors is derived directly from information systems. The extracting of the data is covered in Chapter 9, but in order to conduct such data analysis, it is critical that the auditor satisfy him- or herself that the controls within the computer systems themselves are of a standard that allows reliance to be placed upon the integrity, accuracy, and completeness of data extracted for analysis. These controls are typically classified in two main subdivisions:

- *General controls* may be seen as those controls governing the environment within which computer systems are developed, maintained, and operated as well as controlling the environment within which application systems operate. General controls may include operation of the computer installation if an in-house IT facility exists and the functioning of the system software (operating system, communication system, database management system, and networking system) as well as the systems development standards operational within the organization. General controls are critical because of the pervasive effect they have on all application areas. The nature of the general controls will be influenced by whether the computer systems are run on an in-house basis or in a cloud.

- *Application controls* involve those controls, both manual and computerized, operating within the business area to ensure that transactions are processed completely and accurately. The controls in these areas are normally specific to the business function, resulting in an audit program that will typically involve a certain degree of standard audit tests and analysis as per the examples below.

Audits of Significant Balances and Classes of Transactions

Procurement audits—Audits in these areas commonly seek to determine whether organizational procurement policies and procedures have been complied with. This will typically involve the analysis of purchase orders, clerical, or digital evidence, seeking the following:

- Missing documents
- Excessive voids or credits
- Alterations on original authorizations (clerical or digital)
- Duplicate payments
- Common names or addresses of payees or customers
- Customer name, banking details, or addresses matching the employee file
- Increases in past due amounts
- Increases in reconciliation items

In addition, receiving and inspection records may be reviewed and matched against purchase files in order to ensure appropriate quantities and qualities of items have been received.

Spend analysis involves the auditor in the process of collecting, classifying, and analyzing expenditure data from all sources within the organization. The auditor will analyze the past, current, and forecasted expenditures by department, supplier, goods, or services provided across the enterprise. This analysis allows the auditor to answer questions, such as the following:

- How many suppliers are in use?
- How much was spent with each?
- What was purchased?

- When was it purchased?
- How much was paid?

Although data analysis at this level will not normally disclose paybacks or bribes, data can be analyzed seeking evidence of inappropriate use of sole-suppliers or unauthorized suppliers. By analyzing volumes acquired and comparing this to volumes consumed, purchases of excessive inventory may be identified.

Should there be a requirement, organizationally, to apply specific procurement criteria, data may be analyzed seeking exceptions to these criteria. When commissions or discounts are granted based upon purchase volumes, the auditor may seek to recalculate commissions or discounts due for comparison to discounts or commissions received.

Used appropriately, a spend analysis allows the auditor to assist management in the following:

- Reducing material and service costs
- Cutting excess stocks
- Improving contract compliance
- Elimination of duplicate suppliers
- Receiving regulatory reporting rules
- Reductions in expediting costs

Inventory audits—For many organizations, inventory represents a significant amount of the corporate investment. Manufacturers may have financial risks in the quantities and longevity of raw materials on hand. Inventory audits will normally involve the auditor determining, first, the existence of the inventory as well as the appropriateness of stock levels, buffer stocks, the frequency of stock outages, and use of economic order quantities in restocking.

Policies and procedures surrounding custodial control of inventory as well as those governing the receipt of inventory to ensure its quality, appropriateness, and completeness would also be examined. In terms of data analytics, the auditor may use appropriate tools to examine the records seeking evidence of the following:

- Overstocking
- Stock outages
- Stock write-offs
- Stock usage and slow moving stock

Accounts Payable Audits

In general, an internal accounting service is usually held responsible for verifying vendors, authentication of invoices, and ensuring departmental authorization for goods and services acquired. Audits in this area will normally focus on assessing the adequacy of controls in accounts payable procedures for payments of goods and services and ensuring the information on invoices agrees with that on purchase orders as well as receiving reports. Auditors may also seek evidence that payments were made in a timely and proper manner, that all appropriate time-related discounts were taken, and the access control over vendor and purchase order master files are appropriate and effective. Data analysis in this area would include the following:

- The valuation of invoice records to ensure no significant deficiency in terms of proof of purchase and total invoice amount calculations.
- Access logs to master files are maintained and indicate no unauthorized accesses or modifications of the data in these files.
- Analysis of sales tax records to ensure all appropriate taxes were paid.
- Matching of vendor payment addresses against vendor master files.
- Timeliness of payments made and that no duplicate payments were made.
- All vendors paid were in an active status.
- No unrecorded liabilities exist (checking for unmatched vendor statements and invoices as well as unmatched receiving reports).
- Reviewing cash disbursements occurring after year end.
- Scanning for payment patterns indicating fraudulent activities.
  - Purchases from unapproved vendors
  - Purchases from multiple companies with the same address
  - Vendor records address, banking details, post boxes matching employee records
- Matching accounts payable records against accrued liabilities.

Accounts Receivable Audits

A common audit procedure in the accounts receivable area is to seek verification from customers of amounts due. In many cases, this is not practical, and the auditor will seek analytical evidence regarding the accuracy and completeness of accounts receivable records as well as assurance that the organization received all monies due including interest charges. Tests on data using analysis in this area could include seeking evidence of the following:

- Timeliness of recording of receivables
- General misstatements of accounts receivable
- Corporate procedures for a waiver of interest not being followed
- Analysis of credit memos issued
- Reconciliation of accounts receivable to the general ledger
- Review of accounts receivable reserved amounts to confirm the methods of calculation and verify the reasonableness
- Recalculation of the aging of receivables to ensure compliance with corporate standards and that appropriate follow-up mechanisms are being utilized
- Numeric sequence checking seeking duplicates and missing invoices
- Analysis of receivables by location
- When appropriate, matching billings to shipping reports seeking items shipped but not billed
- Large balances that may be overstated
- Accounts that have been outstanding for a long period of time and may not be collectible
- Receivables from affiliated companies, officers, directors, and other related parties that may need separate disclosure
- Significant credit balances that may need to be reclassified as a liability
- Compared allowance for uncollectible accounts as a percentage of accounts receivable with previous years
- Compared sales returns and allowances as a percentage of gross sales with previous years (by product line)
- Compared gross margin percentage with previous years (by product line)

Payroll Audits

The objective of this type of audit is to provide reasonable assurance that adequate and effective controls are in place to ascertain the integrity of pay transactions.

Control within this area is normally seen as critical within any organization because payroll processing involves the disbursement of corporate assets. In addition to examining current payroll procedures to ensure appropriate segregation of duties and supervisory control exist, data analysis of payroll records may be used to do the following:

- Verify records against original authorized transactions, such as overtime claimed
- Verify the accuracy of calculations by recomputing totals
- Verify electronic payments made against bank transactions
- Analyze checks, seeking duplicates and uncleared checks still outstanding on bank accounts
- Seek data anomalies, such as the following:
  - Employees with unusual names ("do not copy," "duplicate," etc.)
  - Multiple employees having the same address, bank account number, etc.
  - Payments made to employees not on the master file
  - Overtime payments exceeding normal amounts
  - Pay rates exceeding the norm for a specific salary grade
  - Leave taken in excess of the norm for a pay grade
  - Negative gross pays
  - Gross pay less than net pay
  - Employee date of birth indicating age less than the minimum by law

Banking Treasury Audits

Where treasury functions exist within an organization, audits commonly involve three functional areas: the *front office*, the *back office*, and *general management.*

In the front office, where deals are made, management requires assurance that all deals taking place are properly authorized according to organizational standards and are conducted within prescribed dealings limits. Analysis in the front office will commonly include ensuring that the deals themselves are also recorded accurately and completely and that adequate and effective controls over the accounting for the deals are maintained. The back office is responsible for the recording of deals as well as the recording of payments and reconciliation of deals to accounting records. Once again, the auditor may assist by analyzing the historical records to ensure that they accurately and completely reflect transaction movement. General management's role is to ensure the appropriate segregation of duties between the front and back offices, and audits in this area normally look to the adequacy of operational standards and evidence of their compliance.

Corporate Treasury Audits

Today's regulatory landscape is complex and in flux. Virtually all international regulations require organizations to improve their tracking of and reporting against specific metrics. It is now required of treasury and finance teams that they must be able to deliver accurate, complete details on thousands—if not millions—of transactions and do so virtually instantaneously. This data, which changes on a daily basis, must be analyzed extensively while also ensuring data availability, system functionality, and data integrity.

From an internal audit perspective, the auditor must assist management and ensure that their reporting is fully accurate. Finance and treasury staff must be able to respond quickly to unpredictable requests and must be able to address evolving reporting requirements, accommodating rules that may differ between jurisdictions yet may overlap while, at the same time, being able to handle exponentially increasing volumes of data. This means that the audit needs to play a pivotal role in ensuring that the data analysis, particularly of Big Data, may be relied upon. In other words, auditors need to be able to conduct audits of the data analysis process itself.

When finance, for example, uses a predictive analytics solution to detect anomalous patterns that may indicate the presence of fraud, errors, or other irregularities, they must be sure that the analytical procedures are appropriate and effective in detecting these patterns.

9

OBTAINING INFORMATION FROM IT SYSTEMS FOR ANALYSIS

This chapter covers the assessment of IT systems in order to determine the sources of evidentiary data appropriate for analysis as well as the techniques the auditor may use in order to obtain, extract, and if necessary, transform such data to facilitate analysis.

In order to choose the appropriate method for obtaining data, it is critical that the auditor understand the nature and forms the data may take.

Data Representation

Binary and Hexadecimal Data

Binary System   All computer systems store data in binary mode (Base 2). Unlike the decimal system that has 10 digits from zero to nine, the binary system has only two digits: zero and one.

For example, the number 41 in the decimal system represents 100101 in the binary system.

The binary number 11010101 is equivalent to the decimal number 213, which is computed as follows:

$$1 \times 1 + 0 \times 2 + 1 \times 4 + 0 \times 8 + 1 \times 16 + 0 \times 32 + 1 \times 64 + 1 \times 128 = 213$$

Each binary digit is called a bit. Four bits combine to make a nibble, and two nibbles (or 8 bits) make up a byte.

Hexadecimal System   Although all computer data is in binary form, this data is represented in practice in hexadecimal mode (Base 16), which is compact and easy to handle. For example, the number 65 in the decimal system is equivalent to the binary number 0100 0001.

It may be noted that in order to represent hexadecimal digits greater than nine, the characters A–F are made use of, with A representing 10, B representing 11, and so on, with F representing 15.

Data is one of an organization's most valuable assets and may be liable to experience theft, corruption, substitution, or manipulation.

ASCII and EBCDIC

The vast majority of data stored in computer systems the internal auditor is likely to examine consists of characters of text. Because computers store all data (including text characters) only in binary/ hexadecimal format, a coding structure is required for "mapping" characters to the binary/hexadecimal format for computers. There are two coding structures in current use:

- EBCDIC (extended binary coded decimal interchange code), which is the native character set for all IBM mainframes and some minicomputers.
- ASCII (American standard code for information inter- change), which is the native character set for all microcom- puters and most minicomputers

Data is typically structured into the following:

- Files containing
  - Records containing
    - Data elements or fields

Flat-file data can itself be categorized into the following:

- Fixed-length data
- Delimited data
- Variable-length data

Fixed-Length Data Fixed-length files consist of records that have a fixed length, which will always occupy the same space and contain the same number of characters. In this type of file, the same individual data elements or fields will be present. Fields, which are either empty or have fewer characters than the maximum length for the field, are padded up with spaces to achieve equal lengths.

Fixed-length data is the easiest structure for downloading data because it involves no requirement to alter the data in order to make it capable of analysis or manipulation.

Delimited Data   In this case, although all records again have the same individual fields, the fields are of variable lengths with the start and end of such fields indicated by commas, semicolons, quotation marks, and the like.

Variable-Length Data   There are occasions when the auditor may encounter records of variable lengths stored in a single file:

- Different types of records, containing varying fields, are stored together in the same file.
- A single type of record, but with varying fields, is stored in a file. From an auditor's point of view, defining variable-length data is considerably more difficult than handling fixed-length or delimited data. The approach adopted will be dependent upon the analysis software used.

Databases

Back in the early days of computing, data was grouped into similar records and stored in individual files. Programs were written to access such files directly, and each program required a full description of the records and data elements contained within the file as well as the method of accessing the data. This caused significant problems when the organization wished to change its data definitions because every program had to be changed individually.

This problem was overcome by the introduction of *data indepen-dence.* This is a technique allowing diverse users with different logical views to access the same data in different ways. The manner in which this is achieved is by divorcing the definition of the nature and loca-tion of the data from the programs using it.

Some definitions may, at this stage, prove helpful.

Definition of Terms

- *Access methods:* Software logic procedures used to retrieve, insert, modify, and delete data on a storage device.
- *Data dictionary/data directory systems (DD/DS):* Software that manages a repository of information about data and the database environment.
- *Data independence and data sharing:* A technique allowing diverse users with different logical views to access the same data in different ways. This is achieved by divorcing the definition of the nature and location of the data from the programs using it. The definitions, views, access rules, locations, logical views, and other information describing the actual data are located in one file of *metadata* or data about the data. This enables new users with new logical views to be accommodated as well as changing logical views and changing physical representations.
- *Data structure:* The interrelationships of data.
- *Database:* A collection of data logically organized to meet the information requirements of a universe of users.
- *Database administration:* A human function involved in the coordination and control of data-related activities.
- *Database management system (DBMS):* A hardware and/or software system that manages data by providing organization, access, and control functions.
- *Storage structures:* Methods and techniques used to physically represent data structures on storage devices.

The structures may exist in conventional files or may be grouped in a variety of manners to be readily accessed via a *database management system* (DBMS). A DBMS is a software or hardware structure controlling the nature of and access to the information required by a user application system.

Individual database management systems vary widely in data structuring capabilities. Selection among these will depend on both the *entry access methods* (randomizing, indexing) and the *navigational access methods* (read the first, read the next, embedded links, inverted index).

Principals of Data Structures

Data structures are used to model a business (function) in terms of information and follow the general business structure:

- Sequential
- Hierarchical
- Network
- Relational model

All of these database types have generic components, although each component is different for each branded product:

- Data definition language (DDL)
- Storage structure definition language (SSDL)
- Data manipulation language (DML)
- DBMS nucleus and utilities

Database Structuring Approaches

Over the years, the form in which we have looked at data has evolved from the original *sequential approach* to today's *relational approach*. The auditor may still find examples of all such database approaches in the course of auditing.

Sequential or Flat File Approach   In this form, data is stored in the form of one or more data files, which are nothing but simple text files (ASCII or EBCDIC), which can be viewed directly using a text editor and printed without difficulty (Diagram 9.1).

- Fundamental assumption

There is a direct relationship between data.

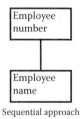

Sequential approach

Diagram 9.1   Sequential data structure.

Hierarchical Approach

- Fundamental assumption

There is some hierarchical relationship between data (Diagram 9.2).

Terminology

- Root segment
- Parent segment
- Child segment
- Twins

Network Approach

- Fundamental assumption

There is some general relationship between data (Diagram 9.3).

Terminology

* Records
* Pointers

Note

* Any structure may be defined.
* Records may contain multiple fields.

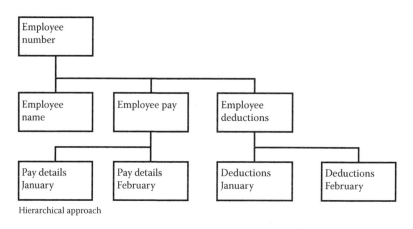

Hierarchical approach

Diagram 9.2   Hierarchical data structure.

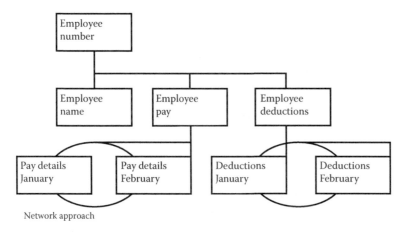

Diagram 9.3   Network data structure.

Relational Model

- Fundamental assumption

There is some mathematical relationship between data.

Employee Table

EMP NO	DEPT NO	NAME
12	15	F Bloggs
25	43	J Smith

Department Table

DEPT NO	DEPT NAME
43	Internal Audit
47	IT

Data Manipulation

SELECT	All Retrieval
UPDATE	Change
INSERT	Create new TUPLE
DELETE	Delete Tuple
FROM	Specifies Table
WHERE	Conditions
AND	Conjunction of Conditions
OR	Disjunction of Conditions

Example

SELECT – EMPLOYEE = NAME FROM EMPLOYEE – DB
WHERE – DEPT = "B03" AND POSITION =
"MANAGER"

The result is always a table.

Inverted File Structure

RECORD	MAKE	COLOR	MODEL
1	BMW	Red	528I
2	Ford	Blue	Laser
3	Ford	Red	Laser
4	BMW	Blue	328i

Can be indexed by Make, Color, Model

MAKE	RECORDS
BMW	1,4
Ford	2,3

COLOR	RECORDS
Red	1,3
Blue	2,4

MODEL	RECORDS
328I	4
528I	1
Laser	2,3

Terminology

  * Indexes and pointers

Big Data

Big Data was first classified in 2001 and has become a popular term to describe the exponential growth of data in both structured and unstructured formats. The data was defined as having three main attributes:

- *Volume*, which is derived primarily in structured form from transaction-based information; with decreasing storage costs, the amount of stored, structured data is now enormous, creating problems in drawing meaningful and relevant analytics. In unstructured form, data may come in from social media in even larger volumes.
- *Velocity* of data throughput creates its own problems because of the need for analysis to be conducted in a timely manner.
- *Variety* of data formats range from structured data in traditional database formats as used in corporate application systems through unstructured formats, such as email, video, audio, and e-commerce transactions.

The sheer complexity of data formats gives the analyst problems in linking and matching information across systems in order to correlate relationships and perform the necessary connections and data linkages to convert drawn data into useful information. By using the ability to extract data from any source, extract the relevant data, and analyze it appropriately, organizations currently seek to ensure time and cost reductions and to enable more effective business decision making.

Big Data analytics are typically used by auditors to, for example,

- Quickly identify high-risk operational areas
- Use clickstream analysis to collect and analyze information on web pages visited, in which order, in order to improve e-commerce analysis or detect fraudulent behavior
- Recalculate entire risk portfolios at high speed

In normal operations, organizations are using Big Data analysis to do the following:

- Optimize work performance areas and logistics
- Broadcast tailored corporate information to mobile devices
- Determine root causes of business defects or failures in near-real time

Once again, when businesses are using data analytics for business decision making, it is critical that the auditors ensure that the data is complete, accurate, and can be relied upon and that the analytic process is carried out with equal integrity. This is covered in more detail in Chapter 11.

The Download Process

Running the auditor's analysis software on the auditee's IT system is frequently impractical due to differences in technical platforms, and it may not be required when the auditor could use existing tools on the auditee's system. The downside of this approach is that the auditor must be familiar with the tools available in the specific client's IT environment, and the use of such tools for audit purposes could cause potential disruption of the auditee's live system with implications for both data integrity and operational performance.

As a result, the more common approach is the extraction of the information data files in which the auditor has an interest and downloading of such to an independent machine under the direct control of the auditor.

As with any other form of audit, the initial stage of any data analysis is a planning exercise in which the auditor will have decided the intention of the audit, the evidence that is being sought, and the nature of the analysis that would be carried out. This information may be derived from the current system documentation where a high-level understanding of the IT processes may be obtained, including a precise understanding of the individual data elements available so that those appropriate for data analysis may be selected. Once the evidence required has been identified, it must be located. This will typically involve research on the documentation of the file structures containing the evidence to be interrogated. Such documentation may be clerical or may be contained within the schemas and subschemas of a database. In the case of non-database files, the auditor will seek a full listing of all potential data files together with their contents and purposes so that for each selected file record layouts may be examined to identify data fields of interest, the type and format as well as the field lengths.

When a database is involved, perhaps the most useful source of information regarding the structures and access paths to the required data may be contained in the metadata held in the data dictionary of the relevant DBMS. From this, the auditor may derive a list of files or tables together with the details of the fields contained and constraints of fields at the table level as well as sort keys, access paths, and data relationships.

The auditor needs this information to ensure the data targeted is clearly identified and located and that false conclusions will not be derived by interrogating the wrong data or even the correct data using the wrong file layout.

The auditor will then decide the mode of data transfer to be utilized and how the data will be verified and reconciled after it has been downloaded. At that stage, it may be possible to decide if any data conversion will be required and what form it should take. As previously noted, doing direct interrogation on the auditee's live system carries the disadvantages of not being reproducible and at the same time placing an overhead on live processing. Once the planning has been carried out to this stage, the auditor should then be in a position to seek authorization for download.

Access to Data

Whether the data is to be attained from live systems, reports, or via downloads, the auditor will need the proper authorities to obtain such information and analyze it in the appropriate way. This may come from user management, executive management, or IT management, depending on the nature of the information and the analysis to be performed. Such authorities should always be granted on a read-only basis. Unless there are exceptional circumstances, the auditor should not have the ability deliberately, or accidentally, to corrupt or change live data. When such circumstances exist, the auditor must ensure the appropriate authorization is documented and retained securely.

Downloading Data

Data may be interrogated directly from live files, but the disadvantage exists that, even as the interrogation occurs, the data contents will move on, and the results will therefore not be reproducible. As a result, most audit data analysis is conducted on copies of live data, which can be stored off-line and the analyses can be repeated as required. The extraction process can take a variety of forms using standard programs available within the system to be interrogated (*utilities*) or by using software specifically obtained for downloading purposes.

For downloading data from the auditee's system, there are several choices available:

- *Magnetic media,* including tapes as well as CDs
- *Incoming e-mail attachments* when data is sent to the auditor from a remote location
- *Direct copy of files over network connections,* which may be in-house networks or over public networks
- *Import via database connectivity using Microsoft's ODBC or OLE DB*

The ODBC (open database connectivity) interface is a Microsoft C programming language interface that makes it possible for applications to access data from a variety of database management systems (DBMSs). The ODBC interface allows maximum interoperability so that audit software or any other application can access data in diverse DBMSs through a single interface. In addition, the software will be independent of any proprietary DBMS from which it accesses data. Auditors can add components called drivers, which interface between an application and a specific DBMS. One drawback to ODBC is that it only provides access to relational databases. OLE DB (object linking and embedding database) provides access to data regardless of its format and location as well as full access to ODBC data sources and drivers.

In all cases in which information is downloaded to the auditor's domain, it is critical that the auditor ensure the following:

- *Accuracy*—The downloaded data is a faithful representation of actual data in which the auditor has an interest.
- *Validity*—The downloaded data is valid from a technical perspective; that is, garbage or nonsense characters have not been included.
- *Completeness*—All the desired data has been downloaded, and conversely, no spurious data has been included.

Data Verification

A variety of audit techniques exist so that the auditor can place reliance on the downloaded data prior to analysis. Perhaps the most common of these is a straightforward count of records to ensure all data has been received. Accuracy of information downloaded may be checked by recalculating totals and comparing them to the original source. These totals may be of genuine numbers, such as valued information, or hash totals, such as totals of telephone numbers. In developing hash totals, the auditor should be mindful that the numbers are themselves meaningless and are calculated only for comparison purposes to ensure completeness and accuracy of downloads.

Once the data is downloaded, additional checks may be made to ensure internal consistency, particularly when data is coming from multiple sources, files, or tables. Obviously, if the original data to be downloaded was inconsistent, the same inconsistency should apply, and that, in itself, may be a significant audit finding.

Obtaining Data from Printouts

When the original data is only available in printed form, it may still be possible to convert it to a digital format or request that the printout be repeated but printed to file rather than paper.

When the printout has been reduced to digital form, the auditor will find that the data structures may require multiple line definitions in order to gain access to relevant information. Mechanics of achieving this will depend on the software used for data analysis, and this is covered in more detail in Chapters 17 through 19.

Sanitization of Data

Once the data has been delivered in a format readable by the auditor, consistency checks may reveal spurious data as well as data in a format more useful for analysis. The auditor may then decide to sanitize the data and convert less useful formats into data that is readily analyzed. This could include the following:

- The removal of unneeded data fields. Data fields will typically remain on the files as downloaded but be removed only from the active view of the auditor. This is important because, should the audit turn into a forensic investigation in midstream, it is critical that the auditor is able to produce the original information in an unaltered form if called upon by a court.

- The conversion of data from one format to another. The data obtained by downloading will be as it is currently held in the system. This can mean that, for example, numerical data is held in a field defined as alphanumeric. In effect, this precludes the auditor from carrying out arithmetic operations on this data unless it is converted into a numeric format. Once again, the auditor would seek to convert the data only as it is to be used by the auditor and not changed in its original version.
- Substitution of data may be desirable when multiple files are to be joined and the common key format is different.

In all these cases, the auditor must ensure that all sanitization activities are clearly documented in the working papers to explain what was done, why it was done, who did it, and what the impact on the analysis was. Again, the intention is that any analysis done could be independently replicated by another analyzer, and therefore, amendments to data must be clearly understood and their validity agreed upon by the second reviewer.

One fault that, unfortunately, is common in such data analysis is the use of editing software to make direct changes to the downloaded data prior to the analysis. As a result of such changes, the auditor may not be in a position to substantiate that the analysis is based upon the data as it was originally presented with only specific and recorded modifications made. If such prior editing is to be carried out, it is critical that the auditor operate on a *copy* of the original downloaded data, noting the changes made and retaining the original downloaded version in a secure manner so that it remains available for independent scrutiny at a later stage if required.

Documenting the Download

As with any audit, careful and comprehensive documentation must be maintained by the auditor in his or her working papers to provide an audit trail of all activities carried out, reasons for those activities, and the appropriate authorizations when required. Such documentation typically includes the following:

- Agreement from the data owner to the downloading process
- The source of the data downloaded
- The date and time of the download
- Where the downloaded data was stored
- The nature of the analysis to be performed and the reasons for it
- Any conversions, sanitization, or cleanup procedures conducted
- Computer log files of the data downloading process

Perhaps the most critical parts of the downloading of data for analysis may be summarized as the following:

- Deciding what information will be analyzed
- Sourcing that information
- Obtaining the information
- Ensuring that the information downloaded is accurate, complete, and fully reflects the live system

After that, the normal audit controls must remain in place to ensure that audit tests are appropriate, correctly carried out, properly interpreted, and communicated effectively. The auditor should also be mindful that company confidential information is now his/her direct responsibility in terms of confidentiality.

10

Use of Computer-Assisted Audit Techniques

This chapter examines typical CAATs in common use and the selection of the appropriate technique based upon the type of evidence and the audit objective. Included are the dangers to the auditor inherent in prejudgment of expected results and the subsequent distortion of the analysis based upon these preconceptions.

In today's environment, data analysis for the auditor will inevitably involve the use of appropriate information retrieval and analysis programs and procedures. Computer-assisted audit techniques or CAATs may be defined generically as computer-based tools that are used to improve the effectiveness and efficiency of the audit process by using the computer as a tool for both gathering and analyzing audit data.

An auditor may use test transaction techniques to review system-level activity, and in advanced auditing, the use of knowledge-based systems will allow less-skilled staff to use advanced audit techniques. It should be noted that the use of CAATs does not change the overall audit objectives, only the audit analysis methodology.

Use of CAATs

When auditors were first faced with the problems of conducting effective audits in IT environments, the initial response was to seek evidence sources allowing the auditor to "audit around the computer." In the long term, this proved unusable in achieving audit objectives when large volumes and complexities of data were involved. CAAT usage was originally in financial and compliance auditing; however, CAATs are increasingly used effectively in both performance and investigative auditing.

In addition to their role in data analytics, CAATs may be utilized during the planning stage of an audit with an emphasis on improving overall audit *effectiveness*, for example:

- When CAATs can be used to identify significant or material trends and patterns, a tighter focus on the ensuing audit activities, whether manual or computerized, may result in a shorter and more impactful audit.
- The ability to examine the data "in the round" prior to finalizing the audit program allows the auditor to expand the audit scope when previously unnoticed anomalies are noted. This type of "free-form" examination will frequently prove fundamental in alerting the auditor to red-flag data patterns in forensic audits.

In terms of improving the overall effectiveness of the audit, CAATs have been demonstrated to afford the auditor the ability to improve audit coverage of risk areas while at the same time generating savings in both time and cost. When advanced analytical techniques are required, the use of CAATs has enabled auditors without advance mathematical abilities to carry out sophisticated analyses with high levels of confidence and has facilitated the introduction of innovative audit approaches.

Standards of Evidence

IIA Practice Advisory 2310-1: Identifying Information indicates that in conducting an audit, evidence gathered should be

- Sufficient
- Reliable
- Relevant
- Useful

The use of computer-assisted audit solutions involves the merging of software into an audit program, including the use of CAATs for verification of the effectiveness of different processes within computer programs and the ability to conduct analyses independently from live systems. The nature of the CAAT used is largely dependent on the objective of the audit and may include the following:

- Techniques for verifying the integrity of the data
- Techniques for examining the accuracy, completeness, and validity of data flows
- Extended data analysis

Before embarking on a series of data-analytic CAATs, it is essential that the auditor gain an understanding of the IT systems in use both from an architectural and risk perspective. Only when this is understood in depth is the auditor in a position to identify the evidence source, decide the appropriate audit technique, select the appropriate CAAT, and when downloading the data, arrange the appropriate download and data verification/reconciliation procedures.

Test Techniques

Test transaction techniques are used to confirm processing control functions and include the evaluation of edit and validation controls, the testing of exception reports, and the evaluation of data integrity controls. Total and calculation verifications may be performed.

The transaction test techniques could include the following:

- *Test data*—This technique involves using a copy of the live computer system through which a series of transactions is passed in order to produce predetermined results. The volume of data that can be handled normally limits this technique, although it may be effective in searching programming logic for defects. An additional drawback is the fact that the results may be biased by the results an auditor expects based on the auditor's prior assumptions.
- *Integrated test facility (ITF)*—This technique, although similar in nature to test data, is effected by creation within the live system of a dummy entity (department, warehouse, etc.) and the processing of test data against the dummy entity *together with the live data*. This technique has the advantages of testing the system as it normally operates while testing both the computer and manual systems. It has distinct disadvantages as well.

- All test transactions must be removed from the live system before they affect live totals, postings, or the production of negotiable documents, such as checks. In addition, there may be a very real danger of destroying the live system.
- ITFs must be used with great care.
- *Source-code review*—This computer audit technique involves the review of the source code originally written by the programmer. In the past, this has meant browsing through piles of printouts. In today's environment, sophisticated searches can be implemented using generalized audit software to establish weaknesses in the source code.
- *Parallel simulation*—Parallel simulation is a technique involving the creation of software to simulate some functional capability of the live system, such as a calculation. The live data is processed through the simulating program in parallel with the live system and the outputs are compared.
- *Online enquiry*—Interactive interrogation can provide comparison data for audit reports and confirmation of corrective action taken and can be an additional source of audit information. Effective use requires few IT skills, but an understanding of the information is essential. Armed with the appropriate access authority, auditors can obtain adequate audit evidence to meet their requirements. However, you must be sure about what you are looking at because it is easy to draw the wrong conclusions.
- *Review of system-level activity*—This involves the examination of control areas with a pervasive influence, such as telecommunications, the operating environment itself, and the systems development function and change control. End-user computing, although not in the same category or general control, can be treated in the same manner as a general threat.

Techniques to examine data flow typically include the following:

- *Snapshot*—This technique is implemented by using a utility that allows the auditor to freeze a program at a given point. It is then possible to check on the values of a transaction at this stage of processing as the program is running. The snapshot is quick and relatively easy to use although it has a limited functionality. For example, a snapshot may involve the addition of a line of code in a program that produced a halt in processing and output the value of a particular variable for audit scrutiny. Some utility software enables a program to be executed in systematic mode, step by step. In this manner, the values of different elements of data can be checked at every step of processing.

- *Tracing*—This technique involves the generation of an end-to-end audit trail to trace transactions through processing. By performing a trace, it is possible for the auditor to see how each line of code impacts any data being processed. If a program calculation is suspect, a trace may be used to identify the part of the program where the error is occurring.
- *Mapping*—This technique involves monitoring the execution of the program to ascertain statistical information, for example, program code not executed, the number of times certain lines were executed, etc. This technique is most commonly used by management to highlight redundant code, but it is a useful tool for auditors to identify unauthorized code used for fraudulent purposes.

For these audit techniques to prove effective, key control questions must be predefined in order to facilitate the use of the technology to analyze the data and provide the answers.

Embedded Audit Modules (SCARFs—System Control Audit Review Files)

In systems where audit trails may only exist as computer records and then only for a short time or discontinuously, it may be necessary for an auditor to have an inbuilt facility to collect and retain selected information to serve as an audit trail for subsequent examination. This obviously makes the collected data a target for destruction or manipulation, and it must be treated as such.

CAATs for Data Analysis

Program-oriented CAATs are intended to focus on verification of different processes in programs. Data-oriented CAATs, on the other hand, will ignore the programs used to generate the data and focus exclusively on data analysis.

In practice, analysis of data is often used very effectively to assess the actual effectiveness of controls instead of relying on analysis of programs. In general, use of program-based CAATs requires a relatively high level of technical expertise with specific knowledge and skills relevant to the auditee's technical architecture and, possibly, the specific programming language used.

In addition, data analysis can be used effectively in performance and forensic audits as well.

Information retrieval and analysis programs and procedures include programs that organize, combine, extract, and analyze information. This includes generalized audit software, application software, and industry-related software. Customized audit software and information retrieval software, as well as standard utilities and online inquiry, may also be used for information retrieval and analysis. When an auditor has computer skills in programming, conventional programming languages may provide a viable alternative, but a lack of such skills does not preclude auditors from using such techniques. The ready availability of microcomputer-based software, which provides computing power without the requirement of technical expertise, puts direct data analysis within the toolkit of any auditor. The primary requirement is an understanding of the business application and how data relates.

A variety of audit software and querying tools are available for data analysis on both mainframe and PC systems. Using such tools, common data analysis techniques include the following:

- *Totaling:* Normally used to prove data completeness and reconciliation to the stated amount.
- *Data mining:* This is a broad-based interrogation technique, which may be used to provide comparisons and trends and to identify specific areas for extended analysis and testing.
- *Stratification:* A technique that gives the auditor a more complete picture of the range of values within a data file, facilitating a more structured and focused approach to interrogations and quickly highlighting potential problems within the file.

- *Sampling:* As noted in previous chapters, this enables the auditor to extract a representative selection of transactions from a file for audit testing.
- *Exception reporting:* This technique involves the selection of records and extraction of data meeting or violating specified criteria for further analysis. The auditor must specify the criteria prior to the analysis.
- *Transaction aging:* This is intended to identify patterns of transactions throughout a period. For example, the period between receipt and payment of transactions by the company can be monitored to ensure all appropriate discounts are taken. Equally, the auditor may seek evidence that payments for invoices issued are received in the time scale laid down by management and that no customer discounts are taken for late receipts. Where late payments by customers attract penalties, the auditor can ensure all such penalty payments due are actually received.
- *Duplicate record checks:* This common option allows the audit identification of errors in payments, orders, invoices, or possible fraudulent activity in these areas.
- *Gap detection:* As with duplicate detection, this may prove a useful tool in detecting either errors or fraudulent activities by identifying missing numbers in sequences, such as payments, credit notes, purchase orders, or invoices.
- *Re-performance of calculations:* This technique is normally used to substantiate the accuracy of formulas used when preparing data. The input data could be reprocessed in a parallel simulation to prove the functioning of controls and accuracy of the calculation process. For example, financial statements, such as balance sheets and cash-flow statements, can be regenerated from the detailed transactions and compared with the printed version.

Generalized Audit Software

Generalized audit software (GAS) is software designed specifically for auditors in order to provide a user-friendly audit tool to carry out a variety of standard tasks, such as examining records, testing calculations, and making computations.

A common audit technique is to take a copy of a file of standard data for later comparison to a changed version of the same data. Once again, GAS can conduct the comparison and analysis.

Selecting, analyzing, and printing audit samples are techniques that can significantly improve the quality of an audit by allowing the quantification of audit and sampling risk. In a high-volume system, these techniques may be the only method an auditor can employ to achieve a satisfactory audit. In such systems, the use of computerized sampling simplifies both the usage and interpretation of results. Most GAS comes complete with sampling and analysis functions to handle the complexities. An auditor will commonly have to handle data that is not in a suitable format for analysis. Summarizing and re-sequencing data may be required to put the information into a more useable format. Once reformatted, the software can also perform the appropriate analyses.

Although GAS cannot resolve all of an auditor's problems, it can help in many of the common problem areas. It is specifically designed for the handling of volumes of data.

The output can be used for further computer processing, allowing audits to be linked together. The time to audit can be reduced and the auditor freed to spend time interpreting results. Because limited programming skills are needed, the two leading general-purpose audit packages are IDEA (interactive data extraction and analysis) and ACL (audit command language), both of which are covered in depth elsewhere in this book. Both these packages include the following functionality:

- *Sampling*—Covering the following:
  - Sample planning, sample selection, and analysis; attribute, variable, monetary unit sampling; sample stratification; and sample selection schemes including random and systematic selection
- *Sequence checking*—Including both gap detection and duplicate transactions
- *Arithmetic functions*
- *File comparison and linkages*

- *Exception reporting*
- *Recalculation and computations*

Both packages are capable of importing data from and exporting data into a wide variety of commonly used data formats, including print format and PDF files.

Although these are the most commonly used generalized audit software packages, it should not be seen that these are the only packages available. Other general-purpose audit software tools include the following:

- Arbutus Analyzer—This package is very similar to ACL but is claimed to be faster in data importing and manipulation.
- SPSS Clementine—This is a data mining toolkit, which facilitates auditors to do their own data mining. It has a visual programming interface, which simplifies the data mining process, and its applications include customer segmentation/profiling for marketing companies, fraud detection, credit scoring, load forecasting for utility companies, and profit prediction for retailers.
- CA PanAudit Plus is designed to help IT, finance, and audit professionals run computer-based audits. It provides a collection of routines that non-computer-literate auditors can execute using English-like statements to design and select statistically valid samples.

Application- and Industry-Related Audit Software

In addition to GAS, audit software is available for standard business applications, such as accounts receivable and payable, payrolls, general ledgers, and inventory management. Such software applications are available as standalone or add-ons to standard GAS packages.

Industry-related audit software is available for specific industries, such as insurance, health care, and financial services. Most of these packages require conversion of input to standard package layouts and the selection of appropriate parameters.

This means that a degree of IT skill is required for conversion. The software itself is normally both cost-effective and efficient.

Customized Audit Software

Customized audit software is software designed to run in unique circumstances and to perform unique audit tests. When output is required in unique formats, customized audit software may be required. Such software is normally expensive to develop and requires a high level of IT skills. It must be handled with care because running the tests may not tell you what you think it does; however, it may be the only viable solution in a unique processing situation.

Information Retrieval Software

Standard information retrieval software, such as report writers and query languages, can perform many common audit routines although it is not specifically written for auditors. This category of software includes report writers, program generators, and fourth-generation languages.

Utilities

Utilities are programs written to perform common tasks, such as copying, sorting, printing, merging, selecting, or editing. These programs are normally parameter-driven and can be used in combination with other software. They are extremely powerful, and the right to use them should be restricted. From an audit perspective, they see data as it exists, which makes their results more reliable.

Conventional Programming Languages

Standard programming languages, such as COBOL, BASIC, RPG, PASCAL, C, etc., can be used to develop effective audit tools but require a certain amount of programming experience. Such programs are normally slow to develop and expensive and may not be reliable because auditors are not professional programmers. They can, however, perform any audit test an auditor can envisage and can be used in conjunction with any other type of audit software.

Common Problems

Auditors should always bear in mind that no CAAT is perfect, and problems will be encountered with each. Common problems the auditor will encounter include the following:

- Getting the wrong data files
- Getting the wrong layout
- Documentation is out of date
- Prejudging results

In addition, audit reliance on CAATs may be affected by the following factors:

- The degree that the auditor is relying on data analysis for establishing his or her audit findings as opposed to the auditor supplementing CAAT analysis with non-computer-based audit tests in order to provide corroborative evidence
- Whether the auditor has conducted a controls review of the IT system in order to assess the reliability of the data entered into or processed by the system
- Whether the completeness and integrity of the downloaded data have been verified by the auditor before reliance is put on the analysis findings
- The extent to which the auditor understands the auditee's IT system and data and has verified that understanding by reference to the auditee's documentation and by discussion with auditee personnel
- The extent of training received by the auditor and the extent of his or her experience in using the specific tool and technique used for the analysis
- The degree of formal audit quality assurance in use for the data analysis portion of the audit including both adequacy of supervision as well as peer review

The auditor's first rule of thumb should be to never believe what the first printout tells you, particularly if you wrote the program yourself. In any application system, the auditor should attempt to identify the controls the user relies on. Bear in mind that documentation is often misleading and that not everything needs to be audited. As a rule of thumb, program logic should mirror the business logic so that if the auditor understands the business needs and controls, system testing becomes much easier.

Audit Procedures

In carrying out an audit of a business system, a predefined generic audit program can be followed:

- Identification of users' control concerns
- Identification of system components
- Identification of system processes
- Identification of known controls
- Identification of known control weaknesses
- Verification of controls
- Evaluation of control environment

The CAAT selected must obviously be clearly related to the audit objective(s). In many planning sessions, there may be a temptation to capture excessive or irrelevant data. Although this is normally avoided, in some cases, it might be easier to download all auditee files, tables, or fields in tables when a more selective approach would require excessive time and resources. This has the added benefit that, should the audit scope expand based on initial findings, the rest of the matching set of data is available.

In general, a more selective approach to data selection is used for financial and compliance audits when the evidence sought is generally known in the planning stage. In performance and forensic auditing, in which the scope may be more expandable, the auditor may choose to "troll" the data, seeking anomalous trends.

Back at the planning stage, the auditor would have put together a business case for using CAATs and had it approved. When it comes to the implementation stage, the auditor must formulate the detailed audit data analytic requirements in order to design and develop the appropriate CAAT.

CAAT Use in Non-Computerized Areas

Not all CAATs are applicable only in computerized areas. Computerized tools may assist the auditor in the following:

- Risk analysis
- Sample selection
- Operation modeling
- Analytical review
- Regression analysis
- Trend analysis

Not all of these need happen on computerized information. By the same token, computerizing the audit does not necessarily mean computerizing the old techniques. New audit approaches are possible and innovative automation can make internal auditing more attractive as a career and thus improve staff stability.

Getting Started

When CAATs are to be adopted for the first time, it is essential that a planned, systematic, and phased approach to their introduction is implemented.

Audit staff should be selected and receive the appropriate training both in the design of CAATs as well as in the use of the specific generalized audit software package in use by the organization. A common problem that may be found in new users of computerized analytical software is a willingness to start extractions and analyses without a clear understanding of what is being sought. The ability to implement the software must be seen as secondary to the auditor's understanding of the risks, control objectives, and control techniques in use as well as the primary controls and sources of audit evidence available.

When staff are entering into the area of data analysis for the first time, a useful exercise involves conducting an audit in a pilot area where the business objectives are well understood and IT systems have already been audited so that the architecture, data structures, and primary evidential sources are already well documented within the audit environment. By using this system, the new auditors are in a position to design the audit program and verify it with more experienced auditors prior to actually embarking on the extractions and analysis. At the same time, an in-house data quality management assurance methodology appropriate to the organizational audit approach may be implemented. As previously stated, drawing erroneous conclusions based upon incomplete understanding of the approach or erroneous selection of technique coupled with the examination of the wrong evidence will destroy the credibility of any future audit data analysis.

This approach also facilitates a mentoring in advanced analysis techniques prior to the auditor drawing conclusions and making recommendations in a live environment. When the auditor feels that they are in a position to commence data analysis in the corporate environment, a major factor will be the obtaining of commitment and support from the highest levels of management.

In establishing the data analysis function within an internal audit, a variety of options is available, including the establishment of a specialist CAAT group to download client data, develop, and run the CAATs on the general auditor's behalf. This has the advantage of using more experienced IT auditors to develop standard analyses scripts, which can then be passed on to less experienced auditors to be run in the course of their normal audit program. The specialist group may also be used to train line auditors in the use of the audit software and interpretation of the results independently.

An alternative approach is the full integration of the use of computer-assisted data analysis as part of all audits and the training of all auditors in their appropriate use. This approach has the advantage of ensuring audit cross-training and removes the vulnerability imposed on the audit function by the loss of specialist staff. It does, however, create additional problems with multiple auditors potentially downloading high volumes of data for ongoing analysis when such analysis is not actually required by the current audit objectives. Even when such analysis is desired within a specific audit, maintaining the confidentiality and integrity of downloaded data files is a significant task in its own right, and excess extraction of data in an uncoordinated function can lead to significant difficulties in determining which data is the latest version and how it will be stored appropriately.

A hybrid approach with line auditors handling simple CAAT-based audits with specialists handling or supporting audits requiring the use of more complex CAATs and more complicated analyses may be seen as appropriate. This approach has the advantage of retaining both domain knowledge of the business objectives of the area under review as well as the technical knowledge of the computer systems and the audit software tool. Critical factors in this decision may include the following:

- The nature and architecture of IT systems within the organization
- The extent of data analytic usage currently and in the future
- The need for similar information to be analyzed on an ongoing basis as part of conventional auditing
- The availability of skills in the use of the CAAT software on an in-house or outsourced basis
- The complexity of the selected audit tool and the extent of IT knowledge required to customize it for in-house use
- The extent of coordination required between an in-house specialist team and the general auditors
- The extent of liaison required with auditees in terms of both attaining access to data as well as gaining an understanding of their business risks and evidential sources

CAAT Usage

In addition to conventional audits and data analysis of general business information, such as the following:

- Payroll records
- Financial accounting records
- Cash disbursements

with which analysis of data can highlight areas of control weaknesses, inefficiencies, or even fraud, audit use of data analysis CAATs will depend on the nature of the industry and organization. As is seen below, the data available for analysis can provide a function of the type of business conducted in areas such as the following:

- Finance and banking
- Government
- Retail

- Services and Distribution
- Health care
- Manufacturing

Finance and Banking

Banks and financial institutions face an enormous and growing risk environment, and IT forms a fundamental part of the process. As such, data analysis is a critical tool both for management and audit in ensuring appropriate governance and effective managerial control. Following the subprime crisis of 2008, a huge quantity of governance legislation was passed internationally with each country's central supervisory bank issuing guidance intended to minimize the risks of enormous losses arising from adverse market conditions, inadequate credit management, and failures in operational business controls for banks.

Internal audits can assist in this process by identifying and reviewing the financial institutions risk management systems in order to identify, within the bank's risk appetite, an effective implementation of appropriate control structures to ensure appropriate compliance supervision, monitoring, and reporting. Depending on the nature of the bank, this may involve reviews of the following:

- The bank's overall loan position as a whole and on a branch-by-branch basis
- Movements within trust accounts
- Movements within suspense accounts
- Internal controls over asset management
- Controls within savings and demand deposits
- Real estate loans and mortgages

For each of these functional areas, audit programs may be designed to interrogate data, seeking analytical evidence of inaccuracies in record keeping or inconsistencies in the application of corporate policies and procedures. For example, in auditing the bank's loan portfolio the auditor may need to analyze the following:

- Loan balances by category and detecting such items as delinquent accounts
- Loan terms offered beyond the norm for the bank

- Loans over or under authorized interest rates
- Loan write-offs or bankruptcies beyond the normal frequency
- Unearned revenues from interest or other sources
- Loans with remaining payments that fail to amortize to calculated balances
- Loans granted in excess of local managerial lending limits

This may additionally include similar inquiries depending on the nature of the bank's loan portfolio. Similar audit programs would address each of the areas in the bank's risk portfolios.

Government

Auditing in a government environment, whether federal, state, or local government, operates with a different perception of organizational risk. Government has two main operation areas: revenue collection and service delivery.

Revenue collection includes such areas as ensuring tax compliance and collection of import duties at both federal and state levels, and service delivery will, once again, depend on the nature of the government processes.

On the revenue side, audit data analysis again comes into play. To many people, tax fraud is not a real crime but a minor peccadillo, comparable to drinking alcohol in the days of Prohibition. As tax legislation changes, and e-commerce changes revenue delivery points, over time, new opportunities arise where the differences between tax evasion and tax avoidance become blurred.

Governments, however, regard tackling taxation fraud as a major imperative in order to protect the following:

- Revenue income required for investment in public services
- Honest, taxpaying organizations from criminal or unfair competition
- Social objectives underlying taxation levels and specific items
- The fight against organized crime or even terrorism funding that benefits from the financial advantages of tax evasion

The reduction of the taxable portion of income has become a major concern to individuals and corporations.

Determining the actual state of tax evasion involves the government auditor calculating a probable tax by comparing the population income and expenditure against those taxpayers whose income is derived in a manner that cannot avoid the declaration and payment of tax, such as a pay-as-you-earn tax system. Based on that analysis, the extent of tax evasion can be generally inferred if the total economic activity can be estimated and declared income deducted.

Indirect taxes, such as a sales tax or value added tax (VAT), are also vulnerable to fraud. When a business charges indirect taxes to the consumer, the taxable portion must be remitted to the appropriate taxation authorities within the country. In the case of VAT, businesses are normally permitted to offset VAT paid for specific goods or services against their VAT collected, and the net amount is then paid to the taxation authority. Depending on the nature of the VAT system implemented, the tax due may be calculated at the time of invoice or at the time of payment. This, itself, can give rise to fraud when tax refunds are claimed for items invoiced when no payment has as yet been made.

Audit data analysis in indirect tax gathering can detect such frauds if executed on a large scale by matching revenues, costs, and profits against a theoretical tax due and comparing it to tax declared and collected.

One of the easier ways to evade indirect taxation payable over to the government is to process sales without recording them. Again this will show up if the auditor compares the ratio of items purchased and sold and finds that sales revenue including tax is not appropriate for the number of items purchased to be sold.

As long as these practices do not become excessive or are spread over a wide variety of suppliers, there is a strong possibility that an organization conducting such a fraud may remain undetected for an extended period.

Other forms of indirect taxation fraud include the avoidance of excise duty on commodities such as fuel, tobacco, and alcohol. Because revenues from these indirect taxes represent a significant portion of the taxation income of all state and national governments, tax evasion in these areas is seen as a significant threat.

Audit analysis and comparisons of purchases versus sales and excise duty declared for payment purposes may indicate a supplier selling goods in a "low-excise duty area" with revenues that do not match.

When it comes to government expenditures, again, internal audits can use data analysis to assist in the areas of

- Budget and project management on capital and operational projects
- Delivery of appropriate social services in the correct manner and at an acceptable cost
- Delivery of health services
- Delivery of infrastructure services
- Ensuring an effective amount spent on armed services and internal security services

With the high values flowing through all government channels, fraud detection is a major aspect of government data analytics for the auditor. The potential for excessive charges, non-delivery of services or items paid for, payment of "commissions" and other forms of bribery within the supply chain as well as the cancellation of debt during revenue collection is massive. Fortunately, such frauds leave behind a data trail, which can be as obvious as a neon sign but will only be seen if someone goes looking.

Inefficiencies in government processes can also contribute to non-delivery of services or massive overspending in achieving service delivery. Once again, appropriate audit use of data analysis can readily identify the red flags indicating such inefficiencies. For example, data analysis of budget and project management could involve the following:

- Monitoring of sole-contractor awards
- Analysis of actual costs incurred in such contracts compared to both contracted costs and costs proposed in unsuccessful competitive bids
- Monitoring of expenditures with respect to budget
- Identification of high value projects that are under-expended
- Identification of high-volume projects that are either unfinanced or unauthorized
- A recalculation of key indicators during the progress of projects
- Recalculation of key indicators on completed projects
- Comparisons of ownerships of suppliers with payroll information to identify employee ownership of vendors

Once again, a similar type of audit program may be developed for other government expenditure areas.

Retail

Retail audits are typified by high volumes of transaction information at comparatively low value per transaction. In many such audits, the primary focus may be on loss prevention and inventory control. Financial auditing within a retail environment may focus on sales analysis, cash disbursements, and accounts receivable as well as the normal general ledger analysis.

As an example, loss prevention analysis could include such items as the following:

- Identification of high-risk transactions and tracking by employee
- Analysis of incomplete exchange transactions
- Analysis of voided transactions followed by no-sale transactions
- Aging of the time difference between check purchases and refunds within a minimal time
- Analysis of selling price differences between stores to identify potential fraudulent transactions

In the same manner, sales analysis may be carried out by, for example, the following:

- Comparisons of sales and profitability reports by region, store, product line, and the like
- Trend analysis of sales over similar periods
- Analysis of orders received but not delivered
- Analysis and identification of high-dollar volumes by region, store, product, etc.

Overall, the analyses will be directed by the nature of the retail operation so that high-value, low-volume retail of luxury goods will be looked at in a different manner from low-value, high-volume retail of, for example, food products. In the same way, the analyses used on durable goods will differ from those used on perishable items with short shelf-lives.

Services and Distribution

Once again, distribution warehousing would require a different approach to analysis based on the differing nature of the business. Areas such as inventory control, sales, and purchase order management become critical performance areas and would be subject to extensive analysis. The inventory management area would include such items as the following:

- Sampling records for physical reconciliation testing
- Statistical analysis of stock item utilization
- Identification of slow moving stock items
- Identification of obsolete stock based upon inventory turnover
- Identification of duplicate stock items
- Analysis of high value transactions

Once again, the normal analyses of items, such as salaries, general ledger, and accounts payable and receivable, would be required.

Health Care

Health care auditing covers a variety of operational areas affecting service delivery to patients, a variety of clinical subsystems, managed care, patient billing, material and drug management and inventory control, and position service delivery as well as information systems security of confidential patient data.

Health care is another disbursement area where fraud opportunities are rife. Within health care, fraud encompasses a variety of techniques adopted in order to defraud those entities that provide the funding for health care. The fraud may be at the governmental level or private health insurance companies and may be conducted by patients or the medical profession.

The US government Medicare system, with a budget of over $450 billion and over 40 million beneficiaries, is seen as a major cash cow for fraudsters. Medicare also suffers a large drawback compared to smaller private insurers because it is required by law to send out payments within a very short time period. This gives the criminal the opportunity to make false claims, take the money, and run, leaving Medicare to chase after him or her, attempting to

- Find the criminal
- Prove that this was the individual making a false claims
- Seek restitution

The timing element means that Medicare is not in a position to check the legitimacy of all bills before payment is made. Thus, Medicare is forced into a reactive mode, responding to tips and allegations rather than being in a position to proactively establish antifraud measures. In this environment, data analytics have to take a more proactive form with the auditors perhaps opting for a continuous auditing approach as detailed in Chapter 15.

Auditing health care involves the audit of current practice against standards in any aspect of health care and includes both clinical and nonclinical audits. The purpose of a health care audit is to monitor to what degree standards for any given health care activity are met, identify reasons why they are not met, and identify and implement changes in practice to meet those standards. These standards should be evidence based. The standards can be clinical, for example, cancer management standards, or nonclinical, for example, record management standards.

In the case of nonclinical audits, analyses may be carried out on such items as the following:

- Patient billing
- Accounts receivable
- Overall charges
- Accounts payable
- Medical claims
- Managed care
- Others as appropriate

Taking as an example patient billing, the auditor may wish to analyze the average days from discharge to bill and from bill to payment, age receivables on date-of-service against invoice date in order to calculate cash flow, identify high-dollar accounts, analyze rejected payments, and similar transactional analyses.

In the case of medical claims, the auditor may need to analyze such items as the timeliness of claim payments. This could, for example, be carried out by analyzing data on claim received and comparing to data on the claim paid. In addition, fraudulent claims or simple accidental duplicate billings may be sought against patient records or provider records.

A clinical audit need not involve extensive data collection because it need not require large numbers of cases. Depending on the needs of the audit, analyses would typically be performed based upon type of illness, treatments prescribed, duration and hospital care, analysis by service provider, and the like.

General Accounting Analyses

In all business areas, normal accounting procedures can also be effectively analyzed for such items as changes within financial ratios, selection of journal entries for audit tracing and analysis, preparation of trial balances, comparisons of ledger transactions to budget reports, cash flow analyses, and the like.

The overall usage of analyses within the business are limited only by the auditor's vision and requirement for relevant audit evidence.

11

ANALYSIS OF BIG DATA

This chapter examines the audit advantages and methodologies for the analysis of Big Data. Big Data is a term given to large data sets containing a variety of data types. Big Data analysis allows the auditor to seek hidden patterns and identify concealed correlations, market trends, and other data interrelationships, which can indicate areas for improved operational efficiencies within business processes.

Although data has always been the kernel of computing, it is the ability to access data on an enormous scale that has turned the tide toward the analysis and manipulation of Big Data, bearing in mind that not all Big Data is useful data. Classifying all data as Big Data can lead to a mindset that old data will be useful someday and should be retained "just in case."

Although conventional volumes of transactional data have been counted in terms of gigabytes or even terabytes, Big Data includes unstructured data, such as text, audio, and video, and may run to petabytes (to 1,024 terabytes) or even exabytes (1,024 petabytes). For example,

- Wal-Mart is estimated to hold more than 2.5 petabytes in the corporate databases.
- E-Bay has two warehouses that are estimated at over 50 Pb.

Deploying a large number of small, cheap servers in a distributed computing system can frequently be more economically feasible than buying a single machine with the same computational capabilities, making the manipulation of Big Data cost-effective.

Used effectively, Big Data will change the way companies both identify and relate to their customer base. In his article, Doug

Laney* classifies Big Data as operating within the paradigms of the three Vs:

- *Volume*—The size of the data
- *Velocity*—The speed of new incoming data
- *Variety*—The variation of data formats and types

This is combined with the amount of simultaneous processing required (*concurrency*).

Studies have shown that organizations that use effective data analysis as a basis for decision making are more productive than those that do not.[†]

Traditional data analysis software, such as spreadsheets and relational databases, was generally designed to be used on a single machine. In order to be able to scale to unprecedented size, systems needed to be built that could run on clusters of machines.

In the commercial sector, Big Data can provide answers to many questions, perhaps too many for the traditional roles in analysis. As a result, having a competitive exploitation of the opportunities deriving from Big Data analytics necessitates a focus on analyst skills and education.

In the governmental sector, the utilization of information and communication technology (ICT) to improve public sector services started with the whole e-government concept. This transformation of government services using ICTs has proven to be a complex and costly task, often associated with the automation of public services combined with business systems integration leading to the Smart City concept.

The initiatives driving such interventions are fundamentally based on Big Data. Public service delivery, in today's world, is inextricably intertwined with civic participation via social media, mobile computing, smartphones, and the like, utilizing real-time, high-volume, unstructured information.

A new concept to enter media is the *Internet of Things* (IoT), referring to the network of intelligent devices, which includes sensors to

---

* Laney, Doug. "3D Data Management: Controlling Data Volume, Velocity, and Variety" http://blogs.gartner.com/doug-laney/files/2012/01/ad949-3D-Data-Management -Controlling-Data-Volume-Velocity-and-Variety.pdf.
† Brynjolfsson, Erik, Lorin Hitt, and Heekyung Kim. "Strength in Numbers: How Does Data-Driven Decisionmaking Affect Firm Performance?" (2011).

measure the environment around them; actuators that physically act back into their environment, such as opening a door; processors to handle and store the vast data generated; nodes to relay the information; and coordinators to help manage sets of these components.[*]

Big Data management has a core role to play in supporting decisions in all of these spheres, due to the ability to profile people and triangulate information about individuals. Thus, Big Data analytics offers the opportunity to address some fundamental concerns within the provision of public services.

Online Analytical Processing (OLAP)

Due to the sheer volume of data involved, conventional two-dimensional database management systems were unable to handle Big Data in an acceptable manner. This led to the development of online analytical processing. Using ODBC, data can be imported from existing relational databases in order to create a multidimensional database with OLAP capability. The multidimensional nature results in formation of an OLAP cube in order to organize the data and facilitate the expression of relationships among data. OLAP servers are available from most of the large vendors including IBM, Microsoft, Oracle, and SAP as well as specialized vendors including Jedox and Infor and software available from the open source community.

Using the appropriate software tools, high-speed query performance can be achieved in high-volume data as a result of indexing, caching, and optimized storage techniques. It does, however, retain the problem that structuring large data volumes into usable formats cannot be achieved instantly, and given the extensive times required for such data loads, OLAP data commonly involves processing only data that is changed rather than reprocessing the full database.

Of recent years, variations on OLAP have included the following:

- *ROLAP*—Working with relational databases and specialized schemas to facilitate interrogation to the lowest levels of detail within the databases to bypass the need for data cubes.

---

[*] Zhang, L., and Mitton, N. "Advanced Internet of Things." 2011 International Conference on Internet of Things and 4th International Conference on Cyber, Physical and Social Computing, pp. 1–8 (2011).

- *HOLAP*—Involving a hybrid solution facilitating both specialized storage for less detailed data and relational databases for a high quantity of data. This allows the interfacing of relational data sources and data cubes.

Interrogation query languages for such servers will depend on the server chosen but will normally include the following:

- *XML (extensible markup language)*—which defines rules for encoding documents and bridges the human-readable and machine-readable gap in a standardized form.
- *OLE-DB (object linking and embedding, database)*—an application program interface (API) from Microsoft facilitating the accessing of data from multiple sources in a uniform manner.
- *MDX (multidimensional expressions)*—a query language utilizing the specialized syntax for handling multidimensional data stored in OLAP cubes. Initially introduced by Microsoft, it has since been adopted by most OLAP vendors as a de facto standard.
- *LINQ (language-integrated query)*—also from Microsoft, this is an extension of C+ and Visual Basic using standard patterns for query of data in a form that is easy for the nontechnical auditor to learn and is intended to support virtually any kind of data storage.

Big Data Structures

When dealing with high volumes of data within a data warehouse environment, the usual query structures may not be applicable. When faced with a typical relational database, audit analysis is usually carried out against the center of normalized database tables associated with each other via primary key (PK) and foreign key (FK) structures. Within a data warehouse environment, a *star schema* is a common means of organizing data. The concept is based on a central detailed *fact* table linked to surrounding dimension tables, thus,

- *Fact table*—A large accumulation of facts, such as sales. These tables are often maintained as *insert only*.

- *Dimension tables*—Smaller tables containing information about the entities involved within the facts tables. These tables are normally static.

An example of such a star schema is given in Diagram 11.1.

As can be seen, the fact table may be used to relate the dimensions to each other and, at the same time, indicates the measures to be accumulated—in this case "total items," "total cost," "total sales value," and "holding cost."

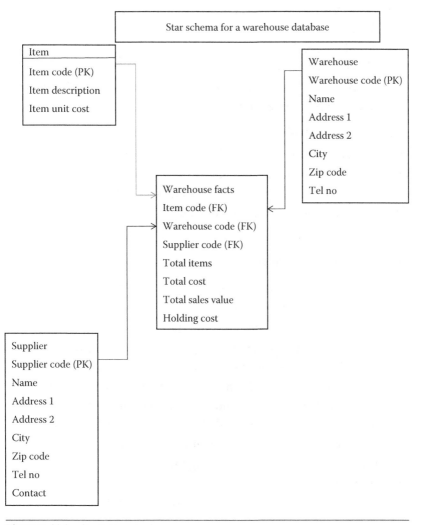

Diagram 11.1   Star table example.

The star schema can then be accumulated into a cube form representing pre-computed results from a given inquiry within a given star schema. Inquiries would correspond to specialized OLAP operations, such as roll-ups, drill-downs, or slice-and-dice.

From an audit perspective, OLAP technology facilitates a multidimensional approach to data interrogation with great analytical flexibility, principally in the following areas:

- Multi-angle data observation—Facilitating fast identification of suspicious aspects within data sets
- Data drilling of suspicious items—Giving the ability to conduct more extensive analysis of data observation items raising auditor suspicions
- Creation of advance data models—Facilitating the precreation of audit data structures to improve audit efficiency by reducing data collection time

OLAP technology should not be seen as the answer to all information analysis problems. Although it is highly effective and efficient in answering *known questions* quickly, it may be difficult to adapt rapidly to new data types and new questions and can prove expensive when data volumes move into a petabyte scale.

Other Big Data Technologies

Other technologies for data structuring are rapidly infusing the marketplace and include the following.

NoSQL databases are designed for huge horizontal scaling with high availability and are typically highly optimized for data retrieval and appending. These databases offer flexibility in the data model, facilitating easy storage and combination of data structures and modification of the data schema without the need to bring down the database. Because of the nature and the focus on scalability, databases can be partitioned or *sharded*, allowing the database to be deployed in-house or in a cloud and facilitating virtually unlimited growth. In terms of performance, NoSQL databases are designed to deliver high performance both in throughput and latency period. The trade-off in such databases can be the traditional relational capabilities, depending upon the package selected. Within non-relational databases, two primary architectures exist:

- *Key-value data stores*—This architecture allows each record in a database to be accessed by a single key, and the data need not match a preexisting schema. Such architectures allow for very fast access performance; however, they generally lack the ability to query data by value.
- *Document stores*—These provide the ability to query against the document itself. This architecture excels when the data to be retrieved is best used in single-document form (such as website content) or when the database schema is very fluid.

Analytic RDBMSs, such as the Microsoft SQL server or Oracle, are designed for bulk load and optimized for fast query downloads. They have the advantage that the technology is mature with a variety of technologies available. The structures are highly efficient for updating data while simultaneously maintaining data integrity and are very efficient for set operations and relational algebra. Problems can occur due to the use of fixed schemas (Schema on Write) and potentially high overheads with full transaction logging used. Inserts of new data can be slow due to the indexing approaches used; however, RDBMSs are based on a tried-and-true design in which each record of data is normalized and ideally stored only once in a single place. This system is effective as long as data always looks the same and stays within a specific size limit.

Hadoop is a low-cost and reliable scale-out architecture ideal for distributed computing, which is emerging as a main player in the Big Data processing market. From an audit perspective, the use of technologies like Hadoop, embracing huge, unstructured data sets and processing data in an ad hoc fashion, enables the use of tools like Hadoop's *MapReduce* framework to answer questions about huge amounts of data.

It utilizes masses of redundant storage capacity across commodity clusters with many distributions available, such as Apache, Hortonworks, HADAPT, and the like. Using Apache as an example, a multitude of applications are available for the Hadoop implementation, including the following:

- *Apache Hbase*—The Hadoop database itself, including random, real-time read/write access
- *Apache Zookeeper*—A distributed coordination service
- *Apache Whirr*—A library for running Hadoop in the cloud
- *Flume*—A distributed service for collecting and aggregating log and event data
- *Apache Pig*—A high-level language for expressing data analysis programs
- *Apache Hive*—An SQL-like language and metadata repository
- *Sqoop*—Used for integrating Hadoop with RDBMS
- *Hue*—A browser-based desktop interface for interacting with Hadoop

Unlike conventional database structures, which require that the data schema be designed before data can be loaded, Hadoop uses "schema-on-read," a concept allowing data to be copied to the file store without requiring transformation into database structures. A serializer/deserializer (SerDe) is used during interrogation to extract the columns—a technique known as *late binding*. This has the advantage that data flow can occur anytime and will appear within Hadoop retroactively once the SerDe is updated to parse the information.

Hadoop, along with the *Hadoop Distributed File System* (HDFS), facilitates the splitting of data processing tasks across a collection of different machines. Users are not required to know exactly what data is available on which specific node within the Hadoop cluster. HDFS is also designed to provide a fault tolerance through data replication. As a result, if a single node in a Hadoop cluster is unavailable, the data will still be available elsewhere in the cluster in a location known to Hadoop.

In a normal Hadoop installation, MapReduce is provided as an interface. It is then possible to write MapReduce workflows using the auditor's preferred scripting language in order to, for example, convert values in massive collections of raw text files from one data type to another for future analysis.

One complication for auditors is Hadoop's use of the specific jargon where, for example, using MapReduce is a three-phase process such that

- *Map phase*—Splits the data into many shards identified by specific keys
- *Shuffle sort*—Aggregates data shards containing the same key on the same node within a cluster
- *Reduce phase*—Takes the shuffled data from individual nodes, processes it on local machines, and produces a final result

This jargon can be confusing to auditors operating in this type of environment for the first time.

Hive

As has been noted above, Hive is an SQL-like language and meta-data repository. Hive has the ability to support queries over a range of source formats, including raw text files. Its basic unit of data is a table in a similar manner to a relational database in that it consists of a two-dimensional "spreadsheet" structure with rows containing records.

Hive provides an SQL-like language (*HiveQL*), which enables functionality (such as GROUP BY, JOINs, and HAVING) in the same way as standard SQL; however, there are some limitations in the type of query as compared to standard SQL because of the differences between the design of a normal relational database and the MapReduce framework. Hive is essentially a system to translate SQL-like queries into Hadoop MapReduce jobs.

As an alternative, multiple open-source derivatives of high-speed query engines are available to run with Hadoop.

Statistical Analysis and Big Data

Due to the sheer volumes involved as well as the velocity and the unstructured nature of some of the data, the ability of auditors to use statistical sampling may be

a. Essential
b. Difficult

Big Data statistical sampling, in terms of volume, intensity, and complexity, exceeds the ability of standard audit software tools to manage and analyze, leaving the auditor faced with two major problems:

- The sheer volume of data may be too big to fit in the auditor's computer prior to sampling.
- The actual data analysis may be too time-consuming using traditional audit sampling techniques.

The auditor is then faced with the need for applying a different form of statistical analysis using scalable computability. Several approaches have been devised, such as the following:

- *Divide and conquer approach*—This approach partitions large data sets into blocks, processes each block independently, and then aggregates the solutions to form the final solution for the whole data set.
- *Subsampling-based approaches*—Subsampling is an alternative method utilizing resampling techniques. For example, the auditor would sample a small proportion of the data with certain weights (subsample) from the full sample. The intended analysis for the full sample would be executed using the small subsample as a surrogate. This approach is known as *leveraging*.
- *Sequential updating approach*—In some Big Data applications, the data come in streams or large chunks, and a sequentially updated analysis is desirable without requiring large storage capacity.

R

One implementation of these approaches may be found in the use of *R*, which is currently one of the most popular open-source statistical software.

R is a system for statistical computation and graphics consisting of a programming language plus a run-time environment with graphics, a debugger, access to certain system functions, and the ability to run programs stored in script files. This allows the auditor to execute data analysis in R by writing scripts and functions in the R programming language.

It is a complete, interactive, object-oriented language designed by statisticians for statisticians although highly effective for audit use. Included within R are objects, operators, and functions that simplify the process of exploring, modeling, and visualizing data.

R is a free software environment for statistical computing and graphics. It compiles and runs on a wide variety of UNIX platforms, Windows, and MacOS. The open-source software most commonly used by statisticians is R.

The R language makes available functions for virtually every data manipulation, statistical model, or chart that the auditor could conceive. Additionally, because a great deal of experimental statistical analysis is done in R within its user community, the latest techniques are usually available first in the R system.

Further details on R may be found via CRAN, the *Comprehensive R Archive Network*, https://cran.r-project.org/.

12

RESULTS ANALYSIS AND VALIDATION

This chapter examines how auditors may confirm the results of the analysis with business owners and, when necessary, revise the audit approach and re-perform selected analyses as appropriate.

The use of appropriately designed and correctly executed analytical procedures carried out on quality data facilitate the auditor achieving audit objectives efficiently and effectively while reducing the extent of alternative detailed audit testing required. It should not be seen that analytical procedures replace the need for good, professional auditor judgment and an in-depth understanding of the organization and its operating environment.

Any conclusions the auditor draws are only as good as the data used to draw them. He or she may have the best analytical tools in the world at his or her disposal, but without reliable data, they're worse than useless because they will inevitably lead the auditor to draw erroneous conclusions or arrive at the correct conclusions without being able to substantiate them. This is true not only for audit purposes; but accurate and up-to-date data is critical for all organizations for managerial purposes.

It is generally accepted that, over a period of time, data degrades or decays in terms of currency, accuracy, and completeness. This may come about as a result of data corruption over time or simply that data is not maintained in a current state. Data verification may be defined as ensuring the accuracy of the items recorded, and data validation addresses the carrying out of standardized and often automated checks on the completeness, accuracy, and validity of the data contents.

Results analysis and validation is a two-stage process involving the validation of the data input to the analysis process, as covered in Chapter 1, followed by the confirmation of the results of the analysis and the analysis process itself with the business process owners.

One critical objective is to ensure that audit evidence acquired when using substantive analytical procedures is relevant and reliable. Given that the primary purpose of internal audit use of analytical procedures is to obtain assurance, in combination with other audit testing, such as tests of controls, document reviews, and interviewing regarding both financial and operational areas, it is essential that evidence obtained is both factual and capable of being substantiated.

Internal audit use of analytical procedures is based on the expectation that relationships among data exist and will continue to exist given no changes to the risk and control environment. It is the existence of these relationships that provide the underlying basis for audit conclusions regarding the completeness, accuracy, and occurrence of transactions and processes.

Audit analytical procedures may be used to identify patterns in data that may form the foundation for multiple audit assertions as well as identifying additional audit issues that may not be apparent from other audit processes. These patterns may indicate risks or deficiencies in internal control that had been previously obscured and that may require revisions to the intended audit approach, including the acquisition of further evidence from independent, non-analytical sources.

Results validation begins well in advance of the actual production of analytical results. The search for valid analytical evidence should not be a haphazard process in which the auditor browses data at random searching for anything that strikes him or her as unusual or worthy of further investigation. Such browsing is inefficient, time wasting, does not inspire auditee confidence, and, worst of all, is normally ineffective.

Rather, the auditor, following a specific audit plan, is seeking evidence that specific control objectives have been achieved, are being achieved, and will continue to be achieved.

Implementation of the Audit Plan

The audit process flows from the business process in that the primary requirements for any audit are to establish first the *business objectives* and then the *control objectives* of a particular audit area. For example, the overall business objective of the payroll department may be to pay employees. The control objectives would include paying the right amount, at the right rate, at the right time, to the right people, in an authorized manner.

The *audit objectives* are typically, but not always, to determine if one or more control objectives have been achieved in the past, are being achieved currently, and will continue to be achieved in the future.

In order to determine this, an auditor must seek the appropriate *evidence* of the achievement or non-achievement of these objectives. Given that many of the controls that management will have implemented will be preventative controls that will not necessarily leave behind evidence of their effectiveness or even of their existence, an auditor may have to look for evidence within detective controls or even compensating controls to establish an opinion on the control objectives.

After identifying the evidence source, the appropriate *audit techniques* may be selected. These techniques may include any of the standard ones, such as observation, questioning, document analysis, computer interrogation, and analysis, which is our particular concern here. Once the techniques have been decided upon, the auditor is then in a position to select the appropriate methodology or tool, such as the use of generalized audit software, use of interrogation software, etc.

Once the techniques and tools are selected, the analysis may progress in the structured format selected by the auditor.

Substantive Analytical Procedures

Analytical procedures may be used to substantiate an audit expectation of probable evidence regarding the achievement of control objectives. These expectations are normally developed based upon results of previous audits, discussions with management, knowledge of the industry trends, and the auditor's observations of the general quality of internal controls. It should be stressed, however, that the expectations must be owned by the auditor and developed independently. Analytical testing should not be expected to achieve results identical to the auditor's expectation, but rather to produce evidence within a previously agreed upon acceptable tolerance of the anticipated results. This tolerance is an indication of the acceptable deviation from anticipated results, including acceptable levels of potential misstatements or tolerable error rates.

The development of an appropriately precise, objective expectation is the most important step in the effective utilization of substantive analytical procedures. When tolerances are developed after the analysis, auditor or management bias may have a significant impact on the subsequent evaluation.

Once the auditor's expectations have been established and agreed upon with management, the analysis can take place with the evidence found being compared to expected values and significant differences identified. When such differences are found, and in particular when such differences exceed expected tolerances, the auditor will typically investigate the causes of such differences, particularly in regard to internal control failures or omissions. If the differences are caused by unexpected conditions, the auditor may be required to reevaluate previous assumptions and expectations and may even redesign the test procedures.

Unexpected conditions may include changes to the degree of reliance the auditor may place upon data provided based on such factors as the source of the data, the age of the data, and whether the data originates from a source previously audited and found to be reliable.

In examining the evidence, the auditor should be in a position to evaluate whether the control objective has or has not been achieved in the past and will or will not continue to be achieved in the future. This would form the basis for presentations of opinions and conclusions combined with the appropriate recommendations and any requisite substantiating evidence in the formal audit report.

Audit analytical procedures will vary depending on the nature of the data and the type of evidence sought but will typically include the following:

- *Reasonableness testing*—Evaluating data against expected norms for either financial or nonfinancial data
- *Trend analysis*—Identify significant variations in data trends observed over a period as compared to the expected trends based on past experience or movements in similar accounts
- *Ratio analysis*—Comparing relationships between data types against expected ratios or over a period of time

Combinations of analytical procedures are common in arriving at audit conclusions with the objective, as always, of obtaining evidence that is factual, adequate, and convincing. The evaluation of the evidence to ensure it is both factual and adequate is a major component of both data and results validation.

Validation

Data validation is the process by which the auditor verifies the accuracy and completeness of information obtained or derived prior to analysis. Inconsistencies identified at this stage need to be examined and, when appropriate, corrected prior to the actual analysis taking place. It should, however, be noted that validation does not prove the accuracy and correctness of data; it can only check the reasonableness of data presented for analysis. However, it must always be remembered that the best analysis possible is at the mercy of the quality of data presented. Data validation is intended to ensure that data obtained for analysis is reasonable, complete, and falls within acceptable boundaries. It does not guarantee the "correctness" of the data.

Data may be validated by a variety of procedures, such as the following:

- *Data type validation*—At its most basic, data type validation is a process intended to verify that the character content of fields defined is consistent with the expected characters specified for data retrieval, such as string characters, integers, or containing the appropriate number of decimal places.
- *Format checking*—Checks that the data obtained is structured appropriately. For example, numeric data fields contain only numeric information, Social Security numbers are appropriately structured, or date fields conform to specific data structures.
- *Length checking*—Ensures that data fields contain information of appropriate lengths without excessive contents or insufficient contents.
- *Existence checks*—Ensures that data does not contain blank fields where inappropriate.
- *Range checks*—Ensure that data obtained falls within specified value ranges.
- *Cross-reference verification*—Ensures the data obtained falls within validity constraints appropriate to the organization,

utilizing the appropriate look-up tables to confirm that data presented for analysis meets the corporate standards for data structures, for example, ensuring that country codes fall within the corporate list of acceptable country code definitions.

- *Referential integrity validation*—This is a technique commonly used in analyzing relational database values, whereby two tables of data can be linked through the use of a primary key and foreign key. This ensures that the referencing data table must always refer to a valid row in the referenced table.
- *Check digit validation*—Ensuring data contained within a field is valid by recalculation of in-built check digits, for example, the last digit of an ISBN code for a book utilizing check digits calculated using modulus 10.
- *Data cardinality validation*—This is a process whereby the auditor verifies that data for analysis is related to an appropriate number of additional records, for example, for a cardinality > 0, a customer order record would require an associated customer record. In the same way, a customer record indicated as "suspended" would have a cardinality = 0 with no customer orders permitted.
- *Hash checking*—This is the calculation of an otherwise meaningless total, for example, a total of customer numbers, prior to data acquisition, to be recalculated once data has been acquired in order to ensure the completeness of data presented for analysis.
- *Data field uniqueness validation*—This form of data validation allows the auditor to ensure the data presented does not contain duplicates by evaluating key fields, such as customer number or employee number, to ensure uniqueness where duplication is not allowed. For example, in the customer master file, the customer number would be the unique field, and in a customer order file, duplicate customer numbers would be permitted.

These checks assist in ensuring that the data presented to the auditor for analysis can, as far as possible, be relied upon to provide accurate and complete data to the analysis process.

High-quality data permits increased confidence in the audit analytical process and reduces the probability of erroneous acceptance of analytical results or the erroneous rejection of the results as an outcome of good analytical technique conducted upon poor quality data. Data validation is commonly seen as an automated process as data is extracted; however, the more complicated the data structures, the greater the need for further manual validation may be required. Overall, the validation process is intended to ascertain the usability of the data in view of the audit tests to be performed and the conclusions intended to be derived.

Data Selection Bias

A critical area in the verification of results is obtaining assurance that no auditor bias was introduced in either the data selection process or the choice of analytical techniques. Any selection or analytical bias can potentially distort the reliability of the results of an analysis. An unbiased analysis must be free from selection or procedural bias. Selection bias may be caused by the auditor's perception of the nature of controls as well as the selection of risk mitigation factors to be relied upon. When the auditor chooses to place reliance on specific components of the organization's risk assessment and mitigation programs, an automatic bias may be introduced into the selection process, resulting in the selected group differing characteristically from the overall population.

Procedure bias may result from the use of incorrect criteria for selection, unavailability of data, seasonal fluctuations that may skew the data, or the use of nonrandom selection when sampling is utilized.

Questionnaire Analysis

When the analysis data is derived from questionnaires, the potential for bias increases and is influenced by the choice of questions selected as well as the wording of the questions and use of analysis based on data derived from Likert scales.

Questionnaires suffer from the same deficiencies as testimonial evidence in that the auditor may receive responses that are accurate or inaccurate, the truth or interpretations of the truth, or simply what the person believes the auditor would like to hear. As a result, the questions must be carefully considered in order to ensure that the answers reflect the true state of affairs. A significant weakness lies in the fact that many audit-based questions make it obvious that the "correct" answer to many of the questions is "yes."

Use of Likert Scales in Data Analysis

A common device used in questionnaires that are going to be analyzed is the use of the Likert scale. This type of scale, named for its developer Dr. Rensis Likert, is a psychometric response scale intended to derive the participants' degree of agreement with the statement or set of statements. These statements use an ordinal scale, commonly a five-point scale with responses ranging from "strongly agree" on one end to "strongly disagree" on the other, with the midpoint of "neither agree or disagree." Occasionally, the auditor may use a scale with more points in order to add granularity as can be seen in Diagram 12.1.

As can be seen above, this type of scale is commonly associated with interval data where the difference between +2 and +1 is the same as the difference between +1 and 0. Although the response levels have relative positions, they are *not* interval scales and cannot be treated as such from a statistical standpoint. That is to say that the average of "strongly agree" and "agree" cannot be said to be "agree and ½." Such data can be analyzed using different analysis methods, such as the use of the following:

- Nonparametric tests utilizing differences between the meetings of comparable groups, such as the following:
  - Mann-Whitney *U* test
  - Wilcoxon signed-rank test
  - Kruskal-Wallis test

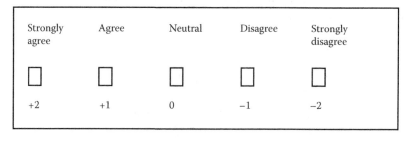

Strongly agree	Agree	Neutral	Disagree	Strongly disagree
☐	☐	☐	☐	☐
+2	+1	0	−1	−2

Diagram 12.1   Typical Likert scale.

- Central tendencies summarized by median and mode but not mean
- Bar charts and dot charts, but not histograms because the data is not continuous

Because they are used primarily to obtain opinion data, Likert scales may also be biased as participants may try to avoid extreme responses and group their answers around a central point. Once again, opinions expressed may be intended to present the auditor with what it is believed he or she wants to hear.

When answers to questionnaires are reduced to nominal levels, such as "agree" or "disagree," then tests such as the chi-squared test may be used.

Questionnaire design is an art in its own right, and a poorly designed questionnaire may result in a data flow that is biased from the onset. Use of jargon within questionnaires raises the question of whether the person completing the questionnaire actually understood the question.

For further details on these techniques see Chapter 7.

Statistical Reliability Analysis

The validity of an instrument refers to whether it accurately measures the attribute of interest. The reliability of an instrument concerns whether it produces identical results in repeated applications. An instrument may be reliable but not valid. However, it cannot be valid without being reliable.

Reliability of measurement involves three factors:

- *Stability*—Ensures consistent results with repeated measurement on the same scale
- *Equivalence*—Determines how much error was introduced by different investigators or different samples
- *Internal consistency*—Considers the consistency or homogeneity among the items of an instrument

External validity measures the ability to be generalized, and internal validity can examine three separate factors:

- *Content or face validity*—Determines whether the measuring instrument provides adequate coverage of the topic

- *Criterion-related validity*—Determines the success of the measures used for empirical estimating purposes
- *Construct validity*—Both convergent and discriminant involve comparison to previously assessed results

Cronbach's alpha (or coefficient alpha) is such a measure of internal reliability.

13

FRAUD DETECTION USING DATA ANALYSIS

This chapter examines the techniques available to the auditor in order to identify the red flags and indicators that fraud may be occurring or may have occurred in the past as well as the obtaining of forensically acceptable data analytical evidence.

A critical element to be borne in mind whenever forensic investigation may become an issue is that the evidence gathered must be in a form acceptable to a court of law. The general rules governing the presentation of evidence in court as detailed within this book will also be affected by the legal environment within which the forensic evidence will be presented.

Red Flags and Indicators

Red flags may be seen as early warning indicators that the risk of fraud in a particular area is either higher than is normally tolerable or has increased over a period. These can be categorized as pressure sources and changes in behavior as well as general personality traits.

Pressure Sources

Pressure sources occur within the environment of the individual. In general, management should be alert for indicators, which could include the following:

- Lifestyle exceeding income capacity
- Medical problems for the employee or a family member
- Loss of job for a family member
- Financial pressures from a variety of sources
- Divorce
- Substance abuse

Changes in Behavior

In some cases, perpetrators of fraud will exhibit changes in behavior that could alert management to the possibility of fraudulent practices occurring and could include the following:

- Sudden increase in the visibility of valuable material possessions
- Decreases in productivity and increases in signs of dissatisfaction at work
- Mood changes and irritability increase
- Borrowing money from coworkers and others
- Refusing promotion
- Refusing to take vacation time
- Working unnecessary overtime
- Carrying large amounts of cash
- Rewriting records for the sake of "neatness"

General Personality Traits

When high levels of fraud have occurred, studies have indicated that certain specific personality traits may be red flag indicators of potential fraudsters. These could include the following:

- Work performance levels considerably higher than the norm
- Dominating and controlling
- Dislike of their work being reviewed
- Maintaining excessively close relationships with vendors or customers
- Exhibiting a strong desire to display material wealth

It should be noted that none of these red flags prove that a fraud has taken place or will take place. They are simply indicators that should alert management to a higher potential fraud risk, particularly when combined with known weakness in internal controls within an area or areas where an employee has sole authority and responsibility.

In addition to these red flags, fraud may occur with no visible indicators pointing to specific individuals, and it is in this area that data analytics may identify patterns indicating the presence of abnormal transactions that may be related to products and services on offer.

Frauds occur commonly in the following areas:

- Purchasing and supplier payment frauds
- Receivables frauds
- Bank accounts/cash accounts frauds
- Payroll frauds

Fraud risks in these areas include activities such as the following:

- Accounts opened specifically to defraud the institution or organization
  - Manipulations of the clearing cycle
  - Abuse of corporate checkbooks and guarantee cards
- Fraudulently altered electronic transfers on client accounts

In order to carry out such frauds, the perpetrator has two main objectives:

- To obtain value
- To conceal his or her actions

To do this, the fraudster must be in a position to remove the funds or other assets. This activity is made easier when the assets are digital assets and the fraudster has right of access to move assets around. In today's computer systems, such access can facilitate manipulation of bank accounts and payment systems as well as manipulation of credit sanctioning and loan administration procedures.

Red flags in these areas may include functional indicators, such as the following:

- Unexplained changes in financial statement balances
- Urgent need to report favorable earnings
- High debt or interest burdens
- Cash flow problems
- The existence of abnormal prices or terms in contracts
- Specifications that can be met by one supplier only
- Dates of tender after the official closing date
- Changes to specification or price soon after contract is awarded
- Clerical documentation not supporting digital transactions
- Erratic inventory levels used to trigger volume discounts

- Unusual or large and profitable transactions toward the end or at the start of accounting periods
- Duplicate payments
- Common names or addresses of payees or customers

When frauds are perpetrated at the technical level, red flags indicating the potential existence of fraud could include the following:

- Operating performance anomalies
- Analytical anomalies

With these indicators in mind, a search pattern using data analytics may become the auditor's tool of choice.

Nature of Computer Fraud

Computer fraud itself takes a variety of forms. In traditional, transaction-based systems, changes to source documents prior to processing but after authorization is a common fraudulent technique involving no additional access to computer systems. In modern online systems, a variety of techniques, including impersonation of authorized users and piggybacking on authorized access as well as the introduction of fictitious transactions are all potential techniques. With the introduction of e-commerce, fraud opportunities have abounded due to the significant size of potential losses as well as the speed of effective asset transfer.

In addition to fraud at the transactional level, computer systems are also vulnerable in areas such as the following:

- Changes to and manipulation of operating system software
- Unauthorized changes to application programs
- Physical substitution of stored data by direct manipulation of digital information using specific tools and utilities
- Use of unauthorized programs

This type of attack may be internal only or may come from outside of the organization using social engineering techniques to gain access or technical attacks using automated attack software, such as network sniffers.

Computer Fraud Protection

In today's world, the exponential growth in the use of computers has put confidential information about all of us on a personal basis, our organizations, and our families in the public domain with easy access from anywhere in the world, and it has opened us all up to the potential for fraud on a massive scale.

Although it is recognized that the primary responsibility for the prevention of all fraud, including IT fraud, is the responsibility of operational management, nevertheless it must be recognized that total prevention is an impossibility, and early detection has a major role to play in assisting management in addressing the problem in sufficient time to reduce the potential for massive losses.

With highly publicized instances of unauthorized online access to mobile information becoming a daily occurrence, it is easy to forget that most computer fraud is not carried out by outsiders, but by authorized insiders and even by executive management. In such instances, preventative controls are highly ineffective, and the use of analytical tools to detect transactional anomalies becomes an imperative.

In order to seek evidence of IT fraud, it is necessary to understand how such frauds can be carried out as well as to understand the architecture surrounding our computer systems and sources of evidence that the auditor can use for appropriate analysis.

At the heart of the computer and the target for most fraudulent activities is the raw data of the organization. If access to this information is obtained (legitimately or by stealth), the organization is immediately exposed to potential fraud. Legitimate users can process unauthorized transactions. Preventative controls are generally ineffective in this situation because the perpetrator commonly has the appropriate access rights and authorities to process such transactions. In addition, legitimate technical users, who have insufficient authority levels to process transactions, may be able to manipulate the raw data directly without the need to utilize the conventional user route to data—that is, transaction processing. Using utilities and other specialized software, technical users may be able to address data directly on magnetic media or in networks in order to change values. In some cases, this form of manipulation may leave no direct audit trail to be analyzed, but direct changes to data may still be detected based on the impact of the manipulation rather than the analysis of transactions themselves.

In today's environment, organizations typically operate in an online, real-time environment in which transactions are entered remotely and access to the data is commonly gained via a variety of intermediary steps. Users may access communications from workstations that are within the organization's physical environment and therefore directly under its physical control. In one alternative scenario, they may connect via remote terminals with which the organization has no direct physical control over who is sitting at the terminal. Another alternative involves the use of mobile devices, ranging from tablets to phones to the "Internet of Things" in which devices that are not normally considered computer terminals, such as refrigerators, stoves, and the like, which use "smart" technology to communicate via the Internet and which, themselves, are vulnerable to penetration. A lack of understanding of the fraud risk in the event that controls are not effectively utilized is to blame for many unauthorized accesses.

Identity theft may be blamed for much of the computer fraud we face today, but this, itself, is frequently due to a lack of understanding of the vulnerabilities exposed and careless use of mobile devices. In addition, social networking can, in many cases, make publicly available a wide variety of confidential data including names, dates of birth, Social Security numbers, and even credit card numbers, all of which enable fraudulent practices to grow.

Cloud Computing

Cloud computing may be seen as a derivation of a traditional client–server approach to computing. Using Internet architecture, a client version of a particular application system may be launched on a user's computer with the bulk of the application and even the data residing on a computer potentially on the other side of the world. This brings decided advantages in the form of wide-ranging access to systems from anywhere in the world and the centralized point of control at the cloud service provider. This form of cloud computing is commonly known as software as a service (SAAS) and is a popular method of reducing both the hardware and software requirements with the cloud's network taking the bulk of the transactional load.

In terms of fraud risk, the locating of both the data and applications within the cloud itself exposes organizations and individuals to potentially serious risks of cyberfraud and espionage as well as potential legal issues regarding future access to the organization's own data in the case of a fraud prosecution.

Information Fraud

Most of the common fraud that has developed and been perpetrated over the years now has a cyber version, which can deliver larger payoffs to the fraudster for fewer risks. Any system involving the electronic transfer of assets may be vulnerable to fraudulent funds transfer or money laundering. The implementation of effective controls can reduce the likelihood of effective fraud penetration with some of the more basic controls still not in common use. In general, outside fraud can be made more difficult with analytic detection eased by ensuring the following:

- *Destruction of confidential scrap* is an easy, cost-effective control intended to prevent ID theft. Modern shredders operate in cross-cut mode, making reconstruction of shredded material virtually impossible, and should be used for any paper products containing personal information. Even credit cards, DVDs, and the like may be shredded by inexpensive, commercially available shredders.
- *Passwords* must all be protected, particularly when used on mobile devices. Mobile phones are some of the most commonly stolen electronic items. In many cases, the primary risk lies in the passwords, PIN numbers, and the like, which have been encoded by the user into the mobile phone itself. When home banking is executed from the mobile device and the financial institution sends a one-time access code to the user, it is common to find that the recipient device of the access code is the same device used for the initial access and the initial password is recorded on the same machine. Users must also bear in mind that mobile phones have video and zoom

capabilities. The person standing behind you in a queue at an ATM speaking on a mobile phone while awaiting his or her turn may, in fact, be video-recording the PIN number of the person using the ATM. In the same way, recording of password entry is also vulnerable to this modern version of "shoulder surfing."

- *Nondisclosure of personal information* either via social media or simply through the response to an electronic request for sensitive information is an imperative. Such information should never be disclosed electronically unless the supplier of such information is fully satisfied that the requester has a right to know. Even then, it would be rare for authorities, such as law enforcement or taxation authorities, to request such information electronically.

Prevention of computer fraud is largely an exercise in keeping outsiders out and insiders where they are supposed to be and doing what they're supposed to be doing. This involves the organization conducting an appropriate fraud risk evaluation exercise in order to establish an appropriate security architecture, which will itself be a combination of the following:

- Operating system hardening
  - Removal of "standard" passwords
  - Removal of redundant security files
  - Implementation of effective change control
- Use of appropriate and effective firewalls
- Effective use encryption
- Network address translation
- Increased security awareness
- Effective user education
- Good personnel policies and practices
- Monitoring of legitimate usage

Seeking Fraud Evidence

When indicators of potential fraud opportunities have been identified, the auditor will typically seek to elicit facts in a fair, impartial, and lawful manner. The overall goals are to confirm whether an instance has occurred and promote the accumulation of accurate evidence while minimizing business disruption. In all cases, the auditor must seek to ensure control over the retrieval and handling of evidence and protection of privacy rights as laid down by local legislation and allow for legal recrimination.

From a legal perspective, evidence is generally defined as anything perceivable by the five senses and includes the following:

- Testimony of witnesses
- Documents
- Facts or data
- Tangible objects legally presented
- Direct or circumstantial evidence

In the case of analytical information, evidence would fall under the category of facts or data. The auditor should always bear in mind that evidence presented in a case takes place in an adversarial arena where the opposing counsel may attack the admissibility of evidence in terms of its relevance, legality of collection, and chain of custody. During initial data analysis, it may not be clear that the evidence being collected will end up in court, and the auditor may find that evidence previously thought to be conclusive may be deemed inadmissible. As a result, all analytical evidence should be treated as though it may, at some future times, become relevant in litigation either in proving fraud or disproving an allegation of fraud. As each piece of evidence is collected, the auditor must maintain an inventory reporting the live data source, location, time of collection, and by whom the item was collected and using what technology. Original data records should be protected against damage, which could destroy future opportunities to derive additional evidence. Originals would normally be stored in a safe or in an encrypted form and should not be altered or written on other than an unobtrusive notation for identification purposes. Any copies made for working purposes should be clearly marked "Copy."

Chain of Custody

To be admissible, auditors must maintain the chain of custody of any evidence that comes into their possession.

This means the evidence obtained must be

- Identified
- Marked
- Inventoried
- Preserved

Any break in the chain of custody may result in the item or analysis being inadmissible at trial. This means that the evidence must be securely stored with access controlled by an "evidence custodian." Securing the location can be as simple as keeping a printout of an analysis under lock and key or retaining a digital version in an encrypted form. From time to time, evidence must be transferred from the custody of one person to another, and the transfer must be documented. Any movement of evidence, including sending it to a crime lab, document examiner, or the police must be accounted for as well. The simplest way to do this is to create an evidence trail within a forensic register that lists each data item by number and description.

Any transfer of evidence must then be noted in the evidence register by the person designated as the evidence custodian, thus maintaining the item's chain of custody.

Starting the Process

In order to begin an analysis as part of a fraud investigation, the auditor requires *predication* or *just cause* or a *valid reason* to suspect that a fraud has occurred. Predication may be defined as *that set of circumstances that would lead the prudent, reasonable, and professionally trained person to believe that a fraud has occurred, is occurring, or will occur.* Such belief normally comes from a tip but can also become apparent during the analysis of data.

In previous days, fraud was commonly seen to leave a paper trail, which could be used to assist an investigator in identifying the individual(s) responsible for conducting the fraud and at the same time estimating the extent of loss. Documents could also be used to link the perpetrator to the crime. In today's world, many systems preclude the production of documentary evidence, relying instead on the analysis of digital evidence.

All that said, this book is not primarily an antifraud book, but rather addresses ways in which data analysis can be used to do the following:

- Identify vulnerabilities in the nature of accesses to systems and processing of transactions
- Identify anomalous access patterns
- Identifying changes to raw data that cannot be backed up by a transactional audit trail
- Identify sources of fraudulent attacks

Common techniques for the detection of fraud indicators in the analysis of information include the following:

- Calculating access statistics from log records, including time of day, terminal usage, GPS location for mobile devices, and the like may identify anomalous access patterns.
- The joining of information derived from differing sources in order to identify common information where commonality should not occur, for example, matching names, addresses, telephone numbers, and bank account numbers on a creditor file against the payroll file. In the same way, the use of the Social Security numbers of deceased individuals may be identified by verifying the validity of an SSN by comparing it to the SSN death index.
- Calculation of operational statistics, such as high/low values or volumes, moving averages, and standard deviations of populations, in order to conduct either trend analysis or to analyze population abnormalities that could indicate the presence of a fraudulent direct manipulation of data.
- Data analysis using Benford's law to identify unexpected occurrences of digits in data sets that are naturally occurring and when such abnormalities could again indicate potential fraudulent manipulation of data.
- Duplication testing to identify duplicate payments, expense claims, health care claims, and other transactions that should be of a unique nature may identify a transaction manipulation either by an authorized insider or by an unknown outsider.

- Gap testing to identify missing transactions or values in data that would normally be expected to be sequential and contain no gaps.
- Verification of transaction dates to identify transactions processed at inappropriate times, for example, expenses incurred in connection with an event processed before such expenses were even possible.
- Classification of data in order to seek patterns or abnormalities within patterns.

A common problem the auditor is likely to encounter is the use of codification structures within data files. In order to improve efficiencies of processing, data is frequently coded in order to save space and processing time. For example, using employee numbers rather than the full employee name within a file may result in it being necessary to extract information from multiple files and combine the data in order to make sense of it from an investigative perspective.

In implementing such coding structures, it is common to concatenate individual pieces of information, each of which has a specific meaning, into one single field. For example, the first three digits of a customer number may indicate the state. Once such information is understood, anomalies, such as an individual claiming a date of birth that does not match his identification number, should immediately stand out in any analysis.

As with any analytical technique described within this book, the integrity and reliability of the information analyzed are essential, and the quality of the data must be established prior to the conduct of the analytical review. This may involve comparing numbers of records, total values, and the like to information sources known to be accurate. When such reliable information is unavailable, reasonableness tests may provide sufficient confidence prior to analysis.

For example, if there are 1,000 employees, each paid monthly, it is reasonable to believe that payroll payments over the year should involve approximately 12,000 transactions. The appearance of 20,000 payroll transactions could be an indication of something wrong although the appearance of 12,010 transactions may prove nothing and may not even be flagged.

When an examination indicates the data to be unreliable, the auditor may decide that this is a sufficient indicator of potential fraud to warrant further investigation. Depending on the nature of the unreliability, the auditor may decide that analytical review cannot adequately be relied upon, and it may have to be forgone and other investigative techniques undertaken instead.

Regardless of the apparent reliability of information, it should always be borne in mind that data analysis is not direct evidence. When anomalies are found, independent verification and double-checking will be required.

When using data analysis to obtain evidence of fraud, a specific jargon has developed, including the following:

- *Evidence media*—the original media to be investigated
- *Target media*—media onto which the evidence is duplicated
- *Restored image*—the copy of the forensic image restored to its original bootable form
- *Native operating system*—the operating system used on the restored image
- *Live analysis*—data analysis conducted on the original evidence media
- *Offline analysis*—analysis conducted using the target media or restored image

Evidence for analysis may also be found within the overall logical file system, including the following:

- Events logs
- Application logs
- Registry and parameter files
- Swap files on disk
- Temporary files
- Printer spool files
- Deleted files

When the possibility of fraud is indicated, there is a danger that management will respond with a knee-jerk reaction of trying to "fix the problem" immediately and as quickly and as cheaply as possible. Rushing the task without fully planning the analytical project will significantly decrease the probability of a successful outcome.

In addition, innocent employees may be wrongfully accused, or the guilty parties may emerge unscathed, and legal claims for damages may ensue against the organization.

From the start of the forensic approach, the assumption has to be that all analytical evidence gathered, whether proving or disproving the existence of a fraud, will be, at some time, required to be presented in court as part of a civil or criminal proceeding. This could involve prosecuting the accused perpetrator of the fraud or with the evidence being produced in a defensive action against improper accusations should an allegation fail to be proven and an action be brought against the company for defamation of character. It may even be required to prove the organization's innocence if a case of fraud is brought against the company.

The forensic analysis starts with the formulation of an action plan in order to determine the scope and extent of the potential fraud. Primary objectives of such an action plan would be to do the following:

- Determine the probable extent and duration of the fraud, quantify potential loss, identify who could possibly be involved, identify the nature and sources of evidence available, and determine how the evidence will be preserved during the course of the investigation.
- Determine the optimal depth and cost–benefit of the data analysis, including special skills requirements and probable information processing resources required together with any new hardware, software, and/or training required.
- Ensure legal compliance with all applicable legislation regarding the acquisition and custody of data evidence during the analytical process.
- Ensure the objectivity of the investigation team is maintained throughout the course of the investigation until final disposition.
- Ensure completion of the investigation in an appropriate time span to mitigate losses or potential damage to the organization's reputation.

The gathering of data may require a multidisciplinary approach in order to comprehend the results of the analysis; however, from start to finish, information should be made available only on a need-to-know basis, and confidentiality of both the raw data and the analysis must be maintained against possible information corruption or disclosure during the analytical process.

Data analytic tools have become considerably more sophisticated in recent years and can be used to scan multiple databases for specific red flags to identify evidence to verify fraud in circumstances indicated by red flags. Most of the generalized audit software (GAS) in common use has in-built capabilities to handle the following:

- *Verification of corporate policies*—Corporate policies regarding financial information, such as pricing policies, discount policies, etc., can be utilized as filtering options to identify data that does not meet the corporate requirements.
- *Searches for duplicate data*—When it is a requirement that data elements appear once, and once only, duplicates can be identified by analyzing the data. The presence of a duplicate may not indicate a fraud, but rather an erroneous double entry of the transaction. In either event, the auditor needs to ascertain the cause in order to report appropriately.
- *Identification of gaps*—Many business documents are controlled by the use of unique numbering, and any missing documents, identified by gaps in sequences, may be red flags for the covering up of fraudulent transactions or, once again, simple errors in processing, which will require audit verification.
- *Record filtering*—Using audit searches to identify anomalies in high-volume databases or transaction systems is comparatively simple using today's interrogation packages. Red flags for anomalous data are easy to detect when the auditor is aware of what would constitute anomalous data. For example, negative stock items in an inventory database would be classified as anomalous. It is a simple matter to identify whether such conditions arise and within which records. In a similar vein, ATM transactions that do not fit value profiles can be readily filtered for identification processes.
- *Transaction tracing*—Data analytics can be used to follow the progress of transactions as they pass through the application system process. Use of the techniques such as a *parallel simulation* can permit the auditor to observe the impact of a given

transaction in the appropriate files. In this process, live transaction data is processed through the auditor's own software simulating the calculations performed within the live application system. The results of the simulation may then be compared to results from the live system in order to facilitate the audit evaluation of the accuracy and integrity of calculations conducted within the normal processing of the live application system.

- *Trend analysis*—When large quantities of historical data are available, data analysis is normally used to facilitate the audit prediction of future events. From a forensic investigation perspective, such analysis can enable the auditor to identify anomalous trends that do not fit predicted patterns and may be indicative of deliberate manipulation or fraud.

- *Ratio analysis*—Such analysis is commonly used by auditors in the determination of whether financial figure movement over a period of time falls within predictable ranges or not. When financial statements are involved (see Chapter 17), *horizontal ratio* analysis is typically used to analyze trends and values of specific financial statement values over time, and *vertical ratio* analysis is used to compare relationships among multiple line items within the financial accounts by expressing all individual line items as a percentage of a given total. Once again, by analyzing movements within these ratios, the auditor may identify where specific values are moving at a rate that is disproportionate to others. This movement could be normal in terms of changes within the business environment or could be a result of fraudulent manipulation of specific accounting values.

- *Correlation analysis*—This form of analysis allows the auditor to examine the relationships among individual data elements, seeking anomalous movements. When there is some consistent and measurable relationship between two values, the correlation coefficient may be calculated in order to determine the strength of the linear relationship. Coefficients will vary between −1 and +1 with a −1 indicating a perfect negative relationship. In this circumstance, when one data element increases, such as items sold, another data element will decrease, such as quantity on hand. The movement therefore shows an exact negative correlation. In a perfect positive correlation (+1), a movement in one data element will result in a matching movement in another. In forensic work, an analysis that indicates a positive correlation of, for example, +0.7, has over a period of time decreased to +0.5 indicates that the relationship has moved, and the auditor will typically seek a causal influence.

- *Regression analysis*—This type of analysis is again used to determine the relationship among data in order to predict the expected movement and one variable (the dependent variable) based on movements within one or more independent variables. For example, if a variable, such as labor cost, increases or decreases in a known manner, and the cost of raw materials also moves in a measurable way, then overall cost movements should also follow a predictable pattern. If the movement is not in line with predictions, some form of anomaly has caused the shift. Once more, this could be due to acceptable fluctuations in other variables or due to some form of fraudulent manipulation.
- *Benford analysis*—This is a form of pattern analysis that is used in the analysis of high volumes of data, looking for evidence of fraudulent transactions. It is based upon Benford's law, which states that the digits in many types of data sets are distributed in a uniform way, and the data can be analyzed in order to find anomalies within the data by comparing patterns of numeric occurrence within specific digits against predetermined frequencies. As can be seen in Diagram 13.1, in any

Digit	First digit	Second digit
0	–	0.120
1	0.301	0.114
2	0.176	0.108
3	0.125	0.104
4	0.097	0.100
5	0.079	0.097
6	0.067	0.093
7	0.058	0.090
8	0.052	0.088
9	0.046	0.085

Diagram 13.1   Benford frequency distribution.

given set of numbers, the first digit of a number will be a one approximately 30% of the time, the number two will occur 18% of the time, and this pattern recurs all the way down to number nine, which is normally found in the first position of a number only 5% of the time.

- Subsequent digits also follow known frequency patterns. By utilizing these known frequencies, large volumes of data can be analyzed to identify abnormalities within the data. It is critical that, when Benford analysis is used, the data selected is appropriate for such analysis. When data is deliberately patterned, such as in SSN numbers, the analysis would be inappropriate because the intentional patterning will not follow normal random distributions. "Natural" sets of data, such as amounts, would normally be expected to follow the Benford predictions of distribution. This would mean that, although individual fraudulent transactions may appear to be genuine, when attempts to commit fraud are utilizing transactions that are high in volume but low in value in order to avoid conventional detective controls—unless the fraudster has specifically designed the transaction values to comply with Benford's law— the frequency distribution will not follow Benford's curve, making possible fraudulent manipulation of data easy to spot.

Detecting e-Commerce Fraud

As with many other forms of fraud, the starting point for detecting e-commerce fraud is an understanding of the nature of that particular type of fraud and sources from which the risks originate. This is particularly true because it now seems to be a critical part of sales and marketing to facilitate the organization's participation in the e-commerce business model. Differing industry classes are entering this world with differing objectives. Some seek to reduce costs and streamline business activities, and others are reducing the overhead of having to maintain large expensive premises. Some electronic traders even manage to remove the need for warehousing and now act as clearinghouses where transactions are routed directly to suppliers who supply directly to customers, and the electronic trader takes a commission.

The use of e-commerce as an information gatherer on customers' preferences and behavior enables organizations to utilize data analytics in order to direct their marketing efforts to targeted customers, allowing cost-effective market segmentation.

Online auctions have effectively created a brand new market. Physical auction houses were generally seen as a specialist consumer area, in some cases, for hobbyists or collectors. With the advent of online auction sites, a new home industry has developed because, for a minimal cost, anyone can become a retailer working from home with little overhead.

Unfortunately, this is one of the hottest areas for consumer fraud with unscrupulous "sellers" advertising nonexistent products, collecting the payment, disappearing, and setting up anew under a different identity with different e-mail addresses and telephone numbers. And data analytics cannot prevent the substitution of inferior-quality goods for those advertised, which is simply an electronic version of the old "bait and switch" fraud. A great deal of effort is put out by auction houses to try and protect customers because one bad consumer experience, spread over the web, can have a major impact on future trading on that site. Increasing use of data analytics as a continuous monitoring tool is proving beneficial in early detection of fraud within these areas.

For organizations dependent on the speed of transactions, such as stock market trading, e-commerce has enabled customers to execute thorough research and then purchase or sell shares in any selected company, in any market in the world, at a fraction of the cost involved in dealing through a full-commission brokerage house. It has, however, also made them vulnerable to high-value fraud, again based on the speed of the transactions and the difficulties inherent in preventing fraud within these areas specifically intended to attract customers.

Online banking offers customers the ability to monitor their accounts and transfer money among their accounts without having to queue within a branch, possibly even at multiple tellers. E-banking permits the payment of bills from home, and banks can give customers the option to receive statements electronically, reducing printing and mailing costs dramatically. Once again, data analytics seeking inappropriate transaction patterns, either in terms of the nature of transactions or even on the geographical spread of such transactions, can assist a financial institution in protecting its customers against such frauds. Continuous monitoring is covered in more detail in Chapter 15.

Multiple versions of e-commerce exist, each with their own particular fraud opportunities; however, the primary control objectives remain the prevention of the theft of customer data and the prevention of fraudulent transactions against that customer data. Neither of these control objectives is 100% achievable, and therefore, effective and early detection becomes an imperative possible only with appropriate data analytics.

Business-to-Consumer (B2C)

In this form of e-commerce, customers deal directly with an organization electronically. Advantages to the customer include potentially lower costs as well as a virtual guarantee that the goods are always in stock. Doing business in this form, however, exposes the consumer by forcing them to disclose confidential information. Identity theft is, perhaps, the most common route via which e-commerce fraud is committed in B2C, and the most common form of e-commerce fraud is credit card fraud.

Business-to-Business (B2B)

Business-to-business is conducted with a different set of objectives in mind. By connecting business partners and creating a virtual supply chain, it is possible to reduce costs while simultaneously reducing resupply times. Fundamental in this e-commerce arena is the verification of suppliers both in terms of quality as well as simple existence. Any Internet user can, comparatively cheaply, create a sophisticated looking website offering heavily discounted component supplies and raw material supplies. Once payment is made, the site is closed, and the fraudster moves on. There are a variety of supplier verification sites available on the Internet, some of which are themselves frauds. At minimum, verification of the addresses, phone numbers, and e-mail addresses must be carried out. E-mail addresses may themselves prove nothing because it is cheap and easy to register a domain name with associated e-mail addresses with the actual owner of the site being almost untraceable in certain jurisdictions. Slightly more sophisticated fraudsters will clone the websites of genuine large companies with subtle changes to web addresses and contact details so that a potential trading partner carrying out cursory checks will believe they are doing business with a reliable supplier. With these risks in mind, it is essential that periodic data analysis of e-commerce trading partners be carried out. The frequency of such analysis will be dependent upon the volumes and values of transactions processed. When e-commerce is the dominant form of doing business within the organization, analysis may be required, using continuous monitoring.

Fraud Detection in the Cloud

The advent of open system architectures and "cloud" computing without recognizing the impact on risk potential and information vulnerability is an open invitation to fraud and theft. For many organizations, the records of their assets now exist only within computer systems, which form part of the cloud. For example, creditors' records, debtors' records, asset registers, and pay information may all be held within the cloud. In terms of fraud risk, cloud computing, if not properly controlled, may exacerbate the risks to information security and privacy because the data as well as the applications may be maintained within the cloud itself. This can expose both the user of the system as well as the service provider to potentially serious risks of data loss or corruption as well as fraud and cyber espionage. In addition, when the data resides in a country other than that of the cloud user, the user may be exposed to legal issues regarding future access to his or her own data and fraud prosecution as well as ownership of the intangible property under the terms of another country's legislation.

Forensic data analysis in a cloud environment will first require access to the appropriate data and will also commonly involve the need to handle data presented in a nonstandard format for which the software must be capable of automatic conversion to analyzable information.

In general, as part of the overall system of internal control, the internal auditor has a role to play in assisting management in establishing a control environment in which fraud is unlikely to occur, but when it does occur, it will be quickly detected. This is in contrast to the approach of the IT forensic auditor whose primary obligation is the resolution of IT fraud with sufficient proof to prove or disprove allegations of fraud. IT forensic auditors must always presume that all cases eventually will end up in litigation, and the quality of evidence gathered must take this into account. Nonforensic internal auditors have not been so constrained, but with data analysis, this possibility must always be taken into consideration.

Once unusual transactions have been identified, the software can then evaluate against known patterns of transaction processing from specific users in order to differentiate between erroneous transactions and those exhibiting, for example, patterns associated with potential fraudulent activity. For example, *fraud chains* are made up of sets of debit/credit pairs that appear normal but, when connected, can net out as a fraudulent transaction. When such transactions are split and hidden among multiple valid entries, the "chaining" may go undetected through normal methods. Only by implementing analysis using advanced fraud chain analytics can such transactions be detected.

Regardless of the apparent reliability of information, it should always be borne in mind that data analysis is not proof of fraud. When anomalies are found, independent verification and double-checking will be required.

Planning the Fraud Analysis

The internal auditor, in planning for a fraud analysis, needs to identify those different areas in which assets flow and where fraud may occur as well as the types of fraud that may be possible in those areas. The risk of fraud and the overall exposure to the organization must then be assessed.

The most critical and sensitive areas will typically be monitored on an ongoing basis (see Chapter 15).

Identification of the sources of evidence and the indicators sought will facilitate the auditor's determination of where to seek the patterns and indicators of potential wrongdoing.

Common Mistakes in Forensic Analysis

In conducting data analysis with the intention that it will be used for forensic purposes, the auditor must ensure that proper documentation is maintained for all processes carried out in the execution of the analysis. Failure to do so may result in evidence being disallowed in court if the auditor is not in a position to demonstrate what was done, by who, when, on what data, and using what tools. Another common mistake of inexperienced auditors is failing to control the digital evidence as mentioned above. In addition, altering date and time stamps on evidence systems before recording them, using untrusted commands and tools, accidentally overwriting evidence when installing audit interrogation tools, or the termination of rogue processes prematurely are all technical mistakes that could call the validity of evidence into question.

14

ROOT CAUSE ANALYSIS

This chapter examines the techniques available to the auditor in order to identify root causes of identified exceptions. This includes the selection of appropriate research techniques in order to identify them and known causes of common exception types.

Root cause analysis is critical in order to identify those control areas where improvements can prevent problems from occurring. The overall intention is to improve the overall effectiveness of business processes while increasing competitiveness, reducing costs, saving money, and generally keeping customers and stockholders happy. This will normally involve the auditor looking beyond the obvious because the evidence found is not necessarily the root cause itself but may simply indicate the symptom. For example, in manufacturing, mistakes in a particular process are commonly put down as caused by equipment failure or human error. Determining the root cause means finding the reason for the equipment failure. Was it due to bad maintenance? If so, what was the cause of the bad maintenance? Was it due to inappropriate maintenance scheduling or poorly trained maintenance technicians or use of inappropriate parts and materials? If it was down to one of these causes, why was the scheduling inappropriate, why were the technicians poorly trained, or why were the wrong parts and materials used? If the cause was human error, was the person careless, poorly supervised, undertrained, overtired; and if any of these is true, what was the root cause?

Root cause analysis is an in-depth process or technique involving a structured and thorough review of the apparent problem and is used to identify fundamental factors underlying the variation in system performance. When it is omitted, the effect is to fix the symptoms without regard to why those symptoms occurred. Commonly, this is because time pressures may be on to fix the obvious problem as quickly or as cheaply as possible without regard to what caused the problem. Used effectively, root cause analysis can help identify the business or process problems faced, eliminate patching of processes resulting in minor and temporary benefits, and conserve resources by focusing on the areas of highest impact.

Once data analysis is complete, you should have identified the criteria that are not meetings the standards. However, it will be necessary to present these results to the audit team to establish the causes of why this has happened. It is only by looking at the root causes that the auditor can identify what changes are required to be put in place as part of the quality improvement plan.

There are a number of tools to assist the auditor in conducting root cause analysis, such as the following:

- *Cause and effect diagrams*—These involve a visual display of possible causes in order to reveal gaps in existing knowledge and to reach an understanding of why loss exists. These may take the form of the following:
  - *The fishbone diagram* (also known as an Ishikawa diagram or a cause and effect diagram)—This is a problem-solving tool that helps identify the particular cause of a problem or a desired effect. A problem or an effect is written in the head of the fish. A common set of major categories of causes are written in the bones of the fish, such as personnel, work methods/ procedures, materials, and equipment (see Diagram 14.1).

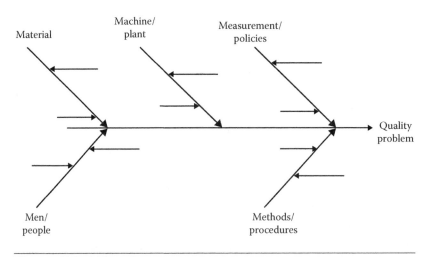

Diagram 14.1   Ishikawa diagram.

- *Process mapping*—Each step of a process is mapped out so that problem areas or bottlenecks in the process can be identified and improved.
- *The five whys*—Asking the question why something has happened five times—each time drilling down further to get to the root cause of the problem.
- *Tree diagrams*—In which the auditor will state the problem with causes listed as branches to the right of the problem. Causes continue to be clarified, drawing additional branches to the right until each branch reaches its logical end.
- *Event and causal factor analysis*—This is an extended version of the Ishikawa diagram and is used for multifaceted problems or for the analysis of long and complex causal factor chains. It is intended to identify anything that shapes the recorded outcome and facilitates the auditor identifying which questions must be asked to follow the path to the root cause.
- *Pareto analysis*—Named after the Italian economist Vilfredo Pareto who, in 1907, described the unequal wealth of the country in terms such that 20% of the population owned 80% of the resources. This technique, used in management, was refined in the 1940s by Dr. Joseph Juran to identify the principle he called the *"vital few and trivial many."* In his initial work, he identified that 20% of defects in the control processes cause 80% of the problems, and identifying that 20% allowed management's focus to solve the bulk of the problems with minimal effort.
- *Change analysis*—This is used when a problem is obscure, typically a single occurrence, and focuses on those items in the environment that have changed since the nonproblematic state. Changes can then be evaluated to determine their contribution to the problematic situation. Change analysis is used to determine *what, when, where, how,* and *who*.

By identifying the root causes, you can then move toward identifying the changes needed to improve, but it should be noted that cause and effect analysis are limited by past existing knowledge, and the auditor must have considered what caused the produced effect in the past. It was Albert Einstein who said, "It's impossible to solve significant problems using the same level of knowledge that created them!"

As a rough-and-ready analysis technique, many auditors simply adopt the five whys, but there are limitations with this technique. It is critical for the auditor to understand first *what happened* before moving on to the *why*. Typically, problems derive from multiple root causes, and the auditor must understand these in order to derive the right questions to ask to determine *why*. Assignment of blame is a common obstruction the auditor will frequently encounter when trying to assess *why*, particularly if the root cause involves human performance. Contributing factors are not root causes although the auditor will need to examine contributing factors in order to determine the root causes.

Although it is critical that the auditor should not leave any loose ends in conducting root cause analysis, it is also critical that the auditor recognize when to stop asking *why*. From an audit perspective, when a point is reached at which a change to control processes will help reduce the impact or likelihood of the problems being observed, the root cause has probably been reached in sufficient depth. In other words, the auditor will, at some point, reach the stage at which he or she can answer the following questions:

- Would the event have occurred if this cause did not exist?
- If this cause is corrected, will the problem recur?

If the answer to these questions is *yes*, the root cause has probably been reached.

Many auditors will say that this occurs when the answer to the *why* question is a person, process, or corporate policy.

Root cause analysis will be most commonly performed when significant or consequential events are occurring particularly when human errors are being repeated during the specific process or when repeated equipment failures are occurring. High priority is normally given to those events that could lead to significant failure to achieve business objectives, result in significant losses to the organization, financial, operational, or reputational, as well as issues that could result in health or safety issues.

Perhaps the fundamental measurement of the effectiveness of root cause analysis is a follow-up action taken by the auditor to evaluate the impact of the implementation the of the auditors' recommendations. If the problem that led to the analysis in the first place has been resolved or significantly reduced, then the root cause has probably been ascertained. If the problem still exists, then the fundamental cause was probably not effectively determined, and the auditor must revisit the analysis.

15

DATA ANALYSIS AND CONTINUOUS MONITORING

This chapter examines the methods and processes facilitated by continuous monitoring to ensure that crucial policies, processes, and internal controls are both adequate and operating effectively. Although this is primarily a management role, the auditor may be required to express an opinion on the appropriateness and effectiveness of the continuous monitoring processes implemented by management. This can also provide the audit with an assurance of the reliability of management's oversight on all internal controls and risks.

Traditionally, internal auditing has focused data analysis on a sample basis and gained insight from transactional data that exists in individual systems in order to perform its work.

Over recent years, however, advances in company-wide data analytical technology solutions are transforming this field. Today, leading organizations are adopting continuous auditing tools to significantly enhance their internal auditing activities.

In a paper, "Continuous Monitoring and Continuous Auditing: From Idea to Implementation"* Deloitte defines continuous monitoring as the following:

> *Continuous monitoring* enables management to continually review business processes for adherence to and deviations from their intended levels of performance and effectiveness.

It goes on to describe it as the following:
• An automated, ongoing process that enables management to

---

* Deloitte Development LLC, Continuous Monitoring and Continuous Auditing: From Idea to Implementation, 2010, https://www2.deloitte.com/content/dam /Deloitte/uy/Documents/audit/Monitoreo%20continuo%20y%20auditoria%20 continua.pdf.

- Assess the effectiveness of controls and detect associated risk issues
- Improve business processes and activities while adhering to ethical and compliance standards
- Execute more timely quantitative and qualitative risk-related decisions
- Increase the cost-effectiveness of controls and monitoring through IT solutions

It further describes continuous auditing as the following:

Continuous auditing enables *internal audit* to continually gather from processes data that supports auditing activities.

The drivers for continuous monitoring include the following:

- *Fraud detection and prevention*—Used effectively, continuous monitoring can assist organizations in improving both the detection and prevention of fraud and other forms of misconduct. When organizations have effective monitoring in place, they are also in a position to potentially reduce the numbers of staff they dedicated to fraud prevention and detection.
- *Enterprise risk management*—Once risk sources have been identified and measurement criteria defined, when possible, automated alerts should be established to notify the responsible individuals and assist them in monitoring their assigned risks. By automating risk monitoring, a repeatable and sustainable detective process forms the basis for management to build upon to create a continuous risk assessment process.
- *Compliance with internal policies and procedures*—Whenever internal policies and procedures exist, indicators may be derived to highlight red flags for noncompliance. By monitoring these on an ongoing basis, management is in a position to explicitly affirm that no significant deviations from the corporate policies and procedures are occurring.
- *Overall regulatory and governance compliance*—With the enormous increase in regulatory requirements across all forms of business, maintaining proof of compliance on an ongoing basis has become an enormous drain on resources in terms

of both financial resources and skilled manpower. As with internal policies and procedures, key performance indicators are readily identifiable, and compliance monitoring may then be placed on an automated basis. As regulations change, it is easier to maintain the key performance indicators than to set a new clerical monitoring mechanism every time. Once again, this gives management the opportunity to demonstrate empirically that the regulatory and governance requirements for oversight are being achieved on an ongoing basis.

Monitoring to ensure the ongoing effectiveness of controls designed to ensure the integrity, confidentiality, and fraud-resistance of IT systems is commonly under-resourced or even ignored by the executives responsible for ensuring effective risk management and good governance. When resources are scarce or the skill to interpret the monitoring is not available in-house, consideration may be given to the possibility of using technology to monitor technology. Technology can also be used to monitor the ongoing effectiveness of the controls themselves. Effective monitoring on an ongoing basis is not only a detective control, but it can also be a deterrent control because incidents of fraud are known to decrease when the expectation of being detected is higher. Continuous monitoring capabilities exist within many standard audit software packages, including generalized audit software, such as IDEA and ACL. Use of continuous monitoring can help the whole data analytic process by

- Providing better access to real-time indicators of potentially fraudulent transactions and allowing improved speed and quality of detection and management response
- Reducing the business impact of errors and omissions by reducing the length of time they go undetected
- Enhancing assurance of corporate compliance with relevant laws and regulations
- Giving early warning of reduced reliability of computerized internal control systems

In high-volume transaction processing systems, continuous monitoring may be the only control viable. When such systems use distributed networks, fluid technology, or virtualized servers, use of continuous, computerized monitoring techniques may be the only way in which relevant, reliable, and timely information can be utilized to monitor the effectiveness of control structures. Using technology in this manner makes possible the 100% checking of every transaction against predetermined indicators of potential fraud, such as high-value transactions, unexpected patterns of transactions, transaction volumes, or values moving against normal trends.

To be effective in detecting fraud or operational anomalies, monitoring of controls must produce information that is relevant, reliable, and timely. Information produced maybe a direct substantiation of the effectiveness of the controls and achievement of business objectives or provide a context or background information against which the direct information can be evaluated, such as performance of key risk indicators or operating and trend statistics.

In order for any monitoring to be effective, there must be a standard or baseline against which the results of the monitoring can be compared. Only then can the auditor detect deviations from the norm in terms of the effectiveness of control operation. In addition, by understanding the existing operations of controls, monitoring mechanisms may be designed and implemented in a more effective manner. Continuous observation monitoring is designed to ensure controls function as intended during times of normal operation and are not necessarily restricted to the use of computerized tools. It is dangerous for management to assume that, once automated monitoring analysis tools have been implemented, management's normal controls of supervision, reconciliations, and the like can be suspended.

Continuous monitoring by use of automated analytical tools, if effective, may give management early alert of potential defects within the operation of the control environment. The design and architecture of such a monitoring infrastructure must be built to meet the needs identified during management's IT risk assessment.

Only once the source of threats to information processing is understood can an effective system of internal controls be designed to mitigate these risks.

It would be neither effective nor efficient to attempt to monitor each control individually. If the risk analysis has been done properly, the control objectives should have been prioritized together with the identification of the key controls designed to achieve those control objectives in the most effective manner. Many of these controls will be preventative in nature and will not necessarily leave behind indicators that can be monitored to evaluate the effectiveness of the controls. Monitoring against control objectives allows management to monitor the effectiveness of multiple controls each contributing toward the control objective in circumstances where it is not cost-effective to monitor each individual control. It therefore becomes more appropriate to identify key control objective attainment indicators that can be monitored on an ongoing basis and evaluated against predetermined levels.

Designing the monitoring architecture is therefore a combination of the following:

- Identifying and prioritizing of risks
- Identifying the key controls intended to mitigate the risk
- Identifying the key indicators that would show that the likelihood of achieving the control objectives is maintaining its strength, increasing, or declining
- Implementing of automated or manual monitoring of these indicators to identify, as soon as possible, any decline in the adequacy of the internal control structures or their effectiveness in achieving the control objectives

Depending on the nature of the risk and the design of the controls, monitoring may be done of the controls themselves or of the degree to which the control objectives are being achieved or a combination of the two.

The process of designing such monitoring mechanisms may, in itself, identify weaknesses in internal control structures when the reliance has been placed purely on preventative controls. Unfortunately, many of the current generation of application systems in use did not have the internal control objectives and structures designed with continuous monitoring in mind. This has led to the implementation of control structures that may be highly effective in controlling risk or may not but that provide management with little or no information one way or the other regarding the achievement of control objectives. This is particularly true in legacy systems developed many years ago that are still running, but it can also be found in some of the latest systems implemented.

Because of the nature of modern systems achieving high-speed, high-volume processing with multiple entry points, the control focus has typically been on preventative controls because the opportunities for human intervention as a result of detected problems are minimal.

Monitoring Tools

Monitoring tools come in a variety of forms and with a variety of primary purposes. Many were not designed initially with ongoing monitoring in mind but can nevertheless be readily adapted to this purpose. For example, computer change control is intended to ensure that, once a program has been put into a live environment, only authorized changes that have been fully tested can be implemented in an authorized manner. Continuous monitoring of live systems can also be conducted in order to identify unauthorized changes and provide continuous assurance of a fixed level of processing integrity.

Generalized audit software and other data analytical tools of the type used by auditors can be utilized by management to monitor transaction streams against known tolerance levels on an ongoing basis in order to determine whether a control designed to prevent certain types of anomalies has been breached.

Error and exception reports can also be monitored electronically using the same tools in order to ensure patterns that could indicate control failures will be detected in a timely manner.

Computer access logs may be monitored on an ongoing basis to seek a pattern indicating invalid access attempts to sensitive areas of systems as well as transaction types that could potentially facilitate a fraud. These analyses can also indicate breaches of corporate policies, such as unauthorized use of the Internet or accesses from unauthorized terminals at unauthorized times.

Management use of GAS to carry out repetitive or continuous analysis of data involves the setting up of scripts to run against large volumes of data on an ongoing basis in order to identify those anomalies as they occur over a period of time. Scripts can be created and tested, then released to run against the data so that management obtains periodic notification when an anomalous condition arises. Alternatively, the script can be run on an overnight basis when notification is not required on a real-time basis and is primarily being used to identify trends and patterns of exceptions.

In terms of continuous monitoring, it must be borne in mind that, with the best tools, most appropriate techniques, and most effective monitoring, the whole process can be rendered ineffective if management ignores the information they provide. Under these circumstances, continuous monitoring may be worse than useless because it can lull management into a false state of security because they have "implemented" continuous monitoring whereas all they may have implemented may be continuous recording. Management must also realize that continuous monitoring is not a preventative control. At its most effective, it is a detective control and will only detect those occurrences that it has been programmed to detect.

Continuous monitoring does not provide a comprehensive, enterprise-wide risk-management approach. It does, however, provide a key component in the corporate risk-management process. Overemphasis on continuous monitoring at the expense of a comprehensive risk management approach can significantly reduce the effectiveness of the overall management enterprise risk management.

To be effective, monitoring requires the active involvement of information system owners as well as the suppliers of common controls all operating within the overall mission and strategic objectives of the organization. When effectively utilized, they therefore become significant factors in ensuring corporate risk oversight and transparency.

The two critical questions that must be answered before such tools can be effectively implemented are the following:

- How much monitoring is required to provide acceptable levels of assurance?
- At what level should the monitoring trigger an alarm that conditions may not be as desired?

Both of these questions need to be addressed as part of the risk assessment process. They are responses to management's decision regarding its level of risk acceptance or risk tolerance. The risk evaluation process should have identified areas where systems are most vulnerable and where corporate objectives can be most easily jeopardized. Levels of significance for indicator movements that should have been established as control structures were designed because without this, the adequacy of the design of the system of internal controls cannot be determined.

When choosing the appropriate tool, in addition to the obvious requirement of cost-effectiveness, care should be taken to select a package that is customizable to meet the organization's requirements and has a history of upgradeability to meet the changing information technology needs of the organization.

Utilization monitoring technology can deliver a powerful punch in the implementation of risk management measures before the event rather than retrospectively after damage has occurred. Depending on the nature of the transactions and their vulnerability, monitoring may take place and be reported on a weekly, daily, or even real-time basis in a higher risk environment.

This type of monitoring overcomes the traditional problems inherent in sampling by using the computer itself to do 100% surveys of data while in process. When monitoring systems were first introduced, the traditional approach was to use field-level comparisons of data to spot abnormalities, such as duplicate order numbers or payments. This was normally implemented as part of the control mechanisms within application systems and was most commonly used to detect errors rather than fraud.

In a modern integrated continuous monitoring system, the objective is to identify overall *similarities* with corresponding *matches* at the detailed level.

Continuous monitoring of transactions can also detect inconsistencies in details, such as revenue recognition where, for example, inventory transfers may be booked as sales or goods may be shipped without invoicing or invoiced without shipping.

Software Vendors

There are a variety of continuous monitoring tools available from different software vendors. The use of the more popular generalized audit software packages is covered in more detail in Chapters 19 and 20, but in addition, specific CM tools include the following:

- *ACL Continuous Monitoring Solution*—Designed to provide flexible and independent control review mechanisms whereby management can review the exposures of business risk, resolve potential problems before escalation, receive timely notification of control breaches and obtain summary reports through an intuitive web-based interface (http://www.acl .com/products/acl-analytics-exchange/).

- *ACL AuditExchange*—A centralized, server-based assurance platform. Provides additional power to the basic ACL Desktop (see Chapter 19) as well as improved analytical processing capabilities in support of continuous monitoring. Automation of analytics is simplified by the use of a built-in job scheduler with management able to control the timing, frequency, and parameters for each analytic. Exceptions found during data analysis may be distributed automatically to the appropriate management levels within the organization (http://www.acl.com/products/acl-analytics-exchange/).
- *CaseWare™ Monitor*—A sophisticated continuous monitoring solution facilitating the monitoring of controls across business processes, divisions, or the complete enterprise. Compliance issues and interventions can be monitored and the consolidated views presented and initiatives, such as ERP, external databases, custom applications, system logs, and legacy systems, can all be monitored and a consolidated view presented. Rules may be prebuilt or custom built for business processes, improving financial performance and response to risk notifications (http://www.caseware.com/products/monitor).
- *Infor Approva*—Provides continuous control monitoring software enabling management to execute repeatable processes to meet the control aspects of governance, risk, and compliance requirements for the organization. It provides the ability to carry out transaction monitoring across business applications as well as across platforms and verify the legitimacy of application process configurations. The software facilitates the definition, identification, and monitoring of risks and controls with the ability to automate testing, track the results, and enable investigation (http://www.infor.com/product-summary/fms/approva-continuous-monitoring/).
- *Infogix Enterprise Data Analysis Platform*—Is a family of software modules enabling the organization to automatically validate operational and financial information, utilizing standardized user-defined business rules. The software modules are intended to improve data quality while ensuring effective monitoring of transactions. The modules provide balancing and reconciliation, facilitate the identification of fraud, and

provide predictive models to improve operational efficiencies and revenue optimization. Use of a rule-based exception research, resolution, and reporting process enables the resolution of exceptions in a timely manner. Information from disparate reporting systems can be centralized and personalized for individual management requirements (http://www.infogix.com/products/).

- *Oversight Systems*—Oversight Systems' continuous transaction monitoring software has, over the last 13 years, developed a proven track record in data analytics, assisting organizations in fraud reduction, prevention of misuse, and reduction in errors within financial operations. The software acts as a virtual analyst aimed at the detection of operational variance within targeted business processes. Analytical capabilities include statistical, behavioral, Boolean, and time-based facilitating the identification of anomalies within corporate data (http://www.oversightsystems.com/solutions).

Implementing Continuous Monitoring

To be effective as a management tool, continuous monitoring requires an upfront investment and commitment of resources. The investment in information technology has already taken place for the organization as a whole, and continuous monitoring should be seen as an add-on to an already sunk cost with the objective of significantly improving the rate of return for that cost. Typically, it does not require a separate calculation of a return on investment because the objective is to maximize the benefit of an investment already made. It frequently finds its initiation in corporate areas involving disbursements so that payments can be monitored on an ongoing basis. In many organizations, the initial champions have been internal auditing utilizing software products, such as generalized audit software already in use. Information technology vendors, recognizing the additional benefits to be aimed at the corporate level are now delivering the CM software products designed to monitor controls already embedded within their ERP system products. For example, IBM now offers a product called *Watson Analytics*, facilitating the discovery of patterns and meaning in the user's data. This approach is cloud-based and offers guided data exploration and automated predictive analytics while at the same time enabling dashboard and infographic creation. ERP vendors, such as SAP and Oracle, are also incorporating CM into their existing systems.

The expanding requirements and legislation regarding governance compliance, coupled with the increasing emphasis on operational excellence are compelling organizations to find ways of proving their adherence to standards on an ongoing basis. Companies are therefore finding CM implementation becoming a crucial component within their regulatory compliance–driven technology component, and at the same time, weaknesses in business processes can be identified, leading to improvements in operational efficiencies and effectiveness.

As a starting point for CM implementation, it is critical that the organization identify the business need for such a strategy in terms of its place within evaluation of risk exposure against risk appetite and the degree of corporate tolerances permissible. The essential building foundation is the establishment of the current internal control environment in order to determine the following:

- How is the system of internal control currently monitored?
- By whom?
- At what frequency?
- How effective is the organization's current internal control architecture?
- What is the overall cost of the current control monitoring architecture?
- Is this cost appropriate to the risk level and risk appetite of the organization?
- What is the role of internal audit as opposed to management?

This facilitates the identification of a threshold setting as well as the identification of the need for real-time alerts. When possible, as with any other control opportunities, it is generally more efficient to incorporate CM into the automation of business processes up front rather than as a subsequent add-on. This has the added benefit that continuous monitoring is seen to be an integral part of systems rather than a nice-to-have to be incorporated if there is sufficient budget and time left at the end of a project.

Most organizations start off continuous monitoring in order to achieve *regulatory control objectives*, such as those relating to Sarbanes-Oxley, Dodd Frank, Basel, and other regulated activities. In addition to the overhead cost reduction, the continuity achieved by the use of continuous monitoring facilitates a higher level of third party confidence in compliance statements. Once the fundamentals inherent in regulatory compliance is ensuring its achievement on an ongoing basis, the next organizational priority is commonly the achievement of *operational control objectives*. Operation processes, such as supply chain management, inventory control, customer financial control over receivables, general control over payables, and the like are fundamental to the effectiveness of business operations. Ultimately, the goal of continuous monitoring is the optimization of business processes to ensure the overall accomplishment of corporate strategic objectives in terms of achieving customer satisfaction, improving market penetration, enhancing risk management, and other strategic initiatives.

The precise architecture will depend upon the nature of the business and business profile.

- *Transaction monitoring*—For example, when preset criteria exist in specific areas of business, such as the price structuring of loans or the calculation of discounts, particularly when the ability exists to override the criteria at management's discretion, the monitoring of transactions against predetermined limits can readily identify exceptions that otherwise may be hidden in the sheer volume of transactions.
- *Operational monitoring*—When an operating manager is controlling a specific operation within, for example, a manufacturing company and is balancing loads on multiple machines within an assembly line–type process, it becomes essential that a real-time awareness of production rates can be monitored in order to avoid bottlenecks in processes, raw material outages, and capacity overloads or underloads in order to optimize factory throughput.
- *Segregation of duties monitoring*—When specific authority levels are required to execute specific tasks, for example, purchases or payables, any breach of that segregation may leave opportunities for fraudulent activities to go unnoticed. By

monitoring on an ongoing basis, the processing carried out beyond an authority level is readily detectable and this can prevent the undetected outcomes of low-volume, high-value fraud. Such analysis could be on a per-transaction basis or accumulative over a period of time.

- *Computer access control*—Prevention of the sharing of access rights can be monitored by the analysis of access logs, seeking evidence of the same user ID being use simultaneously from multiple terminals, cross-referencing the user IDs used on internal terminals at a time when the ostensible user was not physically present, or computer access after hours or at a time when the user was supposed to be on vacation.

To a certain extent, the architecture will also be dependent on the need to migrate from nonexistent control processes or perhaps extensive manual controls that typically have significant problems in adequacy of monitoring, to fully IT-integrated processes and controls that are readily amenable to continuous monitoring.

Overcoming Negative Perceptions

As with any other significant change to existing procedures and processes, the concept of continuous monitoring is likely to be met with lukewarm support from those who see some potential benefit in the future and active resistance from those who perceive continuous monitoring as a "Big Brother" oversight specifically designed to catch them out. Arguments against will include the *perceived impact on the organization* in terms of additional overhead within the IT function and internal audit as well as the impact on managerial authority to make decisions and accept risk. This can take the form of "defending one's turf" against the imposed outsider. Very rarely is continuous monitoring introduced in an organization where there are ample resources, budget, and time available. As such, there are always other areas of managerial priority that require similar investments in time and effort. Continuous monitoring, in these cases, must fight for its resource requirements in terms of putting up a business case by clearly identifying the anticipated return on investment, impact on the corporate risk profile, and ease of implementation using the appropriate tools. At the same time, the benefits promised must be realistic, particularly in terms of time and commitment required.

Potential Benefits

When implemented appropriately and effectively, continuous monitoring can initially replace manual preventative controls, which are never 100% effective, with automated, risk-based detective controls at a greater effectiveness rate. Improvements within operating and financial controls can make significant and demonstrable bottom line improvements and facilitate improved decision-making at both operational and strategic levels.

16

CONTINUOUS AUDITING

This chapter explores the difference between continuous monitoring and continuous auditing, which is a methodology that gives audit results simultaneously with, or a short period of time after, the occurrence of relevant events. This facilitates continuous control assessment as well as continuous risk assessment based upon the ongoing examination of consistency of processes, thus providing support for individual audits as well as allowing the development of enterprise audit plans.

Continuous Auditing as Opposed to Continuous Monitoring

Although there are similarities between the two processes, the primary difference is in the ownership of the process. As discussed in the previous chapter, continuous monitoring is essentially a process in which key business process transactions and controls are constantly assessed and the process falls under management's responsibility. The continuous auditing concept, on the other hand, is owned by the audit function and includes the specific audit process, which is subject to repetitive execution. The process is not new in its conception, but modern usage, in combination with continuous monitoring, has changed the emphasis from simple repetitive audits to the usage of information technology to gain audit assurance on a continual basis.

In its 2005 publication *GTAG 3: Continuous Auditing: Implications for Assurance, Monitoring, and Risk Assessment*, the IIA defined continuous auditing:

> Continuous auditing is any method used by auditors to perform audit-related activities on a more continuous or continual basis. It is the continuum of activities ranging from continuous controls assessment to continuous risk assessment—all activities on the control–risk

continuum. Technology plays a key role in automating the identification of exceptions and/or anomalies, analysis of patterns within digits of key numeric fields, analysis of trends, detailed transaction analysis against cutoffs and thresholds, testing of controls, and the comparison of the process or system over time and/or other similar entities.

In its 2015 second edition, *GTAG 3: Continuous Auditing: Coordinating Continuous Auditing and Monitoring to Provide Continuous Assurance, Second Edition,*[*] the IIA extended the definition to include "the combination of technology-enabled ongoing risk and control assessments. Continuous auditing is designed to enable the internal auditor to report on subject matter within a much shorter time frame than under the traditional retrospective approach."

The closeness of integration of information technology into business processes, coupled with the availability of corporate data on a scale that, even 20 years ago, would have been unmanageable, have opened up opportunities for internal auditing, using the appropriate information technology themselves, to provide real-time oversight of the effectiveness of management's system of internal controls. This has made a drastic impact on the scope and objectives of internal audits as well as the skills and competencies required of today's internal auditor.

Following the shifting emphasis toward risk-based auditing, internal auditing has no choice but to take a proactive approach to both risk management and risk assessment. Management's expectations have moved away from audit assurances of the accuracy and completeness of financial information to searching for a consultative support regarding the effectiveness and efficiency not only within internal controls, but also with regard to operational issues and even strategic risk. This cannot be achieved without the auditor having a full understanding of the processes and information flow supporting those processes within the organization as a whole.

Once this understanding has been gained, the auditor is in a position to make a positive contribution to the overall governance, risk, and compliance within. Continuous auditing facilitates the automation of the bulk of regular substantive testing, freeing up skilled

---

[*] https://na.theiia.org/standards-guidance/recommended-guidance/practice-guides
/Pages/GTAG3.aspx

auditors to focus on the analysis of the implications of testing results on the corporate risk profile. In terms of bottom-line impact, the whole audit process benefits by an improved focus on high-impact business activities while reducing the expensive use of skilled auditors in auditing low-impact areas, which, while still required to be audited, are nevertheless more suited to automation.

In the same manner as continuous monitoring, continuous auditing involves the testing of transactions as close as possible to their time of execution. In today's computerized application systems, many of the managerial controls previously relied upon, such as supervisory authorization of individual transactions, have either migrated within the computer environment or no longer exist. Combine this with the speed of transactions, and it has become a virtual impossibility for management to use detective controls effectively without the active ability to monitor on a real-time basis. In the same way, internal auditing must also utilize such techniques in order to enable the early detection of control failures, either accidental or fraudulent, allowing critical issues to be brought to the attention of management within a time span facilitating urgent management attention.

Implementing Continuous Auditing

As always, internal auditing is seen as part of the third line of defense in the provision of independent assurance. The first line of defense is operational management that owns and manages the overall risk, and the second line of defense is those functions that oversee risks, such as mismanagement in compliance. Continuous auditing applies across all three lines by utilizing technology-enabled ongoing risk assessment as well as ongoing control assessment. To be effective, continuous auditing will involve the use of the analytical techniques detailed elsewhere within this book utilized in a manner reducing the active audit involvement to a minimum. Using predefined measurement criteria, the audit program can take the form of a set of standardized interrogations using preprepared audit scripts to run in a background mode and report on an exception basis. Reporting can take the form of regular notification of minor control deviations or real-time alerts to significant control violations.

Structuring the Implementation

In order to effectively implement continuous auditing, the internal audit function must establish an overall strategy for the process in order to coordinate with the first and second lines of defense in order to establish priorities and ensure management support for its use within the annual audit plan. In today's integrated environment, the integrity and reliability of transaction data as well as master file data forms the critical foundation for all business operations and can be assured via the continuous auditing process. When necessary, amendments to the internal audit charter should be made to ensure the appropriate authorities exist for access to require data.

Once a strategy has been established, access to the data requirements on an ongoing basis needs to be established with the reliability and integrity of the data being evaluated as part of the continual assessment process. It is critical to ensure ongoing management support that continuous auditing should not adversely impact response times and the overall operational performance of IT applications. The internal auditor must also recognize that having such access places the onus on the auditor to ensure that all applicable internal and regulatory requirements regarding the confidentiality of data and information privacy must be maintained. Should any breach of confidentiality or security occur, the auditor must be in a position to demonstrate that such a breach could not have happened while the data was under the control of the audit function. The internal audit function will also require the development or acquisition of technical skills and competencies to define the analytical requirements as well as the development of analytical tests and comprehension of the results of such analysis. As continuous auditing grows and develops, the degree of IT proficiency required will also increase.

Once the nature of the analyses is understood, the metrics for the control performance indicators can be established and agreed upon with management. These performance indicators must relate to the functional control objectives so that the ongoing effectiveness of key controls can be assessed. In a similar way, risk indicators can be identified with appropriate analytics designed to verify changes to the levels of corporate risk being experienced.

During the reporting phase of the audit, the results of continuous auditing must ensure that the need for management action is addressed and any requisite changes to the control environment facilitated.

Implementation of such a program, once again, involves internal auditing in the conducting of risk analysis to identify critical performance areas within the organization, sources of evidence, and key performance indicators that would be measured using the appropriate analytical techniques on an ongoing basis. Once these sources of evidence and indicators have been identified, the auditor will assemble a test-bed of analytical inquiries using the techniques detailed in Chapter 10 and differentiating between anomalies that require an early alert and instant response and those that require a management review or even an audit review prior to management alert.

A pilot audit is carried out by the auditor directly to test the analyses and ensure the appropriate response notifications are created. Once the audit program has been fully tested, amended as necessary, and agreed upon with management, the program can be fully automated and implemented to run auditor-unattended.

It is not uncommon for such a continuous auditing program to eventually be transferred to the ownership of management to become a continuous monitoring program with audit responsibility declining to the extent that the ongoing audit process becomes a risk review to identify significant changes combined with a review of the key performance indicator trigger points to ensure the ongoing relevance to the business risks. Effectively, the internal auditor is seeking to move the ongoing control evaluation back into the realm of management with internal audit playing a supportive role.

The need for ongoing continuous auditing will not disappear, but as continuous monitoring increases, the extent of continuous auditing will decrease, and the nature of the auditing will move toward continuous auditing of strategic and performance issues rather than financial and operational compliance issues. When management is actively involved in the continuous monitoring of transactions and the effectiveness of controls throughout the corporate business systems and processes, internal audit's role within these areas decreases significantly because to continue continuous auditing at that level would be an unmerited duplication of effort and a waste of corporate resources.

In the areas where management deem it inappropriate or inefficient to carry on continuous monitoring, the internal auditor may choose whether the overall risk levels and risk appetite mean that continuous auditing would still be required or whether audit data analysis would be carried out on an as-required exception basis. This choice would normally be influenced by the auditor's evaluation of the criticality of activities being performed and the consistency of the effectiveness of the system of internal control combined with the auditor's assessment of the effectiveness of the continuous monitoring currently being implemented by management.

Perceived Downsides of Continuous Auditing

In attempting to implement continuous auditing, the internal auditor may find resistance for a variety of reasons:

- *Audit access to live data*—Continuous auditing in any form requires audit data analysis to be carried out on master files and against live transaction data. IT auditors will already be familiar with the difficulties in gaining read-only access to live data. The perceptions that the audit will somehow corrupt the data despite having read-only access, will breach confidentiality by allowing outsiders access to confidential corporate data, or will simply slow down processing by carrying out excessive and unnecessary interrogations are all given as reasons to restrict auditor access to off-line copies of data. This, of course, obviates the whole concept and the benefits of continuous auditing.
- *Availability of appropriate audit tools*—Continuous auditing requires the implementation of the appropriate tools based upon the nature, source, and amount of data to be analyzed. Auditors must also be fully conversant with a variety of techniques and tools for conducting the analysis. It is often said that when a person has access only to a hammer, every problem looks like a nail. In continuous auditing, one tool will not fit all, and the auditor will have to have sufficient understanding to be able to select the appropriate techniques and tools to achieve the desired audit objective.

- *Untrained or unqualified auditors*—Use of advanced analytical techniques to make business sense out of large volumes of corporate data requires skills in both execution and interpretation beyond the conventional role of internal audit. For continuous auditing to work and produce the benefits desired, internal auditors must understand the business processes involved, the information flow, the control objectives, the control points, the sources of evidence, and the potential techniques of analysis. They must also be fully conversant with a variety of techniques and tools for conducting the analysis. In addition to having the skills to use the tools and the knowledge of where to look, the auditor needs the ability to understand what the analyses are telling him or her. Even with the best-designed continuous auditing program and the most skillfully implemented audit tests, poor interpretation of results can invalidate the audit conclusions, resulting in ineffective recommendations when recommendations are required or even recommendations made when none are required.

- *The perception that continuous auditing is a technical area*—Although many of the techniques require a high audit skill level, continuous auditing should not be seen as technical auditing but rather as applying varying techniques to the auditing of business controls. At present, many organizations have either postponed the implementation of continuous auditing, have passed it on to their specialist IT auditors, or have even called in specialist consultants to design and set up the whole continuous program. This is a throwback to the old days when the sight of computer terminal made nonspecialist auditors throw their hands up and call for the technical auditors. In today's business environment, *all* auditors must be capable of reviewing the critical systems used by the organization to achieve its business objectives. These will typically involve computer systems and will require the auditor to be able to follow a computerized audit trail, examine large volumes of data, identify key performance indicators, identify key data red flags for fraud, and evaluate the results of audit tests in order to carry out the simplest audits.

Actual Challenges

Over and above the perceived problems, the auditor will face a variety of difficulties during the initial design and implementation of continuous auditing. Much of the data requiring analysis will reside within a variety of legacy computer systems utilizing an array of architectures and technologies and with little up-to-date documentation and no in-house expertise. This can result in data being decentralized and/or duplicated and with significant data degradation occurring over a period of years. The geographical dispersion of corporate data as well as interfaces to external systems with complex interfaces and bridges can result in data that is out of sync and make it difficult to determine what data is in fact "correct."

Data integrity is the foundation on which modern business processes rely. Unfortunately, the responsibility is commonly delegated to officers, such as the CIO or CFO, resulting in strategic decisions being made without a genuine understanding of the underlying factors affecting the integrity of their data, and therefore, the reliability of the raw information used as the basis for those decisions. When data integrity has been compromised, internal auditing can conduct as many tests as they like with no measurable degree of assurance that the results can be relied upon.

Given that continuous auditing is intended to identify problems by recognizing anomalous data situations, the task is complicated even more when the data is, by definition, anomalous. As a result, audit objectives, such as the detection of fraud within data, may be problematic initially, and the full benefits may only be derived as continuous auditing matures and data acquisition becomes standardized.

For some organizations, this means a massive exercise to sanitize their data before either continuous auditing or continuous monitoring can be put into effect. This should not be seen as a by-product of a desire to implement continuous auditing. Rather it is a business necessity if the organization wishes to continue in business as a going concern because, ultimately, lack of integrity in the data entering information systems may be the quickest way to close down a business entity.

Obtaining Support

In order to overcome these perceptions, it is critical that continuous auditing be driven on a top-down basis. When the concept has a business-oriented product champion who is in a position to provide leadership and support to ensure the overall audit approach and strategy fully integrates data analysis as a critical element, the benefits to be derived from continuous auditing can be demonstrated and proved effective.

When the business area to be audited does not buy into the concepts of either continuous auditing or continuous monitoring, successful implementation may be problematic. Some support has come from the Public Company Accounting Oversight Board (PCAOB) when standards modification supported the move from the concept of manual sampling and testing in audits to an automated and comprehensive approach with continuous auditing as the foundation. The primary concept is that, if controls are sufficient, as evidenced by appropriate analysis, specific verification routines become unnecessary and wasteful of resources.

Although it is possible to perform continuous auditing with various types of general-purpose analysis software, there are many advantages to using audit data analysis software that is designed for the purpose. There is already a degree of acceptance of audit use of generalized audit software, which may be built upon during the initial phases of introducing continuous auditing.

During transition, it is essential that planning take place to ensure the people and process issues will be addressed in order to achieve the full intended benefits of continuous auditing. Role assignment to appropriate individuals is fundamental to success. Technical specialists should be expected to deal with the issues of data access or designing a complex analytic, and the nontechnical auditor should focus upon the business design of the tests regarding the specific audit and control objectives. The combination of the two skill levels increases the probability of successful implementation and acceptance because this combination facilitates the confirmation of the validity of both the data and the analysis as part of the design and running of specific tests in order to ensure they address the appropriate audit and control objectives.

A critical area for gaining acceptance of the whole concept is the manner in which false positives are dealt with as well as dealing with the sheer volume of exceptions generated. When false positives are generated, the audit analytic tests may be modified to ensure future exclusion. When an excessive number of minor exceptions are reported (common during the startup phase of continuous auditing), reporting can be tailored to summarize values without specifically addressing individual minor anomalies.

It is impossible to prove a positive return on investment without quantifying the benefits sought and achieved through its introduction in terms of benefits to both the audit as well as the organization as a whole. These benefits may be in terms of reduction of risk, improvements in corporate reputation, improving customer satisfaction, and improving profitability as well as reduction of the likelihood of fraud occurrences.

Maintaining the Support

As with many new techniques, continuous auditing is seen by some organizations as a short-term intervention that will, no doubt, be superseded by some other new technique shortly. In order to maintain the levels of support required to ensure effectiveness, continuous auditing has to demonstrate added value to the organization. The methodology must be capable of repetition with minimal operator intervention; however, it must also be responsive to changes in the business environment as well as to changes in both the risk appetite and risk events to which the organization is exposed. To achieve this, the overall continuous auditing architecture must be seen to be dynamic with a quick response to changing management requirements, revision of priorities, new business opportunities, new technology, and continuous audit activities, which will be challenging due to the scarcity of internal auditors with knowledge in the area. Developing the skills in-house leads to retention problems due to the increasing demand for these skills from other organizations.

In addition, the implementation of the continuous audit process will create a continuous stream of anomalies that need to be examined, and this can overload current resources and may require the involvement of the audit committee in terms of resources.

As auditor skills and understanding develop over time, additional intervention areas will become apparent, allowing an expansion of audit scope into areas previously thought to be not cost-effective to audit and, in some cases, not possible to audit.

Analyses will change as the sources and nature of data to be analyzed change. This does not always mean the introduction of additional analyses because changing risk and operational profiles may facilitate the removal of continuous auditing protocols when the inherent risk has dropped below significant levels.

At the same time, the ability to transfer responsibility from internal auditing to operational management allows a process to switch from continuous auditing to continuous monitoring.

Faced with greater expectations from governance bodies and management, combined with increasing demands from legislation and stakeholders, internal auditing as a value-adding activity will become irrelevant without the ability to adapt to the new business reality.

As more and more organizations implement continuous auditing, auditors and managers need to rethink the traditional annual audit plan and expand their horizons to maintain an audit competitive edge.

17

FINANCIAL ANALYSIS

This chapter examines the process of reviewing and analyzing an organization's financial information in order to evaluate risk, performance, and the overall financial health of the organization. Such analyses could include DuPont analysis or the use of ratios with horizontal and vertical analyses, and they facilitate the auditor expressing an opinion on profitability, liquidity, stability, and solvency.

In any accounting system, the following fundamental principles must all be included:

- Control
- Compatibility
- Cost–benefit
- Relevance
- Flexibility

The quality of internal controls is integral to ensuring that management places reliance on the data held within the accounting system and the quality of analyses derived from it. The accounting system itself must be structured in order to be compatible with the goals and objectives of the organization. As with all control mechanisms, the benefits derived from the accounting system should exceed the costs incurred in developing and maintaining it while the information derived must be pertinent to the objectives of the organization, relevant to its needs, and produced in a timely manner. With the rapidly changing nature of the business environment, it is essential that the accounting system maintains flexibility to meet management's requirements as they develop and mature.

In addition to the use of internal auditors, financial statements are analyzed for the general use of management as well as external users, such as investors, regulatory agencies, stock market analysts, creditors, and the like. From an internal perspective, the primary use of such analysis would be in the planning, evaluating, managing, and controlling of company operations while external users' primary use would be in assessing past organization performance and making predictions about future profitability and solvency based on the current financial positions. Internally, financial analysis may be utilized to compare the financial and operational performances of multiple divisions within the organization as well as to evaluate optimum product mixes as new products are proposed.

Analyzing Financial Data

A critical area for the application of financial and economic analysis is the need to provide a basis for the day-to-day decisions made by managers and employees. From an audit perspective, analytical practice in this area often tends to be overlooked because the pressure of conventional auditing reduces the time for audit interpretation of operational issues and trade-offs.

In conducting business in any form, an organization participates in major activities:

- Planning
- Financing
- Investing
- Operating

Audit analysis of financial data requires an understanding of these major business activities as they are implemented within the organization before sense can be made of the financial records of an organization.

The overall *business plan* defines the organization's purpose, strategy, and operational tactics within which the organization functions. It is the overall business plan that directs management in their efforts by identifying both business risks and opportunities. When analyzing financial data, the auditor needs a benchmark against which to compare the results of the analysis in order to determine whether business objectives have been achieved, are being achieved, and will continue to be achieved, and these are, to a large extent, provided by the business plan. By the same token, the auditor must always be aware that the business plan is a highly mobile entity, and although it is a good starting point for any business analysis, it is not a fixed point and will change constantly as environmental factors change.

In order to achieve the business plan, the organization will require *financing* to raise the funds required to pay for fundamental business needs, such as research and development, marketing, payment of employees, acquisition of materials, and the like. Financing can come from a variety of sources both external and internal with external funding being raised normally from investors or creditors. Audit analysis of funding sources must take into consideration corporate finance requirements, potential and preferred sources of funding, and structures for financial agreements. Without an understanding of why specific financing decisions were made, the auditor's analysis gives no indication of the appropriateness of the results of the analysis. When financing is raised from creditors, two possibilities exist:

- *Operating creditors* are owed money by the organization as part of normal operations and typically include suppliers, employees, and government departments.
- *Debt creditors* are organizations, such as banks, who lend money directly to the organization in the forms of loans, overdrafts, or issuance of bond securities and who will normally charge interest on such debts.

The structure and composition of the current financial position of the organization can be fundamental to any decisions regarding future expansions or funding requirements.

Investing occurs when an organization utilizes funds for the acquisition of assets in order to provide services or produce and sell products as well as the acquisition of equipment, inventory, buildings, intellectual property, information systems, and the like, which are classified as *operating assets* because they are required specifically for the purpose of conducting the business operations of the organization. The term *financial assets* refers to the organization's investment of excess collateral in financial securities, such as bonds, equity holdings in other companies, or money market funds. Investments intended to be converted to cash within a short period of time are classified as *current assets*, and longer-term investments are simply classified as *noncurrent assets*.

Business operations are where the bulk of the finance is utilized and also generated, typically in five major areas:

- Procurement
- Production
- Administration
- Marketing
- Research and development

Business activities are reflected in the financial records and information available for audit analysis within the company. The records themselves are conventionally split into the following categories.

Balance Sheet

This forms the basis of the whole accounting process within an organization following a simple equation that assets = liabilities + equity. The assets may be seen as those resources expected to generate future earnings, including such items as the following:

- Fixed assets, including:
  - Buildings
  - Equipment
  - Plant
  - Machinery
- Current assets, including:
  - Cash
  - Inventories
  - Accounts receivable
  - Marketable securities

Liabilities indicate obligations of the organization and include the following:

- Current liabilities, including:
  - Short-term loans
  - Accounts payable
  - Wages and salaries

- Long-term liabilities, including:
  - Capital lease obligations
  - Bonds
  - Notes and other long-term indebtedness

Equity equals the value of shareholder ownership, which is the residual left over and would include items, such as the following:

- Common stock outstanding
- Retained earnings
- Additional paid in capital

Balance sheets as presented have fundamental shortcomings in that, although it would be useful to have a summary of the values of all the assets owned by an organization, not all of those things that may be seen as "assets" can be assigned a specific value on the balance sheet. For example, an organization's "human capital" may be a critical asset to a service organization in terms of the skills and creativity of the employees, but as an intangible asset, it will normally not be reflected on the balance sheet. Intellectual capital has come to represent a growing proportion of the perceived value of many major organizations. This inability to affix a finite value to intangibles allowed many of the dot-coms to be overvalued by guesswork rather than the traditional accounting approach, which permitted assets to be valued only if they were sold, leading to the concept that there can be no accounting event if no money changes hands. This concept can result in a significant understatement of the value created by research and development outlays. The traditional accounting principle of utilizing the historic cost as a basis for asset valuation because it is a verifiable figure has the disadvantage that no asset can be represented on the balance sheet unless it has formed part of a transaction.

One common difficulty that results from this principle involves the accounting for goodwill in the balance sheet. When a company believes a value exists over and above its tangible assets, it will not appear on the balance sheet simply because it has never been transacted. If the company is acquired by a second organization at a premium value to the declared value, the value of the intangibles, having now been processed through the transaction, can now be recognized and reflected in the balance sheet.

Income Statement

This document presents the financial representation of an organization's operational performance over a period of time with the bottom line *net income* indicating the gross profit or loss sustained by the organization during that period. It summarizes the results of the organization's operating and financing decisions during that time. The operating decisions are applied to parts of the organization, such as production, marketing, etc., and cover such items as sales, revenues, and cost of goods sold as well as administrative and general expenses. Overall, it shows the operating income and earnings before interest and taxes (EBIT). The auditor should be aware that net income does not necessarily equal the actual cash flow. The goal of analyzing an income statement is essentially to determine whether the picture it draws is good, bad, or indifferent. To accomplish this objective, the auditor draws preliminary conclusions and then compares them with income statements of earlier periods as well as statements of other companies operating in similar markets. One complication for non-financial auditors is the use of the *accrual basis* for accounting with which revenues are recognized at the point of sale or delivery of a service regardless of when payment is made. In the same manner, expenses are recognized at the time the debt is incurred regardless of when the payment is made. When conducting an analysis of the financial movements within the organization, it is critical that the auditor understand if records are maintained on an accrual basis as this may have a drastic impact on the results of any analysis. A more effective technique in analyzing income statements is for the auditor to make use of a *percentage income statement* or *common form income statement.* This structure allows each income statement item to be expressed as a percentage of sales and revenue. This gives the auditor the ability to conduct trend analysis of the income statement components against previous periods or years as well as against the income statement from a peer company. Analysis based on this structure facilitates the identification of causal factors for anomalous movements in order to determine whether these movements are control-related or due to movements within the business environment. Income statements are also commonly used in the calculation of executive bonus levels and, as such, may be open to manipulation designed to inflate the apparent earnings in a specific operational area. Some of these manipulations to inflate revenue may be permissible within legal limits, and others are clearly fraudulent. In all of these maneuvers, the intention is to boost reported earnings with no effect on cash flow as is seen further on this chapter.

Statement of Cash Flows

The statement of cash flows is the analysis that traces the flow of funds in and out of the organization. The statement is usually divided into cash flows from operations, investments in the business, and financing. This statement is of comparatively recent introduction, and even its predecessor, the *statement of changes in financial position*, only came into effect in 1971. Cash flow statements avoid accounting confusion, such as depreciation, the amount of which does not represent an actual outlay of cash, and the current year, and are intended to indicate how the firm's operations have impacted its cash position in order to indicate that the organization has sufficient excess cash flows to do the following:

- Invest in new products
- Repay debt
- Purchase additional fixed assets for growth

When cash flow is insufficient, the analysis may identify areas where external financing will be required for such investments or to maintain operations at current levels and anticipated future levels.

In analyzing financial accounts, the auditor must always keep in mind the objectives for producing such accounts and the difference between these objectives in publicly held companies as opposed to private companies. For financial-reporting purposes, a *publicly owned company* is normally producing financial accounts for the use of current or potential investors and normally seeks to maximize its reported net income because this is a common basis used by investors in valuing the organization's shares. As a result, when accounting rules allow discretion, the inclination is to minimize expenses shown to improve the reported net income. This can be done in a variety of forms, such as capitalization of expenditures when permitted with depreciation of the fixed assets of the organization over as extended a period as permissible. As long as the organization can avoid the perception that it is employing liberal accounting practices, such as using depreciation schedules that exceed those of compatible companies, the market valuation of its reported earnings will remain high.

A privately held company, having no need to impress public shareholders, will typically prepare the financial statements with the intention of minimizing the income reported in order to minimize the tax burden for the company.

The auditor needs to be aware of these differing objectives because analyzing an organization and comparing it to a different category of company may distort the impression of the financial and operational performance of the company significantly.

From an audit analysis perspective, cash flow statement analysis can be highly effective in analyzing both publicly owned companies as well as privately held or highly leveraged companies. From the corporate risk perspective, it is critical to know where the organization is in terms of its life cycle—that is, is it

- *Starting up*—In this phase of the corporate life cycle, organizations tend to be heavy users of cash with little revenue yet coming in. At this stage, conventional analysis of financial statements will yield little useful information.
- *Emerging growth*—These organizations have survived the initial startup and are operating in a market characterized by rapid growth although profits may not, at this stage, appear impressive. Amortization and depreciation of fixed assets, coupled with a need to increase working capital as the market expands, can create a heavy reliance on external financing, both in terms of long-term debt and increases in equity funding, leaving the organization at risk in periods of limited access to capital.
- *Established growth*—Such organizations are still operating in a high-growth phase but are operating with higher rates of profitability. Companies operating in this phase are less vulnerable to cash flow fluctuations.
- *Maturing industry*—Companies operating at this stage of development have developed beyond the cash strains imposed by the need for large development programs. Cash flow from operations can be expected to be consistently positive.

External funding is commonly used for acquisitions in order to obtain the economies of scale in corporate operations and defend potentially diminishing profit margins.

- *Declining industry*—Companies operating within this stage face significantly reduced earnings and an inability to generate sufficient cash flow. This commonly occurs when the nature of the core business changes due, perhaps, to technological changes, making the core business products obsolete. When the organization cannot recognize such developments at an early stage and respond appropriately, the ongoing viability of the company is at risk.

By recognizing in which stage of the life cycle a company is operating, the analyzing auditor can more readily identify the key analytical factors impacting corporate risk. In addition, the auditor can express an opinion on the organization's financial flexibility, allowing it to continue to make expenditures even in the event of a downturn in business, thus ensuring its competitive survival.

A balance sheet analysis in a declining market may present a more confusing picture in which, for example, write-offs have lagged behind declines in the profitability of corporate operations, and the asset value may appear overstated. In a similar way, the income statement may still be used to produce an image of impeccable earnings.

Cash flow analysis, as previously stated, gives the analyzing auditor the ability to form reliable conclusions on issues such as the following:

- The ability of the organization to continue to meet its obligations in the event of a significant downturn in its core business
- The ability to continue funding from internal sources if external capital availability is constrained or becomes unacceptably expensive
- The ability of the organization to continue paying shareholders their expected dividends

An analysis of the general cash flow with the various uses of cash identified from most critical to most discretionary will readily identify those areas where cash expenditures can be conserved in difficult times in order to maintain its long-term sustainability. When the organization's debt quality has declined, borrowing may even be prohibited because many bank credit agreements include contracts restricting total indebtedness. Early identification of the indicators of this pattern of decline may facilitate early management intervention in areas that will not impact those operations essential to long-term corporate health and avoid transforming a short-term problem into a long-term inability to survive.

Creative Revenue Enhancements

Revenue and earnings can be improved by, for example, the following:

- Allowing short-term discounts to encourage customers to place orders earlier than they otherwise would. This can create an apparent surge in sales in the current period. Obviously, sales in later periods will decrease by equivalent amounts, but the immediate perception is growth.
- Lowering the credit standards applicable to perspective customers. This will normally reflect as a short-term gain in both earnings and revenues. There would normally be a corresponding increase in credit losses; however, these may not be apparently control-related.

Audit analysis can normally detect structured highs and lows over a period of time. In addition, surprise increases or declines in revenue should be a sufficient red flag for the auditor to conduct a more in-depth examination.

Depreciation Assumptions

By changing the basis on which depreciation or amortization is calculated, expenses may be understated and earnings overstated. Such changes are commonly justified as an attempt to come into line with industry norms. Although this may be true in some cases, most depreciation adjustments, when analyzed, tend to reduce the amounts allocated rather than increase.

Extraordinary Gains and Losses

When an event has occurred that has had a negative impact on financial performance, it may be in the company's interest to suggest that the event causing the loss is unlikely to recur and happened outside of the normal course of business activity. By classifying such a loss as an "extraordinary item" on the income statement below the line showing income or loss from ongoing operations, the organization creates the impression that the loss was abnormal and should not be taken into account in audit analyses of financial information. Strictly speaking, such events should be of a high degree of abnormality and generally unrelated to the normal activities of the organization. To distinguish *extraordinary* items from simply *unusual* items, auditing standards boards around the world issue strict standards regarding which items may not be classified as *extraordinary*. Items such as gains or losses on the sale or abandonment of property or a plant may be unusual, but they would not be permitted to be classified as extraordinary.

Use of Ratios

By themselves, ratios may have no meaning. They become effective measurement criteria when compared to ratios from previous years or ratios from other organizations and similar industries. They do not provide complete answers, but they give indications of where more significant, in-depth analysis is required.

Financial statements are intended to report on the organization's position at a point in time as well as in the past. They may also be used as a basis for planning future activities by anticipating future conditions in order to identify activities that will assist the organization in achieving its future objectives. Ratio analysis provides a means of evaluating and diagnosing performance anomalies as they provide a means of standardizing numbers and facilitating comparisons. Ratio analysis is commonly utilized to identify whether the organization's position is improving or deteriorating compared to the following:

- Previous financial periods
- Other organizations in similar industries
- Leading organizations in similar industries

The variety of different ratios can be deduced or calculated from financial data, including the following:

- *Liquidity ratios*—These are primarily intended to ensure that an organization can meet its current obligations. A liquid asset is one that can be readily converted into cash at fair market value. The primary liquidity ratios using financial analysis include the following:

- *Current ratio*—This is calculated using the ratio of current assets divided by current liabilities. This solution is also known as the *working capital ratio*. The current ratio is a rough indication of the financial health of the organization. The higher the ratio, the larger the proportion of asset value available to pay the organization's liabilities. A ratio of less than one would indicate that, at its current funding level, the organization would not be able to pay to its current liabilities without future borrowing. By the same token, an excessively high ratio (normally taken as greater than three) may suggest that current assets are being used inefficiently or the working capital is not being managed well.

- *Acid-test (quick) ratio*—This ratio ignores assets, such as inventory, that may not be quickly convertible to cash. It does, however, include cash itself as well as accounts receivable and short-term investments. This is normally seen as a better guide to an organization's ability to pay its current liabilities, and the ratio of less than one is normally taken to be an indicator that the organization should be treated with caution. Once again, such ratio analysis must be read with care by the auditor because the nature of the organization, for example, retail stores that typically have high inventory levels, may operate highly effectively with acid-test ratios significantly below one. For such organizations, the auditor would normally extend analysis to include items such as *inventory turnover* and other such asset management relationships.

- *Asset management ratios*—These ratios are analyzed in order to determine how efficiently and effectively the organization is utilizing its assets. Ratios in this arena would include the following:

  - *Inventory turnover ratio*—This ratio measures the efficiency with which inventory turns into sales as opposed to remaining in warehouses. It is generally taken to indicate how many times the organization's inventory is replaced over a period of time. It is commonly calculated by dividing sales by inventory but may also be calculated by dividing the cost of goods sold by the average inventory value at cost. A low turnover ratio may indicate that inventory is being used inefficiently, and when the items are perishable, a high turnover ratio would typically be sought. Once again, this ratio does not tell the full story, and the auditor would need to take into consideration such factors as seasonality.

- *Days sales outstanding (DSO) ratio*—This asset management ratio, also referred to as *days receivables*, is commonly used to evaluate the quality of accounts receivable by measuring the average length of time the organization must wait after a sale before payment is received. It is a measure of the effectiveness of an organization's credit policy. This ratio may be calculated on a monthly, quarterly, or annual basis, depending on the nature of the organization, and is normally found by dividing the value of the accounts receivable during that period by the total value of credit sales for the same period and multiplying the result by the number of days in the period being analyzed. A low value indicates an effective credit policy with fewer days taken to collect accounts receivable. For a small company or an organization without adequate resource to capital, a higher DSO can be problematic, particularly during an organization's startup period when cash flow may be critical.

- *Fixed asset turnover ratio*—This ratio is used to measure the efficiency of an organization's long-term capital investment. It indicates the ratio of property, plant, and equipment (net of depreciation) to net sales. A higher ratio indicates the degree of effectiveness of the organization in using its fixed assets to generate revenues.

- *Total asset turnover ratio*—This ratio measures the value of the total assets required to generate revenue, is an effective indicator of the efficiency of the organization's performance, and is normally calculated on an annual basis. Once again, this ratio may be significantly affected by the market sector within which the organization operates such that retail organizations tend to indicate a higher yield while organizations requiring a large asset base, such as utilities, will typically have a lower asset turnover ratio.

- *Debt management ratios*—These ratios indicate the nature and quality of the organization's use of its borrowings, such as the following:
  - *Total debt to total assets ratio*—This is a *leverage* ratio indicating a percentage of assets that are being financed through borrowing, including both short- and long-term debt and including both tangible and intangible assets. The higher the ratio, the higher the degree of leverage indicated, with an increased financial risk. When this ratio is excessive, an increased risk of bankruptcy exists. Once again, the auditor must be aware of the impact of asset quality on the effective use of this ratio because it does include all tangible and intangible assets together. This ratio can be used most effectively as part of a trend analysis to determine whether the financial risk profile is deteriorating or improving over time.
  - *Times interest earned (TIE)*—This ratio measures the extent to which an organization is capable of meeting its debt obligations. It measures the organizational earnings before interest and tax (EBIT) and divides it by the total interest payable on contractual debt. This indicates how many times a company can cover its interest charges using pretax earnings. Failure to pay such interest can result in creditors taking legal action against the organization with the potential for bankruptcy. Too high a ratio may indicate an undesirable lack of debt or the inefficient utilization of earnings to pay down debt rather than being used for other projects. Once again, the auditor needs to take into consideration the overall organization cost of capital.
- *Profitability ratios*—These indicate the combined effects on operational results of liquidity, debt management, and asset management. Ratios in this area would include the following:
  - *Net profit margin on sales*—This is calculated by dividing net income by revenue or net profits divided by sales. The net income is calculated by deducting all corporate

expenses from its total revenues giving its profit margin in percentage terms. It is a measurement of how much of the income available to common stockholders relates to sales.

- *Basic earning power*—This ratio is a common measurement of efficiency in generating earnings from its asset base in modeling different tax situations utilizing different degrees of financial leverage.
- *Return on assets*—This is a common indicator of management's effectiveness in utilizing assets to generate earnings. Assets, in this case, include both debt and equity because both of these are used to fund the operations of the organization. High ROAs indicate that the organization is earning more money from a lower investment and is utilizing its resources effectively.
- *Return on common equity*—This is a ratio of the net income (before dividends paid to common stockholders but after dividends to preferred stock) divided by the shareholders' equity. Equity, in this case, does not include the organization's *preferred shares*, if any. This issue is typically used for comparing profitability of a company to other organizations in the same industry.
- *Common size analysis*—This form of analysis is achieved by taking all balance sheet items and dividing them by *total assets* and also by taking income statement items and dividing by *net sales* or *revenue*. This type of analysis facilitates comparisons between companies or between time periods within one company. From an analytic perspective, the auditor can determine the impact the various components on the balance sheet or income statement have on the organization's profit.

In using ratio analysis of all kinds as part of their analysis of financial statements, auditors should always be aware of potential distortions of comparative data as well as any indicators within the *notes to financial statements*, which may indicate that the data is not directly comparable to other organizations and may be subject to interpretation. Differences in accounting treatments may also render such ratio analyses inappropriate for comparative purposes. Other influencing factors could include the effects of inflation and seasonality as well as management's attempts to display a specific impression within the financial statements themselves.

Horizontal Analysis

Horizontal analysis involves the use of comparative financial statements to calculate dollar or percentage changes in the specific item in the statement from one period to the next. For example, by looking at comparative balance sheets, the current year's figure may have the previous year's figure subtracted to give the dollar change. The same could be done for the stockholders' equity section or the income statement. Anomalies can be detected, such as sales increasing by a given percentage while net income decreases by a higher percentage. Further examination may indicate cost of goods sold increasing as well as operating expenses, and the auditor may then determine whether these increases are sufficient to more than offset the increase in sales resulting in an overall decrease in net income.

Vertical Analysis

Within a single financial statement, each individual item is expressed as a percentage of a significant total, for example, expressing all income statement items as a percentage of sales. Once again, these can be compared to previous years using a trend analysis.

DuPont Analysis

The DuPont method is used to analyze a firm's return on equity by decomposing it into three parts:

- Profitability
- Efficiency
- An equity multiplier

The equity multiplier is intended to represent the effect of the organization's use of debt financing on its return on equity. As the organization uses more debt, the equity multiplier increases, thus

$$ROE = \text{profitability} \times \text{efficiency} \times \text{equity multiplier}$$

or

ROE = net profit margin × total asset turnover ratio × 1/(1 − debt ratio)

In this manner, a DuPont equation shows how three different areas combine to determine ROE:

- Expense management (measured by the profit margin)
- Asset management (measured by asset turnover)
- Debt management (represented by the debt ratio or leverage multiplier)

A DuPont analysis allows the comparison of these critical performance factors across a variety of organizations as well as seeking areas where the organization may perform better resulting in a more positive return on equity.

As can be seen in Diagram 17.1, return on equity is calculated by multiplying the return on assets by the financial structure. The return on assets (less any interest adjustment) is, itself, calculated by multiplying the operating profit margin by the asset turnover. The financial structure is derived from the total assets over the total equity derived from the debt to asset ratio.

Leverage may be seen as the total assets divided by total equity and is the mix of debt versus equity capital utilized to make profits. This is

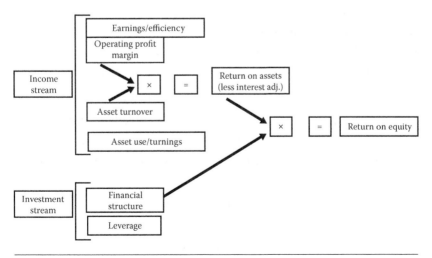

Diagram 17.1   Return on equity calculation.

commonly used by management and auditors to identify whether an organization has the following:

- Sufficient debt
- Too much debt
- Debt capital, which is being utilized effectively
- Debt capital, which is generating profits

Overall, DuPont analysis can be used to identify the following areas in which:

- Revenues are too low for costs
- Costs are too high for revenues
- Assets are unused or underutilized
- Assets are obsolete or inefficient
- Insufficient debt is being utilized
- The wrong type of debt is being utilized

All of these areas are key in auditing operational performance and may be derived directly from analysis of management accounts.

Subsidiary Ledgers

Subsidiary ledgers are formed by structuring groups of accounts with common characteristics. This is done to facilitate the recording process by freeing the overall general ledger from the transactional detail contained within individual balances. The overall details are summarized into a *control account* within the general ledger. The general ledger control accounts must equal the totals of the individual accounts held within the subsidiary ledgers. Perhaps the most common subsidiary ledgers are the following:

- *Accounts payable ledger*—This is a subsidiary ledger containing the transactional records of many different creditors.
- *Accounts receivable ledger*—This ledger contains the transactional records for customer accounts.

From a control perspective, the detailed records in the subsidiary ledgers facilitate the management location of errors within detailed transactions by controlling the number of accounts combined within a single ledger and enabling the use of controlling accounts.

- *Special journals* are also used to group similar types of transactions so that, for example, sales of merchandise on an account basis may be grouped into the *sales journal*, and sales of merchandise on a cash basis may be included in a *cash receipts journal*. The number of special journals used will depend, to a large extent, on the nature of the business and the types of transactions generally processed. The *general journal* is used for transactions not included in any of the special journals.

In terms of usage, within the general ledger, the control account for accounts receivable may indicate that all customers in total owe the organization $5,320. It does not, however, indicate how much is owed by a specific customer. Only by examining the accounts receivable subsidiary ledger can the balance for a given customer be found.

Other transactions that are typically entered into the *general journal* would include adjusting entries, reversing entries, and closing entries as well as those transactions not recorded within special journals.

When, for example, a *perpetual inventory system* is maintained, a single entry at the *selling price* in the sales journal would result in a debit to the accounts receivable and a credit to sales. Another transaction at *cost* would result in a credit to inventory and a debit to cost of goods sold. These transactions would commonly be posted daily to the accounts receivable subsidiary ledger with the summary posted monthly to the general ledger.

A common audit technique intended to prove the accuracy of the ledgers would involve the re-computation of the accounts receivable subsidiary ledger balance and comparing it to the balance in the general ledger's accounts receivable control account.

In a similar manner, an analysis of a cash receipts journal perpetual system would involve the recalculation of the debit columns for cash and cost of goods sold for comparison to the totals of the credit columns for accounts receivable, inventory, sales, and other accounts. Once again, the individual amounts recorded as accounts receivable would be posted daily to the appropriate subsidiary ledger account, and the totals for the individual amounts would normally be posted at the end of each month with the exception of other accounts, which would be posted separately to the general ledger.

When transactions cannot be posted to a special journal, they are recorded in the general journal. When an entry involves both control accounts and subsidiary accounts, there will be a dual posting to both control account *and* the subsidiary ledger.

Accounts Payable Analysis and Reconciliation

Included within the reconciliation and analysis of this sub-ledger, the auditor would normally inspect account balances against line item displays and account clearing, comparing internal posting with customers.

Account balance records typically display totals of transactions per month as well as cumulative values, and these would typically be reconciled against the details held in line item records. From an audit perspective, accounts payable reconciliation encompasses the following steps:

- *Reconciling carried-forward to brought forward*—The internal auditor can carry out checks by comparing the opening accounts payable balance in the general ledger to the closing balance for the previous period.
- *Accounts payable reconciliation*—A common internal audit reconciliation is to compare the accounts payable amount posted to the general ledger to the aged accounts payable detail report as of the end of the same period. Should these numbers not match, the auditor would typically attempt to reconcile earlier periods before attempting to reconcile the current period. If the variance is immaterial, the auditor may decide that the reconciliation has been substantially achieved.
- *Examination of journal entries*—The internal auditor will typically review the accounts payable general ledger account to identify any journal entries made to the account during the current reporting period. When such entries are found, the auditor would follow up in order to determine the source and authorization as well as the justification for such entries.
- *Completing the reconciliation*—At this stage, the reconciliation should be complete, and no anomalies should still exist; however, when variations are still in existence, the auditors

would normally seek to determine whether this is a recurrence of a variation from a previous period. Should this not be the case, substantive testing could be increased to ensure that all accounts payable journal transactions were properly posted into the general ledger.

This form of analysis will initially involve extensive substantive testing when first applied. For subsequent analyses, the reconciliation should be relatively simple and may be executed using standardized scripts developed by the auditor and, preferably, executed by management.

Analysis of Duplicate Payments

Whether by intent or accident, processing of duplicate transactions can cause significant losses to any organization. The internal auditor will typically seek to ensure that appropriate internal controls exist to prevent such duplicate transactions, including management scrutiny of original documentation and supervisory checks and balances. These are all, however, preventative controls and are not 100% effective. As a result, an analysis seeking duplicate transactions, payments, purchase orders, invoices, and the like may form a significant part of ongoing monitoring. Depending on the volumes of transactions and their values, this may be carried out using continuous monitoring (see Chapter 15) or continuous auditing (see Chapter 16) or by periodic analysis in the case of low-volume and low-value transaction flow. Regardless of the type of analysis to be carried out, it is critical that the appropriate form of detective analysis become part of management's overall control structures.

Payments for Goods or Services Not Received

Unfortunately, it has become a common practice for invoices to be received with respect to goods or services not delivered or not authorized. Once again, management controls should exist to prevent such occurrences but, from an audit perspective, an analysis of all invoices received compared to records of goods or services received and further comparing of those to authorized orders placed is essential to ensure the payment is only made in an appropriate manner for authorized goods and services fully delivered and accepted by the appropriate level of management.

Financial Database Analysis

Master file database maintenance is a critical control area requiring appropriate accountability, organization, and approval because changes at this level impact all subsequent transactions related to a specific master file record. Before conducting analysis on the database itself, the auditor will typically seek to determine the appropriate authority levels within the organization for adding new vendors or customers, maintaining existing details, and ensuring the reliability and integrity of database master files and tables.

Over a period of time, the database files suffer from data degradation as a result of errors remaining uncorrected, duplicate entries processed, and unrecorded changes to vendor information as well as customer information. Analysis of a typical vendor master file will commonly identify a number of duplicate supplier records that may require consolidation or elimination. Such duplicates may also indicate a fundamental failure of internal control permitting the creation of duplicate records and this, again, would form the basis of audit recommendations for preventative controls to make the accidental creation of such duplicates difficult and ongoing management detective monitoring controls to identify their deliberate creation more readily identifiable. Appropriate controls within this area would include the following:

- *Vendor and customer name and detail matching*—When new vendors are added to the master file, an analysis of vendor names, addresses, contact details, and bank details, seeking duplicate or similar details may be executed. This can serve as a rough screening to prevent vendors and customers who have previously been flagged as undesirable for a variety of business reasons being recreated as new vendors or customers. Once again, if duplicates are found after such input controls have been implemented, the auditors must determine how the duplicates occurred and who was responsible for such creation. Such preventative controls may increase the amount of management effort required to authorize new vendors and customers, and the auditor must determine the level of risk and whether the amount of effort is appropriate in mitigating the risk. It may be that simple periodic analysis, seeking duplicates carried out on a frequent basis, would be sufficient to mitigate the risk.

Achieving Appropriate Discounts

Many suppliers offer early payment discounts, which can be of significant financial advantage to the organization. When such discounts are advantageous, management must ensure that payment is made in such a way as to take advantage of the benefits offered. An audit analysis comparing dates paid to discount trigger dates and calculating the value of discounts foregone can readily identify the cost to the organization of failure to accept the discounts offered. When the discount triggering dates are not recorded on the invoice but are included in the general terms and conditions for a given supplier, a data analysis linking such suppliers to the invoices paid may be required to determine how much in value terms the organization has lost by later payments.

In a similar manner, penalties for late payments may also be analyzed in order to determine how much extra the organization has incurred in penalties due to inefficiencies or ineffectiveness of the payment process.

Analyzing Accounts Receivable

The accounts receivable revenue cycle includes all business processes, including the following:

- Sales
- Shipping the product or delivery of service
- Customer billing
- Payment receipt

Overall, the auditor will seek assurance regarding the following:

- *Transaction occurrence*—That a transaction actually occurred for a given entity

- *Transaction accuracy*—That the transactions were accurately recorded and processed
- *Transaction completeness*—That all transactions have been recorded and processed
- *Classification*—That transactions have been recorded into the proper accounts
- *Period cutoff*—That transactions have been recorded in the correct accounting period

In addition, *SAS 99–Consideration of Fraud in a Financial Statement Audit* indicates that the auditor should presume the risk of material misstatement due to fraud related to revenue recognition with research indicating that more than half of frauds identified involve the overstatement of revenues. Such improper revenue recognition schemes could include the following:

- Recognition of revenues from fictitious transactions
- Creation of fictitious invoices
- Over-shipment of goods
- Shipment of goods that were never ordered
- Recording of consignment sales as final sales
- Recording shipments of replacement goods as new sales
- Recognition of sales occurring after year end
- Customers given unlimited right to return products

Red flags for such frauds are covered in more detail in Chapter 13.

Data analysis to identify such transactional anomalies may include the following:

- Standard analytical procedures, such as:
  - Ratio analysis
  - Trend analysis
  - Reasonableness tests
- Comparisons of cash flow from operations with net income recorded
- Comparisons of the industry trends and economic conditions against trends within client revenue
- Analytical procedures to identify unexpected movements within the transaction history of a given client

- Unusual transactions at period ends, just prior to them, or just after them
- Comparisons of sales and cost of goods sold against budgeted amounts

In the ledger, receivables are reported at net realizable value, requiring auditors to evaluate the appropriateness of management's estimates of uncollectible accounts in terms of mathematical accuracy and aging accuracy. Audit aging analysis of outstanding accounts receivable can be used to agree details to control account balances as well as to identify past due balances. When the auditor determines confirmation of receivables from customers would be appropriate in order to obtain reliable external evidence of the existence of recorded amounts coupled with the completeness of cash collections recorded, sales discounts taken, sales returns recorded, and allowances recorded, data analysis can be used to select appropriate samples for verification (see Chapter 4). Such external confirmation would normally be carried out, unless the receivables due were not of a material value, if sufficient evidence could be derived using other substantive tests, or if confirmation obtained in such a manner would be ineffective.

18

Excel and Data Analysis

This chapter examines the use of Excel as a powerful data analysis tool. Properly used, data may be sorted, filtered, extracted to pivot tables, or utilized in what-if analyses in order to determine the probable effectiveness of the implementation of audit recommendations. This may be coupled with financial, statistical, and engineering data analysis, facilitating analysis using advanced techniques, such as analysis of variances (ANOVA), exponential smoothing, correlation, and regression analyses.

Management's use of Excel is perhaps most commonly associated with the development of business models covering such functions as the following:

- Risk management models
- Budgeting and forecasting
- Cash-flow models
- Costing models
- Inventory management

Excel is perhaps one of the most commonly available tools in use by auditors with built-in analytical capabilities facilitating a wide range of the tools and techniques covered in previous chapters in this book, particularly in the area of forensic data analysis. From an audit perspective, it has one disadvantage in that the data itself may be corrupted by the auditor's analysis. Nevertheless, its powerful analytical capabilities make it a must-have tool in the analytical auditors' toolkit.

In addition to Excel's own capabilities, for those auditors familiar with the use of ACL, there exists an ACL add-on, which is downloadable free from the Internet and which facilitates the creation and use of ACL add-in tables in a manner that protects the data from those Excel functions that allow the altering of data for those cells that would have been defined as part of an add-in table.

This book is not intended as an Excel training book, of which there are many excellent versions on the market, but rather as a how-to in terms of its use for audit data analysis. Nevertheless, it should be noted that, to make effective use of Excel for data analysis or modeling, a highly technical skill level in the use of Excel is required. In addition, the auditor may require the examination of a financial analysis done by a manager in order to determine whether the analysis can be relied on. In such a case, additional knowledge may be required of any specific accounting requirements for a particular industry. Accounting knowledge required could include the following:

- Knowledge of regulatory constraints that may apply and have a direct impact on the analysis
- The role of cash flow and the structuring of the cash-flow forecast
- How cost of capital may be calculated
- Methods of depreciation currently in use within the organization or the industry

A knowledge of the business entity and its trading practices will also be critical so that the analyst can be clear regarding the purpose of the analysis and the source of information required.

The use of Excel in financial analysis can be broken down into a predefined program, including the following:

- Clear identification of the intention of the analysis. This will commonly involve interviews with the interested parties.
- Identification of the information the auditor already has available or has access to.
- Sanitizing the data to remove known erroneous information that could distort the analysis.

As with all data analysis, the process begins with deciding what information the auditor requires, where that data resides, what its format is, and how the data will be acquired. These have been covered in detail in Chapter 8.

Examples of the techniques discussed below will be found in Appendix 1.

Excel Data Acquisition

Because of the popularity of Excel as a data analysis tool, most common database programs and financial systems have the capability to export data in a format appropriate to later importation into Excel. This can take the form of exporting directly to the Excel format or exporting to a text file, which can subsequently be imported into Excel. An alternative approach to data acquisition is to use Excel's own capability to extract information from an external database or even a web page, for example,

- *Data acquisition from a website* can be achieved by using the Get External Data from Web command on the Data tab. This will open the New Web Query box and allow the auditor to identify the URL of the web page containing the table from which the data is to be extracted, for example, http://www.bls .gov/emp/ep_table_201.htm (see Diagram 18.1), which will result in the following: By placing the yellow arrow next to the table the auditor wishes to import, in this case Table 2.1,

Diagram 18.1   Data acquisition example.

and clicking Import, the whole table will be extracted from the website and imported directly into Excel.

- *Querying an external database* is a method of extracting from an external database only that information which the auditor wishes to analyze, using From Microsoft Query under Other Sources within the Get External Data on the Data tab. This allows the auditor to select an ODBC driver, select a given database, and define the query with the Microsoft Query Wizard.
- *Importing a complete database table* involves, once again, the Get External Data on the Data tab. In this case, the auditor may choose to import from Access or from another source such as an SQL Server, XML, or OLEDB.

Excel Functions

Once again, because this is not specifically a book on how to use Excel, it is limited to the descriptions of Excel functions more commonly used by auditors to conduct analyses.

Excel Database Functions   The Excel Database Functions are designed to assist in the analysis of a large number of organized data records stored in Excel. They are accessed via the Formula tab and inserting a Function from the Database category.

For example, if the auditor wished to analyze the data to determine from an inventory spreadsheet or database the sum of all inventory values purchased before or after a certain date, the DSUM function could be used. In the same way, the DCOUNT function could be used to compute the number of records on the data list for those criteria.

These functions perform basic operations, such as sum, average, count, etc., but in addition handle criteria arguments, facilitating the performance of the given calculation for a specified subset of the records in your database with other records in the database being ignored.

Included among these are functions such as the following:

- *DSUM*, which calculates the sum of values in a field of a list or database that satisfy specified conditions
- *DAVERAGE*, which calculates the average of values in a field of a list or database that satisfy specified conditions

In all cases, the functions use the same syntax:

- *DSUM (database, field, criteria)*

where

- *Database* specifies the full range of the cells containing the list. It *must* include the row of field names in the top row.
- *Field* specifies the field whose values are to be calculated by the database function. This is specified either by enclosing the name of the field in double quotes (such as "Purchase Price") or by entering the number of the column in the data list counting from left to right with the first field counted as one.
- *Criteria* specifies the address of the range that contains the criteria that will be used to determine the values calculated. This range must include at least one field name that indicates the field whose values are to be evaluated and one cell with the values or expression that will be used in the evaluation.

A full list of the database functions and their use may be found in Excel Help under Database Functions.

Excel Financial Functions   Excel financial functions may be subdivided into the following:

- Payment functions
- Price functions
- Investment value functions
- Interest rate functions
- Internal rate of return functions
- Yield functions
- Asset depreciation functions
- Duration functions
- Dollar functions

In conducting a financial analysis, these functions may be extremely useful to the financial auditor in, for example, verifying depreciation values, recalculation of loan amounts for verification purposes, and calculation of future values or present values.

Once again, full details of the uses and syntax may be found in the Excel Help screens.

Financial Analysis Using Excel

The three basic financial statements, as covered in Chapter 17, commonly form the starting point for many financial analyses of organizations. Perhaps the most useful tools for financial analysis are the financial ratios. These are commonly used by management in planning, goal setting, and performance evaluations. From an external analysis perspective, ratios may commonly be used as part of the due diligence review in forecasting the financial performance of a proposed investment or acquisition as well as in the decision of whether to grant credit to an organization. Financial ratios abound, and the decision as to which ratios to place greatest reliance on remains with the analyst. As described in Chapter 17, the five main categories of ratios are the following:

- Liquidity ratios
- Coverage ratios
- Efficiency ratios
- Profitability ratios
- Leverage relationships

All may be readily calculated using Excel's analysis capabilities.

DuPont Analysis

As covered already in Chapter 17, *DuPont analysis* is a method of evaluating the return on equity (ROE), which is a critical measurement for an internal auditor conducting a financial analysis. The overall formula for this is given as the following:

$$ROE = \frac{Net\ Income}{Equity} = \frac{Net\ Income}{Total\ Assets} \times \frac{Total\ Assets}{Equity}$$

This is derived by breaking the ROE down into its components. The equation for return on assets (ROA) is the following:

$$ROA = \frac{Net\ Income}{Total\ Assets} = \frac{Sales}{Total\ Assets} \times \frac{Net\ Income}{Sales}$$

As such, the ROA may be seen as showing the combined effects of profitability and the effect of the usage of assets. To improve profitability, expenses must be reduced or sales must be increased relative to total assets or a combination of the two.

The linkage between ROA and ROE permits the evaluation of the amount of leverage utilized by the organization, which, within the ROE formula, can be indicated as the following:

$$\frac{\text{Total Assets}}{\text{Equity}} = \frac{1}{1 - \text{Total Debt Ratio}} = \frac{1}{1 - \dfrac{\text{Total Debt}}{\text{Total Assets}}}$$

This is frequently known as the *equity multiplier.*
By combining the equations, it can be seen that

$$\text{ROE} = \frac{\text{Net Income}}{\text{Total Assets}} \Big/ \left(1 - \frac{\text{Total Debt}}{\text{Total Assets}}\right)$$

From this, it can be seen that potential investments, each having the same ROA, will not necessarily have the same ROE because more use of debt will result in a higher ROE.

Using Excel to conduct a DuPont analysis can indicate that the organization's ROE can be improved by the following:

- Increasing the total asset turnover
- Increasing the net profit margin
- Increasing the amount of debt relative to equity
- Any combination of these

By conducting such an analysis in combination with ratio analyses, the auditor may make recommendations to improve the areas where movements and ratio analysis have led to significant downturns in the ROE.

Z Score Analysis*

This technique uses multiple discriminant analysis to identify those organizations potentially at risk for financial distress or bankruptcy. For publicly listed companies, using the following formula:

$$Z = 1.2X_1 + 1.4X_2 + 3.3X_3 + 0.6X_4 + X_5$$

---

* Altman, E. "Financial Ratios, Discriminant Analysis and the Prediction of Corporate Bankruptcy," *J. Finance*, September 1968.

where

X_1 = net working capital/total assets
X_2 = retained earnings/total assets
X_3 = EBIT/total assets
X_4 = market value of all equity/book value of total liabilities
X_5 = sales/total assets

Altman concluded that an organization with a Z score below 2.675 should have an expectation of severe financial distress within the following year and possibly even bankruptcy should the Z score be less than 1.81. As with all analyses, such predictions are by no means guarantees.

For private firms, this formula is problematic because the market value of firms is, necessarily, not certain. The book value of equity can be substituted for market value, but the coefficient must be changed to reflect that many publicly traded firms show market value several times the book value. Indeed, when Altman recalculated coefficients for privately held firms, all the coefficients changed resulting in a model of

$$Z' = 0.717 X_1 + 0.847 X_2 + 3.107 X_3 + 0.420 X_4 + 0.998 X_5$$

With the exception of X_4, variable definitions remain unchanged; however, the cutoff points for predictions indicate the bankruptcy prediction score would be required to be less than 1.21, and financial distress would be indicated with the score calculated in the range of 1.23 to 2.9. Once again, these are predictions and not guarantees of performance.

Graphing and Charting

Although audit use of data analysis is a very powerful tool, presentation of the results of such analysis is critical to the acceptance of the auditors' findings. Excel offers a range of graphs and charts in order to convert numerical information into a visual presentation.

Creating a graph is a simple exercise involving highlighting the cells containing the information to appear in the drive, including the column labels and labels if they are to appear in the graph. By clicking on the Insert tab, the auditor may choose from a variety of chart types and sparklines which will best illustrate the message the auditor wishes to convey. General use of charting in visual presentation is covered in more detail in Chapter 22.

ACL Add-On

For auditors who find working in Excel to be complicated when one goes beyond the standard functionality or who are already familiar with some of the capabilities of ACL, a free, downloadable piece of software from ACL* allows some of the functionality of that software to be incorporated within the standard Excel package. It enables the auditor to do the following:

- Create read-only versions of information, formulas, and cells to avoid errors
- Select samples for testing or investigation
- Summarize and filter, stratify, and age information in Excel

Once the package has been downloaded and installed, it may be enabled or disabled within the Microsoft Excel Ribbon at the auditor's discretion. The software itself is designed to integrate seamlessly in order to facilitate data analysis while documenting and tracking the progress of the investigation. The starting point of an ACL add-in analysis is the identification and protection of the data to be investigated by defining it as an ACL add-in table. The data to be analyzed needs to be selected as normal, then the Define Data button is clicked. At this stage, the auditor can also choose to create a new worksheet to operate within.

In addition to the normal data selected for the ACL add-in table, multiple computed columns may be added, for example, to input a custom formula in one cell and automatically apply it to the other cells within the column.

Any activities the auditor carries out within this table will have no effect on the raw data itself as the data to be examined is now read-only and cannot be accidentally changed. Numeric data is totaled and headers are frozen so that they may be seen while scrolling the data. At the side of the column headers is an arrow key. This key allows

---

* http://www.acl.com/products/acl-excel-add-in/

this column to be sorted or to be filtered based on a variety of value options, such as the following:

- Greater than
- Equal to
- Not equal to
- Top 10
- Greater than average
- Lower than average

Once the table has been created, an ACL add-in is created on the right-hand side containing table, column, and row details, and all of the ACL buttons are now activated, permitting the auditor to summarize the data, grouping and counting the rows for each unique value in a column. Optionally, subtotals may be calculated of the number of rows for each unique value and the percentage of the total count and carried out with the unique values being sorted. Options exist to output to a pivot table or a pivot chart.

A common analytical technique available is the option to age numbers by grouping values in a date column into a range of aging periods and subtotal amounts as well as counting the number of entries in each period. This can be carried out even if the data is not presorted into date order. Once again, the output can be formed as a pivot table or chart if desired.

Another option under the Summarize tab is the stratification of the data. This permits the auditor to group values within a particular numeric into a specified number of equal intervals and count the values within each interval.

Data can be sampled using random selection and outputting selected items to a new ACL add-in table for further analysis. Selection is done on a without-replacement basis (i.e., each item will be selected only once) and output to the new table. The seed key for random selection may be specified by the auditor so that a future repeat of the exercise using the same seed key would result in the same items being selected. Alternatively, the seed key may be generated directed by the ACL add-on itself. In either event, both the seed key and the sample size are recorded in the history of the ACL add-in table created.

In order to maintain a full set of audit working papers, notes may be added to multiple rows to indicate the analyst's intention as well as variables selected.

When the analysis is complete, the auditor may save the table on his or her computer or network. Alternatively, the auditor can send an ACL add-In table by email.

When sending or saving ACL add-in tables, it should be noted that only the active worksheet is sent or saved and that any data that the auditor has excluded with filters will not be included in either the saved or emailed ACL add-in table, although the history of the original table will be included. The email option will only work on a computer with Microsoft Outlook installed.

The ACL add-on permits the generation of reports that can either be printed or integrated into working papers for future reference. The report will include the table history but excludes any column or row notes.

For auditors who do not wish to develop the skill set to carry out advanced analysis using Excel's own analytical capabilities, the ACL add-on may provide adequate analyses for many audit purposes. Auditors who require more extensive analysis and would prefer to use generalized audit software (GAS), may select from the growing range available. This book covers the two most common GAS packages, namely ACL and IDEA.

19

ACL AND DATA ANALYSIS

This chapter examines the use of ACL Analytics, which is one of the most commonly used generalized audit software applications presently in use and is a powerful tool for a nontechnical auditor to examine data in detail from a variety of sources with a variety of standard audit tests and present the results in a range of high-impact presentation formats.

ACL is a prime example of generalized audit software facilitating the extract and analysis of data independent of IT. It allows the auditor to handle high volumes of data and facilitates 100% testing of large populations, thus increasing the probability of detecting data processing errors and omissions as well as intentional fraud. As with all such analyses, it is critical that the auditor understands the data that will form the basis of the analysis and knows how and where to obtain the data. As a quality measure, it is also important to be aware of which are the critical fields for analysis as well as the statistical expectations within those fields. During the data acquisition process, the auditor should ensure the validity of those key fields, including the use of valid codes when appropriate.

Access to Data

Once again, the auditor is likely to encounter the stumbling block that the IT department will be reluctant to give auditors direct access to data within the computer systems. IT departments have legitimate concerns regarding audit access into live databases, including the following:

- The danger that auditors may inadvertently corrupt live data.
- Audit tests may cause the live system to crash, causing processing disruption and corporate damage.
- Audit queries may significantly impact the speed of processing in critical systems, resulting in client dissatisfaction.

Interrogation of live systems contains a major audit disadvantage in that, while the analysis is being conducted, the data contents will move on as further transactions are processed. This means that the results of audit analysis may not be reproducible, and the auditor may end up with assertions that can no longer be substantiated.

The solution to these problems is for the auditor to work on a copy of the live data as at a point in time. This allows the auditor to repeatedly work on the same data over a period of time and retain it for future analyses should they be required. As one problem is solved, another is created, however, as the auditor must now accept responsibility for the confidentiality and integrity of the data in his or her possession. Maintaining this level of control typically involves the use of encryption techniques whether or not the analysis will eventually be used in a forensic environment. The auditor must be in a position, should a breach of confidentiality occur, to demonstrate conclusively that the breach could not have happened from the data under the auditor's control. ACL Analytics is a component of ACL for Windows, which also includes the Analysis App window, Project Manager client, and the ACL for Windows launcher. Prior to version 10.0, ACL Analytics was called ACL Desktop, but for the sake of simplicity, this book will continue to refer to the whole system as ACL.

Importing Data into ACL

ACL Analytics 12 for Windows considerably simplifies the task of importing the data, including the abilities of handling the following:

- *Client–server capability*—ACL can be networked with a mainframe version of ACL, ACL for OS/390, to operate as a "client–server" system for transparent access to mainframe data, which may in the form of flat files, VSAM files, or IMS or DB2 databases.
- *Data with electronic definitions*—Data accessed through ODBC data sources, as well as dBASE data and SAP data, is recognized and imported automatically by ACL. Likewise, delimited files with embedded field names are also recognized and imported automatically.

  ACL can also import data with external electronic file definitions, such as AS/400 FDF specifications, COBOL copybooks, and PL/1 file definitions as well as external file definitions for flat, sequential, VSAM, and IMS data files.

- *Data definition wizard*—Even when electronic file definitions are not available, the ACL data definition wizard attempts to identify field types and field boundaries.

The preferred method for importing data into ACL is using the data definition wizard. The wizard has the following steps:

- *Selecting the data source*—The auditor will specify whether the data file is to be obtained from disk, tape, through ODBC, or using an external electronic file definition. When ODBC or an external electronic file definition is available, the definitions for individual fields may be imported directly. When this is not the case, ACL will take the auditor through the process of defining the data being imported.
- *File analysis*—ACL will then analyze the file in order to determine certain properties of the file and will seek confirmation from the auditor as to the file format, character set, and other file properties. ACL will then analyze the file structure in order to identify the file as either a single record type data file, multiple record type data file, or as a print image file.
- *Field analysis*—The fields in the data file will be highlighted using vertical lines, acting as field separators. These field separators indicate ACL's best estimate as to the start and end of individual fields. The auditor is then faced with a choice of accepting, deleting, or moving field separators or creating new separators.
- *Defining field properties*—The auditor will then edit the field properties such as field name, data type, number of decimal places, and the like.

Once the data has been imported appropriately, it is essential that, prior to analysis, the auditor must ensure that the data to be examined is complete and covers the appropriate time scale intended. This generally involves an initial stage of analysis in order to generate statistics on the key fields including the following:

- Record counts
- Calculation of totals and, when appropriate, key subtotals
- Average, minimum, and maximum values when appropriate

The statistics then need to be compared to a known set of accurate information, for example, from reports from a live system. Within ACL, this would normally be carried out using the Classify and Summarize commands within the Analyze menu.

At this stage, the auditor may also choose to conduct high-level analyses seeking anomalous data, such as a search for equal-value dollar amounts or even the use of use of Bedford's law (see Chapter 13) to seek anomalous number patterns. When anomalies are found, the auditor may choose to extract all identified records of a suspect nature or only a sample for further investigation.

Anomalous records could include both transactions and master file entries that indicate violations of the organization's policies and procedures or legal violations of statute. Such violations could include items such as the following:

- Customers with account balances exceeding their credit limits
- Excessive use of sole vendors
- Vendors with unusual or overseas bank accounts
- Dormant vendors
- Duplicate vendors
- Duplicate employees
- Invalid Social Security numbers on employee records
- Excessive use of overtime
- Loans that are past due
- Transactions over corporate limits
- Multiple transactions to a single vendor in the same time period at, or just below, transaction valued limits

Naturally, what constitutes an "anomalous" record will depend on the nature of the information being processed, and it is up to the auditor to predefine the extent of anomaly that would be of audit significance. Deciding this will typically involve meeting with management to discuss the nature of the business area and the types and regulations regarding transactions. In addition, existing documentation on the nature of the systems themselves as well as past reports produced by the systems may be reviewed. In conducting such pre-analysis reviews, the auditor should be aware of specific control issues that may exist surrounding segregation of duties, independent reviews and reconciliations of records, and the degree of access control exercised over computerized records.

Joining and Merging Tables

Within ACL, there is the capability of joining fields from two tables with differing structures but containing a common key field into a third table. For example, the auditor may choose the detailed records from a purchasing table and join the vendor name from the vendor table where the vendor numbers on both tables are equal. A common mistake in carrying out this kind of join is choosing the wrong file as the primary table. If the primary and secondary tables are not correctly specified, the joined table will be incorrect but may be plausible. In our example above, choosing the detailed transaction records as the primary table and conducting the join would result in a table containing all of the detail records with the vendor name included in each record. Reversing the tables and using the vendor table as the primary table would result in a table containing all of the vendors and the first transaction record for each vendor. In addition, it should be noted that secondary tables need to be sorted in ascending order of the key fields in order to ensure correct matching.

When joins are being conducted, the auditor has the choice in creating the new table of selecting the following:

- *Matched*—The new table will contain one output record for every record in the primary table that can achieve a match in the second table.
- *Unmatched*—The new table will contain only records from the primary table that do *not* have a match in the secondary table.
- *Matched, all primary, all secondary*—This will create one output record in the new table for every record in the primary table with a match in the secondary table and also one record for every unmatched record in both the primary and secondary tables.
- *Matched, all primary*—The new table will contain one record for every record in the primary table that has a match in the

secondary table and additionally a record for every unmatched record in the primary table.

- *Matched, all secondary*—The new table will contain one record for every record in the primary table that has a match in the secondary table and additionally a record for every unmatched record in the secondary table.
- *Many-to-many*—The new table will include selected fields from both primary and secondary tables for which the key fields match. In this case, if more than one key field matches in the secondary file, all matched records will be used.

When two tables have identical records structures, for example, January transactions and February transactions, the auditor can use the Merge command to combine the two tables. It is essential that both tables be sorted into the same order prior to the merge.

Starting the Analysis

Now that the data has been successfully imported into ACL, the temptation is to immediately start analyzing and drawing conclusions from the results. If unchecked, this can lead to considerable amounts of wasted time and the arrival at erroneous audit conclusions because the analysis methodology remains untested at this point. An alternative approach is to extract a smaller sample of the full database and test the analysis on that sample. It is considerably faster to "dry run" the analysis on 1,000 records rather than several million records. The dry run can be executed and the results verified prior to embarking on an extensive analysis with results that may be difficult to verify. Once the auditor is satisfied that the data for analysis is full and accurate and that the analysis will produce the desired results, good or bad, the analysis can then be extended to the full database.

Analysis Options

From the analysis menu, the auditor has a variety of tools to select from, including the following:

- The ability to count total fields within records.
- The ability to derive basic statistics on fields or to profile them.

- Data can be stratified over a number of intervals with variable interval start points and end points.

- *Classify* command use gives the auditor the ability to do a quick data scan and summarize based on the unique value of a character field while sum-totaling specified numeric fields. This command is commonly used to determine areas for future analysis, such as high-value transactions, high-volume customers, single vendor purchases, and the like.

- The *Histogram* command may be used to produce 3-D vertical bar charts showing the distribution of records based on the values of a particular field or expression.

- The *Age* command produces age summaries of the data, facilitating the valuation of trends in values and volumes as well as verifying aging of outstanding balances and the like.

- *Summarize* can generate reports on any number of unique key character and date values allowing numerical fields to be totaled and counted for each key value.

- *Cross-tabulate* facilitates the analysis of data fields in a tabular form of rows and columns and even the identification of items of specific interest.

- The *Perform Benford Analysis* command will generate a digital analysis using Benford's formula as noted in Chapter 13. In addition to the straightforward analysis, this command also includes the Z statistic, which is used when the sample size is large and the data is assumed to come from a normal population of which the variance is known. For each significance level, the Z test has a single critical value (for example, 1.96 for 5% two-tailed).

- *Look for Gaps/Look for Duplicates*—These two commands are commonly used by auditors to identify errors in sequenced databases. The Gaps command may be used to find gaps in either numbers or dates. If the field on which the Gaps command is used contains both numbers and characters, characters are ignored with only the numeric values being tested for gaps. In the same manner, the Duplicates command may be used to test for duplicates within key fields. In either event, the auditor may wish to use the Examine Sequence command to check for sequence errors in the key fields prior to using either Gaps or Duplicates.

In addition to these essential analytical tools, ACL offers auditors the capability of using sampling techniques, including both monetary unit sampling and record sampling as covered in Chapter 2. The auditor can use ACL to calculate the minimum sample size required to meet the auditor-specified criteria as well as to evaluate the impact of any errors detected within the sample.

ACL Tools

ACL also offers a variety of tools enabling the auditor to generate random numbers, examine table histories, create editable scripts from table histories, and the like.

Fraud detection has already been covered extensively in Chapter 13. Suffice to say that ACL facilitates tests comparing employee details with vender details as well as seeking anomalies within vendor files or potential ghost employees.

ACL Scripts

An ACL script is a series of commands intended to perform a specific task or multiple tasks. Using scripts, the auditor can assemble multiple ACL commands to be run in an unbroken sequence or to be run repeatedly. They have the added advantages of portability and shareability such that an experienced ACL auditor can create analytical scripts that can then be executed by an auditor with less experience.

At its most fundamental level, scripts assist auditors by allowing them to do the following:

- Save and repeat commands
- Share best audit practices with others
- Ensure consistency of audit approach and inquiries
- Create interactive audit inquiries that can be run by non-auditors

Scripts may be created that are interactive, allowing the executing auditor to specify his or her own input criteria.

Scripts can also run unattended and can therefore be scheduled to run at periods of low IT usage, such as overnight when there is high availability of IT resources. Once again, this book is not intended as a detailed ACL user guide; nevertheless, it is important that the auditor knows what scripts are and how they can be created. Scripts may be

- Created or edited in the ACL Script Editor
- Created using the Script Recorder
- Created from a table history
- Created from log entries
- Copied from another ACL project
- Exported from the project to be later used in another ACL project

ACL Script Editor

For those familiar with ACL scripting, perhaps the most common way is to utilize the script editor to write a new script. From the File menu, the auditor will select New and Script. Commands can then be entered manually or by clicking on the Start Syntax Capture tab in using the menus for Data, Analyzer, or Sampling as if the commands were being executed normally. The commands and parameters will be copied into the script but not executed until the auditor gives the instruction to run the script.

Alternatively, the auditor can copy the commands directly from the command log and paste them into the script. Once the auditor is satisfied with the script, it can be closed and saved.

Script Recorder

As an alternative to direct script editing, the auditor can select to Set Script Recorder On from the Tools menu. All commands issued will be recorded to a script and will be saved when the auditor chooses Set Script Recorder Off. This script can then be imported into the Script Editor for subsequent amendment.

Creating from a Table History

As normal practice, ACL records all steps the auditor takes and all commands executed and creates a script within the table history.

With the table open, the auditor can select Create Script from Table History from within the Tools menu and save the script.

Creating from Log Entries

ACL maintains a command log file for all commands issued as well as the result of the commands. In addition to serving as part of the audit working papers so the audit activities can be retraced and repeated as required, scripts can be created directly from the log file. By clicking on the Log tab in the Overview tab, the auditor can select the commands to be exported, and by right-clicking and selecting Save Selected Items, the auditor can choose to save to a script. Within the Overview tab itself, the scripts can be seen and selected with a right click for further editing.

Exporting a Script

Should the auditor choose to keep the script for future use within other projects, right-clicking the script in the Overview tab will allow the auditor to Export Project Item. The script can then be saved as a separate *.aclscript* file for further subsequent use.

Copying from Another ACL Project

In order to import a saved script, from the Overview tab the auditor will right click on the ACL project entry and select Copy from another Project and select the project or folder containing the script. The editor can then import the script(s) using the Import dialog box.

Continuous Monitoring/Auditing in ACL

In Chapters 15 and 16, we covered the audit and management use of continuous monitoring and continuous auditing. In conducting either of these, an ACL auditor would typically create and use a script to, for example, identify ex-employees who retain access to network resources.

The script for this would typically involve commands to do the following:

- Import data
- Extract data
- Create ACL tables
- Joining tables
- Export data

The script itself can be created using any of the above techniques above. Sample scripts for use in ACL are also available and downloadable from AuditNet.*

Data Visualization

As covered in more detail in Chapter 23, Data Visualization facilitates a graphical representation of table data created by analytics to quickly identify data trends, patterns, and outliers. ACL has the capability of applying both filters and conditional formatting within its Visualization page.

---

* http://www.auditnet.org/tools/script-library-for-data-analytics

20

IDEA AND DATA ANALYSIS

This chapter examines the use of IDEA, which is the second most commonly used generalized audit software in use. Like ACL, it is a powerful tool for a nontechnical auditor to examine data in detail from a variety of sources with a variety of standard audit tests and present the results in a range of high-impact presentation formats. This chapter assumes that readers have downloaded the software and data files of the demo version at http://ideasupport.caseware.com/public/downloadidea/.

This is the latest version and is a fully functional version, but it is limited to 1,000 records. Once installed, the applicable files will be found in a Project called *Samples*. Other files used may be found in a Project called *Tutorial*.

This chapter aligns with the downloadable software and covers practical uses to which this software can be put. The actual usage of IDEA is covered in more detail in Appendix 3.

CaseWare IDEA®

IDEA is produced by CaseWare, a Canadian company. It has been on the market since 1987 and provides auditors with the ability to display, read, analyze, manipulate, sample, or extract data from data files obtained from virtually any source from mainframe to personal computers, including reports printed to a file or printed reports scanned to a file. Imported data is protected with read-only rights, and data files can range in size to more than 2 billion records with physical file sizes in the exabyte range.

IDEA is a computer-based data interrogation and analysis tool primarily used by auditors, forensic investigators, accountants, and IT support staff. It facilitates analysis by enabling the extraction and manipulation of data so the auditors may examine it to seek the following:

- Anomalous items
- Erroneous calculations
- Gaps and duplicates within data
- Trends within data over a period of time
- Erroneous cross-matching of data among systems
- Statistical sampling

By introducing IDEA into the overall audit program, significant improvements in coverage as well as the scope of investigations can be achieved. Data can be profiled to identify exceptional or anomalous items in a manner that would be unachievable without the use of appropriate generalized audit software. IDEA is one of the easiest to learn analytic tools for auditors.

As mentioned in Chapter 10, generalized audit software comes with standardized, prefabricated audit tests and gives the auditor direct control over the interrogations and analyses conducted. Because of the standardized nature of the software, each use can be a one-off, or the analysis can be utilized as a standard interrogation program that is executable by a non-specialist auditor. Such programs may be created by recording the activities performed within the analysis as a script macro. It may then be saved for future execution by an auditor running IDEA, or by saving the macro as a source code file; it can then be compiled into an executable program that can be executed without the presence of IDEA, either by other auditors or by management. Such compiled programs can also be called by schedulers to provide continuous auditing or continuous management capabilities.

General Usage

In general, IDEA can be used for detective examination of files, seeking unusual patterns of data, verification of processing controls through recalculations of values, direct file interrogations, and standard audit analyses, such as the following:

- Trend analysis
- Time series analysis
- Data correlation
- Gap detection
- Aging of transactions
- Benford's law analysis

Data extraction may be executed as the following:

- Direct extraction
- Indexed extraction
- Extraction of top records
- Extraction by key value

Data, whether extracted or not, may be summarized, stratified, converted to pivot tables, or reported graphically.

When multiple files or data sets exist, the files may be joined using common keys, multiple versions of the same file may be appended to each other, and databases with common numerical keys maybe compared to each other.

Sampling

IDEA may also be used to calculate appropriate sample sizes, perform extractions, and analyze the statistical validity of results produced. Statistical sampling techniques available include the following:

- Attribute sampling
- Variable sampling
- Monetary unit sampling
- Random selection
- Stratified selection
- Generation of random numbers

When sampling is used, it is critical that auditors can accurately plan their use of sampling techniques, extract the sample data correctly, and evaluate the results accurately. IDEA facilitates all of these approaches.

These techniques are examined in more detail in Appendix 3 specifically for IDEA users. In this chapter, we restrict ourselves to the acquisition of data within the IDEA software package. IDEA can import data from a variety of sources, including the following:

- AS 400 databases
- dBase files
- Microsoft Access
- Microsoft Excel
- ODBC-compliant databases
- Print report and Adobe PDF files
- SAP/AIS
- Text files
- XML data

This chapter, although not intended to be a course on how to run IDEA, examines the more common ways for importing data. From within the initial IDEA screen, the auditor can select to gather information from data files using the Import box within the Home tab. This opens up the Import Assistant and allows the auditor to select the file format, location, and name.

Excel

We start with one of the more common file structures from which auditors obtain information, namely Excel files. In this case, the auditor will select Microsoft Excel within the Import Assistant. To the right of the File name box, the auditor may click on the ... box in order to select a data file. In this case, we will use the file named "Sample" within the Source Files .ILB subdirectory. This will take us to the Microsoft Excel importation screen. As can be seen, this file contains a collection of data sheets available for import. At the moment, only the web log sheet is selected. As can also be seen in the Preview area, row one contains the field names. As such, the auditor will click in the area *First row is field names* and give the output file the name of the web log, then click OK. The file has now been imported into IDEA with the information definitions taken from Excel directly into IDEA.

Access

Microsoft Access may be imported directly from the Import Assistant using Microsoft Access format or using the ODBC input format. If ODBC is selected, the auditor must then choose *Next* in order to select from the ODBC drivers installed on the auditor's machine. This allows the auditor to select the source of the Access database—in this case again from the Source Files .ILB subdirectory. The database name in this case is ACCESS. The auditor is then given a list of the available tables; in this case, there is only one, and the auditor will choose it. This file contains a table of customers, and therefore, we will choose a file definition name of "Customers." As can be seen, the field definitions have been imported directly from the ODBC database into IDEA.

Print Report and Adobe PDF Files

From time to time, the auditor will find that the only source of information available is a straightforward printout. When such a printout is available in a file format such as a .prn or .pdf file, the file may be imported as a *Print Report and Adobe PDF* file via the Import Assistant.

For example, we will import a file from the tutorial folder named weblog.prn. The imported file will appear in the *Report Reader* screen and will look like a conventional print on the screen. The auditor should take note of the report headings, date information, and log transactions. The first stage of the process is to identify the detail line—in this case, the line with the *user name* field. This line will become our Base Layer. In order to define the Base Layer, two types of layers are possible:

- Standard Layer—Contains data that is in columns
- Floating Layer—Contains data not in columns

Once the initial layer has been defined, the auditor may choose to exclude subsequent layers. In this case, the auditor will highlight the first line containing the Site information and will choose to create a Standard Layer. The line will then be copied to the *Field Editor* at the top of the screen between the yellow bars. The auditor must then define what distinguishes this detail line from other types of lines in the report. In this case, the field unique to this line is the Time field. In order to select all occurrences of this detail line in the file, the auditor must define a *Trap*. It will be seen that, in the field editor area, the Time field consists of numbers and colons. In the *Anchor Editor* area immediately above the Field Editor, the auditor will place a colon immediately above the last colon of the Time field. As can be seen in the data area, all such detail lines have now been highlighted in blue. Other trapping options include the following:

- Numeric traps *N*
- Space traps *S*
- Nonblank traps *X*

The data fields may now be defined by highlighting them in the Field Editor area. In this case, the auditor will highlight the Time information. Field details will now be shown on the right-hand side of the screen. The auditor can change the name of the field to "TIME." In the same way, both the Duration and User fields may be defined and renamed, ensuring that sufficient space exists within the field editor for each field. Once the auditor is happy with the definition of the fields within this layer, it may be saved using the big *green* tick.

This has now defined the fields in our Base Layer. To these, we must now add the fields in the other layers. In order to define the date fields as a separate layer, we will, once again, highlight the data fields in that layer and create a standard layer in order to bring the first record into the Field Editor area. In this case, because we only wish the date, we can anchor it using—in the Anchor Editor above that character within the Field Editor area. Only certain of the data lines have been highlighted because only certain of them contain the date. The data itself may then be highlighted within the Field Editor area and the Field Details changed to include a name of "DATE." In this case, because we wish the date field to repeat itself in every record, the auditor will also move down to the Field Detail *blank cells*, which will now be changed from *Leave Blank* to *Use value from previous record*. Once again, when the auditor is happy with the definition of the fields within this layer, it may be saved using the big *green* tick.

The final layer we are concerned with will be created by highlighting the data fields in that layer and creating a standard layer in order to bring the first record into the Field Editor area. In this case, because we only wish the site, we can anchor it using :// in the Anchor Editor above those characters within the Field Editor area. The data itself may then be highlighted within the Field Editor area and the Field Details changed to include a name of "SITE." Once again, when the auditor is happy with the definition of the fields within this layer, it may be saved using the big *green* tick.

In order to check that all of the data has been defined as required by the auditor, by clicking on *File* and *Preview Database*, the auditor can examine the results of the extraction. If the data is as required, the auditor will typically import the data into IDEA using *File* and *Input Report Into IDEA*. IDEA itself will prompt the auditor to save the template so that a similar file may be imported without repeating the definition stage.

In such an instance, during the file importation stage, the auditor can identify the *option definition file* prior to importation.

Text Files

Occasionally, printed output will be available in a print text file. In order to successfully import this type of file, the auditor will need an up-to-date file layout describing the file structure, fields, field type, and length. In this case, we will use a file called Sales.txt, which is to be found in the Tutorial/Source Files .ILB subdirectory. The file definition is as follows:

FIELD NAME	TYPE	START	LEN	DEC	MASK	DESCRIPTION
INV_NO	N	1	7			Invoice Number
TRANS_DATE	D	8	8		YYYYMMDD	Transaction Date
PAY_TYPE	C	16	4			Type of Payment
SALESMAN	N	20	3			Salesman ID
CUST_NO	N	23	5			Customer Number
PROD_CODE	C	28	2			Product Code
AMOUNT	N	30	11	2		Trans Amount

With this definition available, the auditor can now proceed to define the fields within the file layout.

When the file has been selected, the Import Assistant will analyze the file in an attempt to determine its nature—whether it is a fixed-length file, a delimited text file, or an EBCIDIC fixed-length file from a mainframe. Once this has been determined, Import Assistant will analyze the record length. If the figures are shown in vertical columns, then the analysis is probably correct. The auditor may experiment by changing the record length to see the impact on the data displayed.

The next screen gives the opportunity to the auditor to define the field boundaries as per the record layout provided. Again, Import Assistant will attempt to estimate where the field boundaries lie and may not always get these correct. In this case, it may be seen that a field boundary line is sitting after position number one. To remove this boundary, a double mouse click on the boundary line will remove it, and a single mouse click will insert a new boundary line. As can be seen, the boundary line for the invoice number is now in the correct place; however, the next field is the date, and that has an additional boundary line after the number two. This again must be removed with the boundary line lying between one and the AMEX. The third field is the payment type, and this is correctly bounded. The next field is the salesman, which will require an additional boundary line after 101. The customer number comes next with the boundary line after the 254, followed by the product code for the next two characters. The last field will be the amount, which is correct in its positioning.

As can be seen in this exercise, it is essential that the auditor have an accurate and up-to-date layout of the file to carry out this exercise. The next screen gives us the opportunity to name and define each of these fields. The first field shown (NUM1) may now be renamed as INV NO. As can be seen, it has been interpreted as a numeric field with zero decimal places. If this is incorrect as per the file layout, the type may be changed to Character or whatever is appropriate. Clicking the second field (CHAR2) allows the auditor to change the name to TRANS DATE. We can see from the record definition that this is a date field and will need its type changed. Changing this to Date causes IDEA to request a Date Mask. The layout tells us this is YYYYMMDD, and this must be entered as the mask.

The next field is the payment type, which is being correctly identified as a character field but will require the field name to be changed.

This is followed by the salesman, which the file layout tells us is numeric with zero decimal places. Following salesman, comes the customer number with five numeric digits and no decimal places. The product code is two digits but has been defined as numeric. We know from the file layout that this field should be a character field and can change its type accordingly. The last field is the transaction amount which has been correctly defined as numeric with two decimal places.

When the auditor is happy with the definition, the *Next* button permits the auditor to add virtual fields to the imported file.

Once the file has been imported, the auditor may proceed to the analysis itself as described in Appendix 2.

21

SAS AND DATA ANALYSIS

This chapter examines the use of SAS, which is perhaps one of the most commonly used large scale statistical analysis systems in use. SAS consists of a suite of software programs developed by SAS Software to provide the ability to access, analyze, and report on high volumes of data across a variety of business applications. Dating back to the 1970s, its primary use is for decision making and business intelligence support. SAS is designed to access databases as well as flat, unformatted files. The software offers a large array of statistical functions; however, SAS tends to be programming oriented. To be effectively used, its features should be achieved with SAS programming language, and each procedure includes several statements. For example, compared to Excel, executing a graphic procedure in SAS is much more complex.

Where SAS comes into its own is in the field of data management. Because the SAS system is highly structured and strict to data, it is both flexible and trustworthy, and users may manipulate data in almost any format possible.

SAS analytics can allow the auditor to examine large volumes of data to uncover hidden patterns, correlations, and other insights as its analysis of variance (ANOVA), general linear model, and extensions are robust and powerful. SAS has a specific module for predictive and prescriptive analytics, which is capable of gleaning important information from large databases using sophisticated and powerful data analysis techniques. SAS comes in a variety of system modules, including the following:

- *Base SAS* provides the ability to access data from multiple sources in a variety of formats with the ability to handle data manipulation, SQL, and descriptive statistics.
- *SAS/STAT* provides routines for both univariate and multi-variate statistical modeling.

- *SAS/OR* allows the building of mathematical optimization models for operational research purposes, utilizing both linear and nonlinear programming techniques. This makes it ideal for network analysis in the audit frame.
- *SAS/ETS* is the econometric and time series module facilitating model building and time series analysis.
- *SAS/Access* contains a series of interfaces for different vendor databases.
- Other modules include *SAS/AF, SAS/Graph, SAS QC, SAS/Share,* and *SAS/Connect.*

SAS can create outputs in a variety of forms, including Adobe PDF, Microsoft Word, PostScript, Rich Text Format, or as an SAS data set for use in later audit procedures and analyses.

Operating Environment

SAS operates in a number of different computer architectures, including both mainframe and personal computers, running under a variety of operating systems, including Windows, Linux, and Mac OS X. A free downloadable version (SAS University Edition)* may be used to gain familiarity with the package. It operates in a virtual environment, such as Oracle's VM VirtualBox Manager, also freely downloadable. On opening SAS University Edition, the auditor will start within the initial SAS Studio screen.

Many people program in SAS by using an application. SAS Studio is different because it is a tool that you can use to write and run SAS code through your web browser.

SAS Studio is a developmental web application for SAS that the auditor may access from within his or her web browser rather than using another application on the auditor's PC desktop or SAS server. In using SAS Studio, the auditor connects to an SAS server that has been installed on the local machine. From there, it is possible to access data files, libraries, and existing SAS programs as well as to write new programs. In addition, the auditor may use the predefined tasks in SAS Studio to generate an SAS code directory.

---

* http://www.sas.com/en_us/software/university-edition.html

When a program or task is run, SAS Studio processes the SAS code on an SAS server. The SAS server can be a server in a cloud environment, a server in the local environment, or SAS installed on the auditor's local machine. Once the code is processed, the results are returned to SAS Studio in the auditor's browser.

The SAS Studio main window contains a navigation pane on the left-hand side of the screen and a work area on the right. The navigation pane facilities access to audit files on the server and file shortcuts. The work areas are where the auditor will find the data, code, logs, and results.

Importing and Analyzing Data

Before you can import the data, you must be able to access the data file from SAS Studio. If you are running SAS University Edition from virtualization software, such as VirtualBox, VMWare Player, or VMWare Fusion, you must save these files to a shared folder. A folder called My Folders is created on installation. Subfolders may be created using the *New* button in the navigation pane. Data may be imported by clicking the Upload button in the navigation pane.

Data may be imported from a variety of different types of data files, including the most common file types the auditor is likely to encounter, such as the following:

- Microsoft Access database files using delimited files, such as files with comma-separated values
- dBASE 5.0, IV, III+, and III
- Stata files
- Microsoft Excel files
- JMP files
- SPSS files

For certain types of data, the auditor may be required to pre-analyze the file by right-clicking on it and choosing, for example, to view a delimited file as text to identify the delimiter and choosing the *New Options* button from the heading line to define the field delimiter. From the Navigation Pane, files may be opened by either double-clicking on the file in the navigation pane or by selecting the file and dragging it into the work area. Once a file has been dragged into the work area, the auditor may examine the code resulting from the importation. By clicking on *RESULTS* within the *CODE/ RESULTS* tab and then clicking on the *Run* tab, the file will be imported into an SAS table. This can be viewed in the *OUTPUT DATA* tab.

Is now up to the auditor to do the following:

- Amend the table properties.
- Add filters.
- Explore the data in the table using *Tasks* within the navigation pane, such as the following:
  - Data tasks
  - Graph tasks
  - Combinatorics and probability tasks
  - Statistics tasks
  - Forecasting tasks
- Develop the auditor's own code via *Tasks, Utilities, SAS Program.*
- *Snippets* are prewritten coding to perform a variety of inquiries. The auditor may choose to use *Snippets* to, for example, create standardized analyses (the coding will need to be tailored to the auditor's own requirements—these tailored snippets can be saved directly under *My Snippets* for future reuse).
- Within *Libraries*, the auditor may access a variety of libraries, including SASHELP, to assist in the programming and execution of SAS code.

For those auditors who prefer to write their own coding, one recommended reference manual would be *SAS Essential—Mastering SAS for Data Analytics,*[*] which is based on SAS 9.4 and covers both the SAS programming language as well as the commonly used SAS procedures.

---

* Elliot, Alan C., and Woodward, Wayne, A. (2016). *SAS Essential—Mastering SAS for Data Analytics*, 2nd ed., Hoboken, NJ: John Wiley & Sons.

SAS Usage

SAS and Fraud Detection

SAS integrates effectively with several of the common approaches used by organizations to assemble fraud detection models, including the following:

- *Anomaly detection*—When alerts are triggered based on statistical deviations from the norm.
- *Business rules*—When alerts are based on management's general experience and the application of the appropriate business rules.
- *Predictive models*—These use alert triggers that are established based on scores derived from event characteristics that have been seen to be indicators of prior fraud events.
- *Analysis of social networks*—A more integrated method by which alerts are triggered based on known individuals suspected of fraudulent behavior and associated with a current event or transaction.

In recent years, the use of simple business rules as an alert-triggering mechanism has declined based on the availability of high volumes of data available for analysis and for the development of more predictive means of identifying fraud potentials.

Enterprise Case Management

With high visibility corporate frauds continuing to erode public trust and confidence in commercial, financial, and government transactions, a plethora of new antifraud laws and regulations have erupted, but despite their intentions, they have not been prescriptive on the design of controls to reduce the likelihood of impact of fraud. Effective fraud risk management, already covered in detail in Chapter 13, is intended to provide the organization with the appropriate tools to manage the risks across the full corporate spectrum.

Enterprise case management addresses the need for the integration of risk reduction and governance requirements across the previously compartmentalized organizational data. Operational risks cross all organizational departmental boundaries, and failure to address them as such opens the cracks for fraudsters to carry out their fraudulent activities. The need to integrate structured data from conventional IT transaction processing systems with unstructured data from social networks, emails, and the like has become a driver in the development of enterprise case management tools.

These tools extend the traditional department-centric solutions by integrating multiple source systems into integrated dashboards for tracking and evaluating individual cases from initiation to resolution. In addition to the derivation of forensic evidence, these systems will enhance the continuous process improvement required for fraud elimination. The integration of data across organizational boundaries facilities the correlation among cases and allows the seeking of commonality of indicators.

SAS enterprise case management is designed for forensic investigation and operation mismanagement, but it can be an effective tool for the internal auditor. Its ability to track cases across functions and business units facilitates not only fraud reduction, but also the ability to recommend streamlining of business processes to improve bottom line profitability. The system is designed to integrate data from multiple systems, standardize data forms, and apply quality data rules consistently across the organization, allowing the auditor to conduct either fraud or operational analysis and maintain a full and effective audit trail on incidents across the organization, including remedial action taken on discrepancies found.

22

ANALYSIS REPORTING

This chapter examines the types of reports an auditor may produce, depending on the nature of the findings as well as the audience for such a report. At the macro-analytic level, this could include business impact across the organization, and at the control and transaction levels, the report would be aimed at operational management in order to ensure the implementation of appropriate internal control structures.

The reporting phase of the review includes the documentation communicating the final results. The overall objective of the analysis was to examine the information in order to identify status, trends, causes, and business impacts discernible from the information examined. It is the reporting phase of any analysis that will persuade management to take any appropriate action that is required. The best analysis in the world may prove ineffectual if nobody understands the meaning and impact of what has been uncovered or fails to take appropriate action.

Conventional Internal Audit Report Writing

IIA Practice Advisory 2440-1: Recipients of Engagement Results provides guidance for internal auditors with respect to their reporting responsibilities as follows.

> Final engagement communication should be distributed to those members of the organization who are able to ensure that engagement results are given due consideration. This means that the report should go to those who are in a position to take corrective action or ensure that corrective action is taken. The final engagement communication should be distributed to management of the activity under review. Higher-level members in the organization may receive only a summary communication. Communications may also be distributed to other interested or affected parties such as external auditors and the board.

Audit Reporting

Results of the audit analysis may be reported orally in the form of interim reports, but at a minimum, a written report will be required at the end of the analysis. Unfortunately, the report is written at the end of the project when time is constrained, and the report becomes an add-on to the analysis and is seen as something to get out of the way as quickly as possible. This frequently results in reports that are rushed and of poor quality. From the start of the analysis audit program, the auditor should already have a mental picture of the structure of the report. The findings at that stage will be unknown, but the scope and objectives of the analysis as well as the future recipients of the report should be known, and all analysis should have been carried out with the communication of the results in mind. Adequate time must be budgeted from the start for report preparation in order to ensure the production of a high-quality, fully communicative analytical report.

Internal audit reports according to IIA Standards should be

- Accurate
- Objective
- Clear
- Concise
- Complete
- Constructive
- Timely

In general, written analytical reports should include a statement of the purpose of the analysis as well as the scope, analytical results, auditor's opinion, and recommendations for potential improvements. Depending on the purpose and scope, acknowledgement of satisfactory performance as well as the auditee's reply to the auditor's opinions and recommendations may also be included. Audit recommendations may take the following forms:

- *Make no changes in control systems, processes, or procedures—* When internal controls are believed to be adequate for a given level of risk and the risk itself is effectively controlled or when processes and procedures are achieving the desired objectives, there may be no necessity to make further changes.

- *Improve internal control structures or redesign processes or procedures*—When current processes, procedures, or internal controls are deemed to be inadequate or ineffectual, the auditor may choose to recommend improvements or to assist management in their redesign.
- *Improve the risk/return ratio*—When current processes, procedures, or controls leave the level of residual risk at an unacceptable level and it is not cost-effective to attempt to improve the situation, an alternative solution may be to seek ways in which the overall return, financial or operational, may be improved while accepting a given level of risk.
- *Transfer of risk*—In areas where analysis indicates that excessive risk exposure beyond the organization's risk appetite is currently being faced and when improvements are impractical in the current processes, procedures, or control structures, management and internal audit may prefer to examine methods by which the corporate risks may be transferred either via insurance or by outsourcing higher risk operations.

Given that the issued audit report is a reflection of the competence and professional image of the whole internal audit department and internal auditing as a profession, reports should be reviewed and approved by the internal audit manager before they are issued. This image will be reflected not only in the report's technical soundness, but also in its clarity, tone, organization, and style. The report must always communicate the auditor's message in an unambiguous way so that the reader of the report gains a clear understanding of the findings and relevance of such findings.

General Audit Reporting and Follow-Up

The ultimate value of any audit analysis rests in the improvements made by management to the overall business situation as a result of the internal auditor's analysis. Improvements will normally only be implemented when the individuals who are appropriately authorized and empowered to take effective action have been convinced that action is required, that they are the individuals responsible for acting, and that the recommendations made are appropriate and will address the causes rather than the symptoms of problems identified.

Audit reports are typically distributed to a variety of individuals for a variety of purposes:

- Executive management may use the audit analysis as reported to gain insights into the performance of specific operations or the overall status of internal controls within that area.
- Executive management may also use such analyses for business decision making in selecting between alternative courses of action and assessment of the likely rate of return.
- Operational management may use the analysis to determine the adequacy and effectiveness their operations in achieving specific performance objectives.
- Shareholders or investors may use the results of such analyses in order to determine the attractiveness of investment in this particular organization.

The reporting of the audit analysis may therefore be required to serve the needs of a universe of users with different needs and objectives in their utilization of findings.

Clear Writing Techniques

The purpose of any audit report is to communicate, inform, persuade, and influence the reader; therefore, the auditor must utilize appropriate clear writing techniques to ensure communication is effective. For many report readers there may be no direct contact with the auditors and no opportunity to ask follow-up questions if the message is unclear. As such, the report must anticipate the readers' beliefs and expectations and the types of questions different readers may raise and answer them within the body of the report itself.

Persuasion itself involves the auditor in an exercise of creating a win–win situation. Many audit findings require management to make changes or otherwise take on additional work. To do this requires the auditor to present the case that management will find beneficial to themselves.

Persuasive writing involves careful word choice, the development of logical arguments, and a cohesive summary. In order to ensure the message is persuasive, the auditor must avoid antagonizing the recipient of the report while ensuring that the opinion and recommendations are effectively communicated.

Putting together a persuasive report involves the following:

- *Clarifying relevant audience perspectives*—It is important that the auditor address the report to those individuals who will be making the appropriate decisions and ensure that the report is designed to address *their* specific concerns.
- *Establishing the facts to support an argument*—Only when the auditor understands what is critical to the audience can he or she truly choose the facts to be presented in a format designed to persuade and influence.
- *Prioritizing, editing, and sequencing facts in order to build an argument*—An argument intended to persuade an individual to move from a given position needs to be structured and sequenced so that specific individuals can follow the logic and build to the same logical conclusion.
- *Formulating and stating audit conclusions*—Audit conclusions should be stated clearly and unambiguously phrased in such a way that the reader will not be alienated or forced to adopt a defensive position by perceiving the conclusion as a threat.
- *Identify potential emotional reactions both positive and negative from the readers of the analytical report*—Again, the wrong word or phrase can build a resistance artificially by antagonizing the reader. The tone of the report may have a significant influence on how the reader perceives the message.
- *Maintaining the focus on logical arguments*—By keeping the focus on logical arguments, the auditor can avoid emotions entering the reader's mind and confusing the issues.
- *Address potential objections*—In any analytical report, there is always the possibility of another view of the situation. Ignoring this can, once again, alienate the reader. A more effective and persuasive approach is to acknowledge the alternative view and indicate why the view proposed by the auditor is the correct one.
- *Ensure consistency*—In the executive summary, state the auditor's opinion up front and be consistent in backing the opinion up with facts, evidence, and proof.

Improvements to business practices will come about as a result of the acceptance of audit recommendations and their implementation, and this will not happen if the report recipient reacts negatively to the manner in which the opinions are expressed. When the analytical findings indicate control deficiencies, the auditor should ensure that it is poor business practices that are criticized rather than individuals.

When consideration is given to the number of reports crossing an executive's desk per day, in order to be persuasive, the report must first be read. Bulky reports containing high quantities of verbal padding can effectively condemn the analytical report to the trash can. It takes practice to write a short, high-impact report such that findings will be accepted and recommendations implemented.

In writing persuasive reports, sentences should be kept short with one primary idea per sentence. Long sentences tend to be dull and boring with the message confused, leading to the reader of the report becoming bored and starting to skip through the report seeking words and phrases of interest to him or her. As report-writing experience grows, the auditor will soon be able to see at a glance if the sentence is becoming too wordy. As a rough rule of thumb, the auditor can try reading a sentence aloud. If the auditor runs out of breath before the end of the sentence, it is too long.

Again, sentences can be longer because of the form of verbs used by the auditor. Passive voice verb constructions, such as "were asked for during the audit," result in phrases that are longer than active voice verb usage, such as "the auditors requested." Active voice verbs tend to be more conversational and assist in making sentences more readable. When the auditor deliberately wishes to be extremely formal in writing style, such as during a forensic report, a passive voice style may be appropriate. This tends to emphasize that the report expresses a professional judgment based upon the evidence gathered rather than a personal opinion.

A common fault in attempting to write persuasively is to choose "consultant"-type words and phraseology in the belief that it will impress the reader. Phrases such as "paradigm shift," "blue-sky thinking," "scope-creep," "mutually exclusive and completely exhaustive," and the like may be crystal clear to the report writer but totally confusing to the reader. Once again, the reader should not have to guess what the auditor's message is. Despite having said that fewer words may have more impact, the writer should never sacrifice clarity in the name of brevity. Some reports describing complex analysis carried out by the auditor can become over-focused on the techniques used and the skill of the auditor while the actual conclusions are abbreviated into cryptic jargon. If at all possible, jargon should be avoided because the report may be read by both the technically minded and the nontechnical. In such cases, once again, the reader may have to guess what the auditor meant by the jargon, and the message becomes confused.

Subheadings

In the same way as long sentences can become boring, so can long paragraphs or even sections of reports. The use of subheadings and even white space can break up the monotony of long report sections. When the report is intended for multiple audiences, subheadings may facilitate *scanning* of the report by the reader seeking those areas of particular interest, although some auditors feel that, having put all of the time and effort into preparing the report, all readers must read the full report and scanning should be discouraged. The alternative may be that readers simply skip the bulk of the report or do not read it at all.

Basic Report Structures

Most analytical audit reports will follow a similar pattern, depending on the departmental standards of the organization, but they will typically include the following:

- Executive summary
- Background, scope, and objectives
- Summary of major findings
- Audit opinion
- Detailed findings and recommendations
- Technical appendices if required

Executive Summary

Most reports originating from internal audits include an executive summary indicating the most significant issues and findings from a business perspective. The executive summary provides the overall context to the report and indicates operational areas where executive attention may be required or areas of specific executive interest. If there are no major findings within the report as a whole, this summary may be all that is read. The order of any opinions that are expressed should be directly related to areas of executive interest of corporate risk. Executives tend to be interested in the findings and business impact of the findings rather than how technically clever the analysis was.

Background, Scope, and Objectives

Without explaining to every reader the background of the area under review and the nature of the analysis undertaken, it is nevertheless important that the reader understands, from a business perspective, what was examined, why it was examined, and the significance of what was found.

Summary of Major Findings

Auditors may occasionally get confused regarding what is a major finding. A major finding is any significant item relating to the primary control objectives within the organization as a whole and the area under analytical review. The degree of significance will be based on management's prioritization of business and control objectives and not on the technical complexity of the audit techniques undertaken. Remember that this is a summary and must address, from the reader's perspective, the question "Do I have to do anything, and if so, what?" If the answer to that question is that nothing has to be done by the executive reading the report, the summary of major findings must make that clear. For example, in a primary control area, the summary of the major findings may be that, "There are no major control or business-related problems in this area, and any detailed findings should be treated as fine-tuning to an already well-controlled area."

Audit Opinion

One of management's common requirements in carrying out analytical reviews is the expression of an audit opinion—typically of the adequacy and effectiveness of the internal control structures or the degree of achievement of business and control objectives. In expressing this opinion, the auditor must bear in mind that the opinion is expressed on the achievement of the control objectives of *management* and not of the auditor. The level of adequacy regarding the internal control structures is again management's evaluation of adequacy based upon the corporate risk appetite. Given that audit analytical results are by their nature a mixture of good and bad, the audit opinion, if badly stated, can result in management overreaction to findings, resulting in significant portions of the report being ignored.

Detailed Findings

The detailed findings of the analysis will normally constitute the body of the report. It is at this stage that many reports go wrong with the focus being on what the auditor found and what is recommended. These are two of the four elements that make up an audit finding, and overemphasis on just these two can lead to an audit finding being misunderstood or misinterpreted. The four distinct elements of an audit finding include the following:

- *Condition*—The condition indicates what the auditor found as part of the analysis—that is, what the evidence showed.
- *Criteria*—The criteria is a standard against which the evidence is measured—that is to say, what is supposed to happen.
- *Cause*—The cause should indicate if what allowed the condition to happen is breach of the criteria—that is to say, what failure of internal control or lack of internal control allowed the condition to occur.
- *Effect*—The effect should indicate the impact on the business of the condition arising.

It is comparatively easy to get these confused when writing the report. If the criteria was that all purchases must be appropriately authorized, was the condition "unauthorized transactions were permitted" with the cause of "not all purchases were signed" and a result that "unauthorized purchases took place"? Or should the findings rather be that the condition was that "unauthorized purchases took place" with the cause of "management failure to comply with authorization procedures" and the effect that "a $250,000 loss was incurred due to unnecessary purchases"?

In many cases, it is easiest, in putting together the finding, to start with the effect on the business and work backward from there:

- What was the financial or operational impact on the business? (effect)
- What evidence supports the auditor's evaluation of the impact (condition)
- What control was intended to prevent or detect that impact? (cause)
- How does that compare to what is supposed to happen? (criteria)

Overall, the detailed finding is intended to provide sufficient information for the reader of the analytical report to interpret the nature of the finding, the relative importance to the organization of the finding, what should be done about the finding, and by whom. The amount of detail required within the report is dependent on the audience being communicated with in terms of their knowledge level and comprehension of the audit finding. It is during the preparatory work that the auditor will have identified how much analysis will be required to obtain the appropriate evidence and to express an opinion and how much detail will be required to communicate that opinion.

Recommendations

In order to write a persuasive recommendation, the auditor must ensure that the linkage between the recommendation, the cause of the problem, and the impact on the business is clearly demonstrated. Many objections to auditors' recommendations come as a result of the auditor simply stating that "the following must be done." A more effective recommendation would follow the lines of "implementation of improving the following controls will assist management to achieve the following business benefit." The business benefit has already been stated in the detailed findings as part of the *effect*, but restating it within the recommendation ensures that the auditor has thought through the recommendation and is happy that it addresses the actual *cause* and will achieve a demonstrable benefit. Before the report is published, it is important that it be reviewed and discussed with management to ensure that nothing has been omitted or misinterpreted in the analysis and that, whenever possible, audit findings and recommendations can be agreed upon with management.

Management's comments are commonly placed after each recommendation within the report. When management agrees with findings and recommendations, the management comments should include the estimated date of completion for any actions or interventions required. When management disagrees with findings and recommendations, that again should be included in management's own words. This gives the auditor the opportunity to indicate that potential objections have been considered prior to reporting. It should, however, be remembered that the report expresses the auditor's opinion and, as such, the auditor may include a paragraph on "Audit reply to management's comments" in order to reemphasize the opinion if required.

The Technical Analytical Report

Writing technical reports differs somewhat from the standard audit report in that the tests may have been complicated in audit terms, but the report is phrased in business terms. In developing analytical reports, the auditor needs to be able to describe how the population was characterized and any assumptions that were made regarding the population and its analysis. The sources of the data that have been analyzed and any problems encountered in the data during the exploratory analysis need to be explained, and should any problems have been encountered, the auditor must explain how the data was sanitized and how outliers were treated. This information need not necessarily be represented within the technical analytical report itself; however, it must exist within the auditor's working papers and be available to substantiate the report if required.

As with any other report, presenting the results of the analysis involves determining what the critical business areas or risks to be addressed are, what the auditor's conclusions are, what evidence substantiates those conclusions, and as above, what the critical message to be communicated is.

In writing a highly technical report of a complicated analytical review, the nature of the audience must again be assessed. When the audience themselves are proficient in the area being analyzed, for example, an analysis of financial results is to be presented to the finance department, a specific level of technical expertise can be assumed. When the analysis has to be presented to the main board of the organization, such background knowledge cannot be assumed, and the results of the analysis must be interpreted into the business language acceptable to the board. If the insights as a result of the analysis are obvious to the auditor, do not assume that they will be obvious to all readers. The rule of thumb is, "If in doubt, spell it out." It is essential to put the insights that the auditor has derived into the context of the scope and objectives of the review. Assuming that everyone in the audience understands all of the background is a fundamental flaw in many data analytical reports. To guard against this, it may be useful for the auditor to present the insight first and then the evidence supporting the insight. This ensures that the auditor is not presenting the evidence and then assuming that everyone understands what it means, why it is critical, and what must be done about it.

Data analysis can reveal insights previously unknown to management. There may be significant management decisions hinging on the results of the analysis, and the business decisions may be critical to the ongoing profitability or even survival of the organization. Continuity of a department may rest on the adequacy of the analysis and understanding of the report. In such a case, the auditor should expect resistance from those with a vested interest in maintaining the status quo with no changes.

When it is known in advance that the recipients of the report come from a variety of backgrounds, there are different requirements in using the report, for example:

- General management
- Potential investors
- Financiers and bankers

It may be necessary to segment the report into specific sections to address the requirements of the various users. For example, a potential investor or financier may require a brief section covering the organization as well as the specific product or service under evaluation, an explanation of the analytical goals, and an overview of the mechanics of the analysis. This would not normally be required within the section for general management.

If the report is segmented for multiple audiences at the same time, it is important that the auditor determine who the *primary* audience is and what their likely response will be as well as the different forms of *secondary* audiences that may make use of the report.

- *Primary audience* is typically the first level of management able and empowered to take effective action based on the results of the report. This audience will typically read the executive summary, the summary of major findings, the audit opinion, and the detailed findings and recommendations. For this audience, the report will be presented in order of the most critical to least important business and control objectives in their particular sphere of operations.
- *Secondary audience*—The *executive* will, in all probability, read through the executive summary and possibly the audit opinion. This is the audience for whom subheadings are critical because it is the report writer's job to make it easy for this audience to find those information elements of specific interest to them.
- *Secondary audience*—The *recommendation implementer* will typically examine the detailed findings and recommendations together with any technical appendices. It is at this level that the auditor may find most of the resistance to proposed changes as recommendations may be found to be "impractical," "unworkable," "too expensive," "not properly thought through," and the like. Knowing this audience allows the auditor to structure the supporting evidence within those sections of the report most likely to be challenged.

When a technical analysis has as its primary audience operational management and recommendation implementers, the report needs to be structured as a form of internal communication to start a dialogue with those individuals on the best way to implement improvements to bottom line contribution. For these individuals, critical components may include the following:

- The data analyzed
- The methods utilized for analysis
- Results of the analysis
- Conclusions drawn from the results

Results of the analysis can be made more effective if presented in a graphical or visual form as covered in Chapter 20.

Polishing and Editing the Report

As previously mentioned, the audit report must always be seen as a reflection on both the competence and professionalism of the internal audit function. As such, the report must look as professional as possible. A rigorous review prior to issuance to ensure both the accuracy of the analysis report as well as the appearance, readability, and overall ability to be comprehended becomes nonnegotiable. It is important that the report be reviewed by an auditor who was not involved in the overall analysis in order to ensure that the message is getting across cleanly and so that presumptions of clarity can be challenged.

The report will normally be signed off on by the in-charge auditor, and this can lead to reports becoming written with the in-charge auditor as the target audience. In many cases, this results in reports that go into too great a level of detail because the in-charge auditor may not be conversant with the detailed work undertaken and may expect to see it in the final report. This level of review should have taken place in the review of working papers, and the overall structure, style, and focus of the audit report should have been discussed and negotiated with the in-charge auditor at that time. It is at this stage that the management expectation for content, organization, level of detail, peculiarities of the expected audience, and overall style should be negotiated.

The final review before sign-off should be a review of the degree to which the recipient will comprehend the message and will be likely to take any remedial action recommended.

Editing of reports can, if not properly organized, become the biggest bottleneck in report production and issuance. It is a common cause of auditor frustration when the auditor sees changes being made for what they believe to be "cosmetic" reasons, adding nothing to the value of the report.

Editing may be carried out for the following reasons:

- Substance
- Readability
- Correctness
- Style

Of these, the most care needs to be taken when editing for style. Style is a matter of our own personal preferences, words, and phraseology we commonly use and, to a certain extent, the clichés we use in everyday speech. Because this is so personal, editing for style requires a high degree of tact, and the editor must be careful not to impose his or her own personal style. Generally, it is desirable to avoid editing style whenever possible, and if it is necessary, a specific style of writing should be chosen to enhance the impact of the report on the specific audience targeted.

Over time, excessive editing can lead to a belief within the audit function that there is no point in putting effort into writing a professional report because "it is just going to be changed anyway." This means that the editor has to consider such factors as:

- How critical is the change?
- What would be the quickest way of getting the change done?
- Who would make the best revision?
- Would the author be receptive to change?

This could result in the editor making the change him- or herself because ultimately it will be going out under the editor's name. This is one of the fastest ways to kill the auditor's pride in authorship and willingness to put effort into the audit report. The in-charge auditor needs to apply the appropriate levels of editing in order to build the writer's pride of authorship. This involves discussions with the writer and understanding of the writer's preferred personal style of writing as well as the editor's own style and an earlier discussion on what particular style would lead to the most acceptable report to the recipient.

When the final audit report involves the coordination of several writers' efforts, people normally have found that the writing style varies within the report, depending on who the writer of that particular section was. This is where style editing comes into its own to ensure consistency of flow within the whole report.

Distributing the Report

Because reports are commonly distributed to a variety of managerial levels, it is critical that the auditor clearly identify the primary and secondary audiences as previously mentioned. The full distribution list is normally known early in the audit process, but during the course of the audit, degrees of executive interest may change depending on interim findings. Auditee chains of command may cause communication problems on the basis of "you don't tell my boss anything until you have cleared it with me" while simultaneously being told "you don't discuss anything with my subordinates until I have cleared it." Such internal political ramifications leave the auditor in a position of not being able to discuss preliminary findings with anyone at all. When such problems occur because of auditee chains of command, the most effective means of communication may be to use internal audit's own chain of command to escalate the report distribution authority to as high an internal level as possible.

Many reports have to be issued to remote locations, and the delivery method should take into account the confidentiality of the reported information. Hand delivery may be preferred, either by the auditors themselves or using courier services, however there may be circumstances in which that may prove impractical. When reports are sent by email, confidentiality and message integrity become major considerations. This analysis contains information that is confidential to the organization and may be highly damaging if it falls into the wrong hands. When email is used, appropriate encryption techniques must be implemented to ensure that only the correct and authorized recipient can have access to the report, and no unauthorized changes can be made in an undetected manner.

Confidentiality is still an issue after the report has been delivered to the appropriate recipient, and company-sensitive reports should be indicated as such on cover sheets.

Following Up

Having completed a successful analytical review, it can again be a major source of auditor frustration that no action seems to be taking place regarding recommendations made within the report. The follow-up after report issuance is a critical element in ensuring effective action is taken. When management accepts the findings of the report but decides for a variety of reasons to take no action, if this is within their realm of authority, then the auditor has no requirement to keep raising the findings. Under the circumstances, management is accepting the risk of not taking action, and no follow-up may be required. Given the mixed nature of the audit findings, it is to be expected that management will accept some of the risks detected and implement controls for risk levels that are seen to be unacceptable. In such a circumstance, follow-up investigation is required with management's degree of risk acceptance being recorded. When management accepts the findings and promises action but takes no further steps, any problems detected will continue and may well increase over time.

As such, it is important that all audit reports be followed up in a timely manner.

When remedial action was promised within, for example, 60 days, the follow-up should occur shortly thereafter. The follow-up is not necessarily a repeat of the original analysis although this may be easy to effect by repeating the scripts involved in the original analysis. The critical element is for the auditors to determine what action was taken and whether it was effective. The *proof* of the effectiveness of the action taken may be evidenced in further analysis, but the auditor's concern is not simply to determine that the numbers have changed, but *why* they have changed—that is to say, what change to the control environment or operational environment resulted in the numbers changing, and can the continuity of environmental and control changes be ensured?

When the auditor believes that management's actions have not adequately addressed the overall control or business objectives, the auditor may seek guidance from the in-charge auditor regarding the departmental standard for rejecting the auditee's corrective measures. The internal audit function does not wish to become the overall approver of management's actions. The critical element is not when the audit's recommendations have been implemented as proposed but whether the control and business objectives have been achieved and will continue to be achieved under the circumstances now prevailing. It is a management decision, and resources should be organized to achieve objectives, and operational management should focus on the operational controls themselves. Internal audit's focus should be on control objectives and principles of control. If the internal audit or feels management's corrective actions have not addressed the fundamental problems, this should be reported in terms of the business and control objectives that are still under threat.

23
DATA VISUALIZATION AND PRESENTATION

This chapter examines ways in which the results of data analysis are presented to management in a comprehensive manner. In many cases of audit data analysis, the analysis may be excellent, but the communication to the decision makers is frequently lacking.

Communication skills are the foundation for creating rapport with management and auditees. Being a good communicator can pave the way to acceptance of audit findings and implementation of their recommendations, and communication breakdowns can lead to conflict, frustration, stress, and ineffective auditing.

Data visualization and presentation tools and techniques allow the extraction of data from various formats and turning it into charts, tables, and pivot tables that allow audit presentations to have considerably higher impacts on decision makers.

With the increase in the collection and analysis of data, it has become increasingly difficult for decision makers throughout organizations to understand the relevance among the multiplicity of variables without a visual representation of the analytical results. Data analysis can only be deemed to be successful to the extent that the information can be comprehended by the human being and appropriate conclusions drawn.

Communication Modes

A communication mode is the medium or channel through which an idea is expressed. Human beings have three basic modes of communication:

- *Verbal*—In which we communicate via the spoken word or in written formats.
- *Visual*—Visual communications involves the transmission of information using symbols and imagery. This is the mode in

which we communicate via what we see. In human terms, this would include communication via a visual aid in a form that can be looked upon and includes graphic design, use of images, and screen-based design.

- *Kinetic or nonverbal*—Here we communicate based on interpretation of body movement, that is, nonverbal behavior related to body movement, gestures, and facial expressions.

Most human beings have one primary communication mode in which they are most comfortable to both give and receive information. Typically, they will also have a secondary mode and, in some cases, a tertiary mode. In general, the most effective form of communication has a large visual component because that is the most common primary mode. In business visualization, the auditor must take into consideration the three basic provisions of any communication:

- *Appeal*—The degree to which the communication engages its audience
- *Comprehension*—The understandability of the information to the targeted audience
- *Retention*—The degree to which the audience will remember the data presented in a visualization

Normally, for audit presentation purposes, it is the degree of *comprehension* that dominates, followed by *retention* and last *appeal*. This is a reversal of the normal commercial priorities of communication in which *appeal* dominates followed by *retention*, and *comprehension* tends to trail behind.

To differentiate the simple use of computer graphics from visualization, the role of visualization is to convey a variety of insights into a given process by creating images involving the manipulation of data produced by that process by decomposing the process into a *pipeline* with each stage in the process having its own specific elements:

- Data acquisition of the initial data set
- Data enriching, transformation, and sampling to enrich the data set
- Mapping the data to visual representations in 2-D or 3-D shapes
- Rendering the final visual representation or image

Data visualization involves the presentation in a graphical format of abstract information in order to discover and understand the information that resides in complex data. Numerical data is abstract in that it does not have a physical form, but by using the attributes of visual information, such as the following, the data can be made more comprehensible and easier to absorb:

- Length
- Size
- Shape
- Color

As such, data visualization techniques make it easier and faster for people to grasp the meaning and underlying trends contained within data elements when they are presented in the forms of graphs and charts as opposed to large volumes of written reports or laid out in spreadsheets. The use of visualization techniques enables the analyst to see patterns that were not previously obvious. Even within high volumes of data, patterns may be identified easily.

In most analyses, the sheer volumes of data offered for analysis make it difficult for patterns to be recognized immediately without the use of visualization techniques and software. When the information is presented in hardcopy, the problem multiplies. Data visualization permits the presentation of the data in a form in which a manager or executive can easily interpret trends and relationships and facilitates interpretation of underlying causes. From an audit perspective, visualization assists the auditor to do the following:

- Identify operational areas where improvements could be made
- Identify revenue or expense areas requiring management attention
- Focus on areas of high risk or impact
- Identify those factors that are likely to have the highest impact on the achievement of corporate objectives

Generating the best visuals for displaying data requires the auditor to follow some basic guidelines:

- Understanding the audience and the type of visual communication medium most acceptable for the message to be delivered.

- Use of a technique that conveys the information in the simplest form for the most effective absorption by the audience.
- Deciding on the kind of information the auditor wishes to convey and what he or she wishes the audience to comprehend.
- The auditor must understand him- or herself the data to be visualized, including its cardinality and size.

Choosing Visuals for Impact

As stated above, understanding the audience is a critical component of choosing the visual mechanism to achieve a specific impact. This involves the identification and selection of the data to be analyzed as well as the level of detail required to be presented. Data granularity, the level of depth represented by the data, may be held in a database at the atomic level of detail even down to the transaction level. In general, the information contained within the overall data warehouse is at too high a level of granularity for general management usage. Management typically requires a lower level of granularity facilitating a summary view of data and transactions. The actual manipulation of the granular data and the summarization can be handled by a combination of the hardware and software architectures utilized. In some cases, for example, in processing a large volume of web data, this may involve a *granularity manager*, which is capable of taking large volumes of granular data, processing it, and producing a subset of that data in a summarized, well-organized fashion.

The problem still remains, however, of deciding the level to which the data needs to be summarized. For visualization purposes, understanding the user's needs involves understanding the data in order to determine the correct shape and format in which to present the data in a context understandable by the viewer. To achieve this, the auditor will require an in-depth understanding of the source of the data and how it is likely to be interpreted by the intended audience. As with all such analysis, the value of the visualization is dependent upon the accuracy and completeness of the atomic level data as well as the appropriate generation of the summarized data. Drawing from the old IT adage of "rubbish in, rubbish out," if the raw data behind a visualization cannot be relied upon, the visualization itself may be misleading to the extent that significant business decisions will be made based upon the image presented without a managerial challenge to the veracity of the auditor's visualization. This means that whenever such visualization methodologies are used, an effective data governance process must be in place, tested, and proven effective.

Once the data has been sanitized and summarized to the appropriate degree, the auditor must then choose the method of presentation. All manner of graphs and images may be chosen, but the big question remains: Which image will present the information in a convincing form to effectively communicate the issues to be presented to management? There is a tendency to seek out overcomplicated graphs. For example, a report on the top 20 states by population can produce a bubble chart, such as in Diagram 23.1.

Diagram 23.1, although an accurate graph, does not convey the relative size of the top 20 states, yet a simple line chart as in Diagram 23.2 gives a clearer representation of their respective sizes.

And a radar graph, such as in Diagram 23.3, is virtually meaningless.

This was a comparatively easy exercise involving only 20 states. When dealing with extremely large amounts of information across multiple categories, producing a meaningful visualization requires clustering the data into a higher-level view with less granularization in order to render the image understandable to the reader.

In Diagram 23.4, you can see the effect of running the data through IDEA's Visualization module to extract a standard bar chart.

In some cases, such as these examples, the numbers themselves are not that difficult to interpret; however, more complex data representations do not communicate well when presented as a table.

The representation of such information in diagrammatic or image form of that enabled by visualization techniques makes it possible to communicate data outliers and trends more effectively. If structured appropriately with the audience in mind, management and the auditees will be in a position to identify those issues requiring urgent attention by simply viewing a chart. Data outliers can be easily overlooked if hidden in a large volume of numeric data presented in tabular form. When outliers form an insignificant part of the data as a whole and have little impact on the overall conclusions to be drawn, the auditor may choose to omit that data either from a chart or from the raw data itself. Any such removal needs to be documented together with good reasons for omission and the impact on the analysis as a whole.

2015		Population estimate for 1-Jul-15	Percentage of total U.S. pop.
1	California	39,144,818	12.18%
2	Texas	27,469,114	8.55%
3	Florida	20,271,272	6.31%
4	New York	19,795,791	6.16%
5	Illinois	12,859,995	4.00%
6	Pennsylvania	12,802,503	3.98%
7	Ohio	11,613,423	3.61%
8	Georgia	10,214,860	3.18%
9	North Carolina	10,042,802	3.12%
10	Michigan	9,922,576	3.11%
11	New Jersey	8,958,013	2.79%
12	Virginia	8,382,993	2.61%
13	Washington	7,170,351	2.23%
14	Arizona	6,828,065	2.12%
15	Massachusetts	6,794,422	2.11%
16	Indiana	6,619,680	2.06%
17	Tennessee	6,600,299	2.05%
18	Missouri	6,083,672	1.89%
19	Maryland	6,006,401	1.87%
20	Wisconsin	5,771,337	1.80%

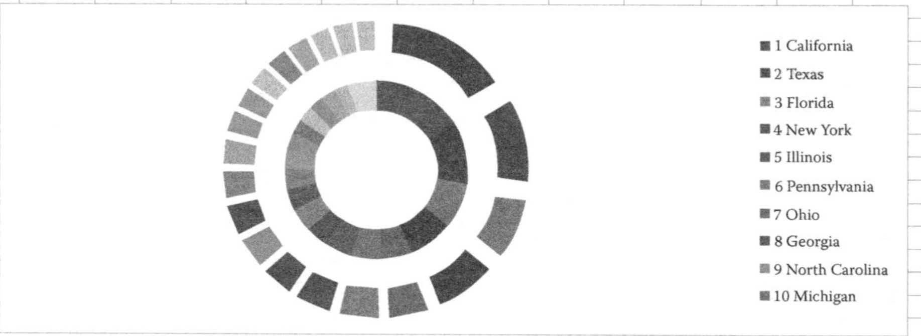

■ 1 California
■ 2 Texas
■ 3 Florida
■ 4 New York
■ 5 Illinois
■ 6 Pennsylvania
■ 7 Ohio
■ 8 Georgia
■ 9 North Carolina
■ 10 Michigan

Diagram 23.1   Bubble chart example.

2015		Population estimate for 1-Jul-15	Percentage of total U.S. pop.
1	California	39,144,818	12.18%
2	Texas	27,469,114	8.55%
3	Florida	20,271,272	6.31%
4	New York	19,795,791	6.16%
5	Illinois	12,859,995	4.00%
6	Pennsylvania	12,802,503	3.98%
7	Ohio	11,613,423	3.61%
8	Georgia	10,214,860	3.18%
9	North Carolina	10,042,802	3.12%
10	Michigan	9,922,576	3.11%
11	New Jersey	8,958,013	2.79%
12	Virginia	8,382,993	2.61%
13	Washington	7,170,351	2.23%
14	Arizona	6,828,065	2.12%
15	Massachusetts	6,794,422	2.11%
16	Indiana	6,619,680	2.06%
17	Tennessee	6,600,299	2.05%
18	Missouri	6,083,672	1.89%
19	Maryland	6,006,401	1.87%
20	Wisconsin	5,771,337	1.80%
21	Minnesota	5,489,594	1.71%

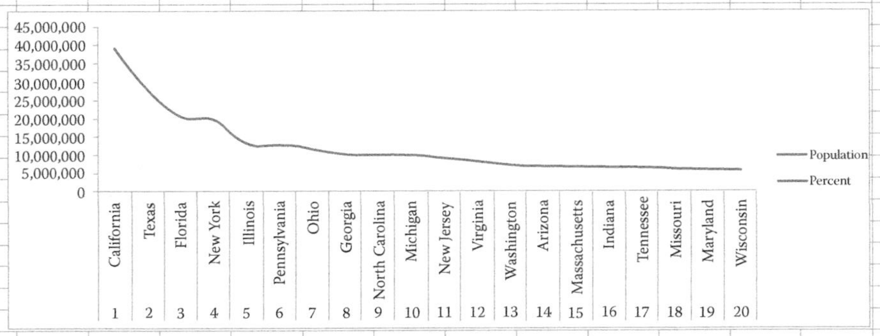

Diagram 23.2 Line chart example.

2015		Population estimate for 1-Jul-15	Percentage of total U.S. pop.
1	California	39,144,818	12.18%
2	Texas	27,469,114	8.55%
3	Florida	20,271,272	6.31%
4	New York	19,795,791	6.16%
5	Illinois	12,859,995	4.00%
6	Pennsylvania	12,802,503	3.98%
7	Ohio	11,613,423	3.61%
8	Georgia	10,214,860	3.18%
9	North Carolina	10,042,802	3.12%
10	Michigan	9,922,576	3.11%
11	New Jersey	8,958,013	2.79%
12	Virginia	8,382,993	2.61%
13	Washington	7,170,351	2.23%
14	Arizona	6,828,065	2.12%
15	Massachusetts	6,794,422	2.11%
16	Indiana	6,619,680	2.06%
17	Tennessee	6,600,299	2.05%
18	Missouri	6,083,672	1.89%
19	Maryland	6,006,401	1.87%
20	Wisconsin	5,771,337	1.80%
21	Minnesota	5,489,594	1.71%

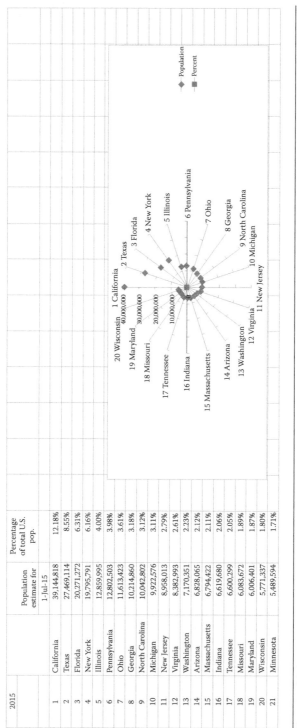

Diagram 23.3 Radar graph example.

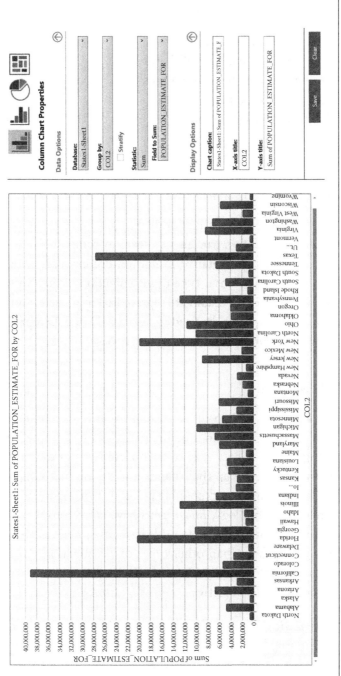

Diagram 23.4 Bar chart example.

As with all visualizations, the form selected must satisfy specific criteria, including the following:

- Represent quantities accurately
- Indicate clearly the nature of the relationship
- Make it easy to see the ranking of values
- Make it easy to compare quantities
- Make it easy for viewers to understand how the information should be used

Non-Quantitative Visualization

So far, we have covered visualization techniques in terms of quantitative values. Visualization can also be used to bring clarity to relationships that are not quantitative in nature. For example node-link relationships may be used as a type of visualization of data in which entities are captured as nodes and are represented by a circle, and links indicating relationships may be used to depict 2-D or 3-D representations of networks, human-based or computer-based.

Big Data Visualization

One of the key areas of impact for visualization is a presentation of information from Big Data in a manner that can be comprehended. A typical Big Data database may consist of millions of rows of data, leading analysts to throw up their hands and decide that sampling is the only technique that could possibly be used. With more advanced use of dashboard technology, *infographics* have come into more common use in order to represent data with fewer assumptions about the viewer's knowledge base than other types of visualization. There are multiple types of infographics that exist with different applications depending on the audit objective:

- *Statistical distributions*—These are intended to reveal trends by illustrating how numbers are distributed.
- *Time series*—Graphics of this type show sets of values over a time period in order to illustrate trends over time.

- *Networking*—These are used to indicate relationships among data elements.
- *Hierarchies*—These can be illustrated as natural hierarchies or assembled as artificial hierarchies using a variety of techniques.
- *Mapping*—This is an obvious way to represent geographical data but can also be used to depict space over a period of time using flow maps.

Differing types of visualization can be used to present information from Big Data in a variety of ways to a variety of audiences for a variety of purposes. The audit analysis is not simply to provide the same data in different diagrammatic representations to the same audience, but to allow multiple audiences to draw their conclusions based on the presentation of information from a common source that best represents their knowledge requirements.

As with most other analytical techniques covered in this book, the whole exercise is a waste of time and money unless there's comprehension by the people using the analysis. This means the organization must invest as much into the training of the people who are intended to benefit from the visualization as it does into the technology and techniques to be utilized.

Using Visualizations

With an understanding of analytical techniques, analysts can dissect data to uncover a variety of business insights. However, unless they are aware of the information required to fulfill a specific job function, the presentation via dashboards of the metrics may not be appropriate for that particular audience because a different organizational role will require different views of data. From an audit perspective, the probability of a single auditor being an expert in statistics, programming, and visualization design is slim and the learning curve steep.

The users of the data presented need to understand not only the meaning of the data, but the implications in terms of their job role and the changes within the organization dictated by the information as presented. The intention is that these dashboards should serve as flexible frameworks to be interpreted as requirements change and user needs vary.

Choosing the Tool

Data visualization tools vary from IBM Cognos Insight, through Microsoft Power View to SAS Visual Intelligence and a plethora of other products. One of the most critical elements to be taken into consideration in selecting the appropriate tool is its ease of use by employees who are not required to be IT gurus. For many users, this is seen to be almost as important as the quality of data analyzed. The actual functional capability in terms of graphical capability is of less importance because software suppliers tend to leapfrog over each other so that whatever innovation supplier A provides in the current version of their software, supplier B will add, plus extras in the next version of theirs.

Most advanced visualization products offer features such as dynamic data, animation, actionable alerts, and the ability to personalize dashboards to meet the requirements of the universe of users. Dynamic data capability, the ability to update visualizations in real time as data sources, such as corporate databases, are updated has become an essential. In the same way, the ability to drill down by simply clicking on a part of the chart must now be mapped onto other charts as usual navigations around optional views. The use of actionable alerts has become critical, particularly in larger data structures, because no user can keep an eye on all indicators at all times. When users can tailor triggering parameters based on criticality, volumes, values, and other key elements, visualization has now moved into the realm of continuous monitoring (see Chapter 16).

Using as an example IBM's Smarter City software, IBM identified the need to address citizens' demands for values, such as the following:

- Convenience
- Security
- Disparity
- Opportunity

All this needed to be matched by civic leaders delivering the following:

- Roads and buildings
- Infrastructure including water and power
- Health care and lifestyle choices
- Education and employment

To achieve this, it was realized that civic leaders had to go beyond the conventional silo approach to service delivery and that this was only possible if data could be integrated from a variety of sources, including such areas as health care providers, universities, civic groups, and businesses. The intention was to leverage information to enable better decision making while allowing problems to be anticipated and resources and processes coordinated to operate at optimum effectiveness.

The system is designed to be modular and cover areas ranging from public safety through transportation to intelligence operations. It was also realized that the existing silos to be covered would continue to grow, and therefore, expandability would be a major requirement.

To make all this work, the information had to be leveraged with real-time visibility of key data elements, and performance variations needed early recognition through appropriate trigger points to mitigate and manage any incident that could impact the overall effectiveness of operations. The system had also to coordinate resources and processes to enable rapid response and effective reaction should such instances occur.

The overall design was based on the evolution of the management of situations faced by organizations and their response moving from the following:

- *Contingency theory–based*—Where solutions to problems were based on the skills of the available responders at the time of the incident. This form of incident response is problematic in that there is little ability to share information, meaning that, should an incident escalate, more physical resources will be required, but confusion and information overload are probable.

- *Fusion center–based*—Where representatives of different response silos are centrally located, and word-of-mouth communication can easily take place. This situation, although an improvement on the contingency theory structure, nevertheless leaves the response silos utilizing discrete sources of data with integration being problematic and still relying on the individual responders.
- *Intelligent operations center (IOC)*—When the information from different domains are integrated so the event response can be coordinated centrally, information is readily available to all participants in a visualization form appropriate to their needs and with the ability to track responses in real time to ensure continuous improvement.

As with all integrated visualization systems, the need existed for it to be able to do the following:

- Collect data from multiple sources, both internal and external, into a standardized structure with the information normalized to provide a common view
- Identify appropriate filters to recognize triggering occurrences based on their significance and impact
- Create visualizations of key performance indicators, alerts, and other significant events coupled with visualization through geospatial mapping
- Identify patterns and trends warranting direct management intervention
- Facilitate cross-silo decision making and collaboration
- Identify and flag potential cross-silo conflicts

The resulting system uses visualization techniques in providing the following:

- Entity-wide dashboards
- Data modeling and integration
- Geospatial mapping
- Model simulation and visualization
- Domain-level analytics
- Incident alerts and directives

Without the use of these visualization techniques, the result would have been an enormous analysis of vast quantities of data but with very little capability to do anything about what the data represented.

Internal Audit Usage

Although the above is an example of the utilization of visualization techniques in the management context, in an internal audit context, it can increase user autonomy by allowing the discovery of relevant insights with minimal IT intervention by making visible the overall big picture with the ability to drill down for details required to make fully informed decisions. Use of audit visualization techniques allows a better identification of impacts on the overall corporate risk assessment and facilitates internal audit focus on the areas of most significant return. The very scope of audit testing can be rationalized based on indicators that can be visually seen to be of the greatest need and impact. Implementing visualization as an everyday internal audit tool would most effectively involve the development of an appropriate KPI dashboard to be integrated into the overall risk-based internal audit approach. This would allow the auditor to enable continuous auditing and to identify control deficiency trends on a real-time basis. The actual visualization type could be any of the standards, such as the following:

- *Classic waterfall*—Demonstrate how an initial value may be increased or decreased by a series of intermediate steps.
- *Geospatial*—Provide comparisons overlaid on a map backdrop facilitating techniques, such as heat map alerts for areas reaching trigger points.
- *Strategy trees*—This is a method of dramatically indicating the overall objective and sub-objectives as well as key performance indicators on a hierarchical basis.
- *Pareto analysis*—This type of chart can indicate how a specific group of the specific population, normally the top percentage, contributes to profitability, risk, or other criteria corresponding to the percentage of the population making up that value.
- *Box plots*—Box plots facilitate the comparison of the spread of related data point values within a given operational dimension.

- *Bubble charts*—These are commonly used in scatter scenarios when multiple variables are in use. The individual data points are indicated by both the size and location of the data markers (round bubbles). These are commonly used to show correlations among value types.
- *Scatter graphs*—These are perhaps the most common form of graphical representation of data points in which points themselves indicate individual values.

This list can include any other graphical representation appropriate to conveying the message.

Making Visualization Effective

The most critical component of any visualization is the overall *quality of data*. Data must be sanitized before integration because the very summarization process involved in visualization can cover up inaccuracies and incompleteness in the data, resulting in misleading visualizations. For the auditor, it must always be borne in mind that *audit bias* can also distort the message by contaminating the visualization with the auditor's own beliefs and values. A problem in visualization design, at least in the early stages of utilization, is a temptation to *overload the design* for the viewer with visual representations that become confusing. In the same way, *representing information in an inappropriate way* can result in a misinterpretation of the data by both the auditor and the eventual user of the information.

The degree of acceptance by management and auditees as measured by the ongoing usage of internal audit visualizations is, perhaps, the most effective measurement of how successful the implementation of audit visualization has been.

24
CONCLUSION

Data analysis for auditors involves the use of techniques to convert data to numerical forms and subject them to the appropriate statistical analysis so that appropriate audit conclusions can be drawn regarding the achievement of business objectives and control objectives.

The intention of this book was to bring the auditor to a state of knowledge regarding the following:

- The acquisition of data
- The variety of analytical techniques available to assess data
- Transformation of data into more readily analyzed forms when required
- The use of advanced computer interrogation software
- Handling of large volumes of data
- Handling of varieties of data structures

We have examined univariate analysis (the analysis of a single variable), which does not involve relationships between two or more variables and whose purpose is more descriptive than explanatory, such as frequency distributions as well as maximum and minimum responses. We then moved on to looking at sampling from an audit perspective. We examined judgmental sampling and differentiated it from statistical sampling. Although both are valid within audit practice, it is primarily statistical sampling that lends itself to use in internal audit data analysis.

Through the use of generalized audit software, such as ACL and IDEA, as well as packages, such as Excel, this book has attempted to provide internal auditors the understanding of the procedures and techniques available to the auditor as well as some of the more commonly used tools in audit practice today.

Although it is recognized that the use of audit software facilitates the testing of complete sets of data rather than simply testing samples, what is possible is not always what is desirable. Again, it must always be recognized that data analysis assists auditors in identifying anomalies and trends and understanding the linkage between cause and effect within the business processes; it nevertheless must always be seen as an aide rather than the final product. Data analytics, *when used as part of an integrated audit program*, can lead auditors to a better understanding of the management processes required to achieve business and control objectives as well as the deficiencies within those processes.

This facilitates audit making recommendations that can demonstrably support management in improving the control environment leading to a greater probability of achievement of business objectives. As such, data analytics do not replace the auditor's interpretation of results and assessment of their impact, although the introduction of smart systems is intended to optimize the use of auditors by automating whenever possible, including interpretation of results.

Where Are We Going?

As the pace of business accelerates and management increasingly seeks access to decision-support information on a more timely basis, both audit and reporting models must adapt to support these changing needs.

Internal audit standards currently require consideration of the use of data analysis in order to gain in-depth understanding of corporate business practices, but this will evolve as the role of internal audit moves further and further toward the auditor as a consultant instead of the conventional compliance role. This is in line with the increasing complexity of national and international regulations with which compliance involves an in-depth understanding of information flow within the organization, and management is increasingly asking internal audit the question, "How?"

Within our traditional internal auditing role, computers have traditionally been used to improve the efficiency of audit processes incrementally rather than to improve audit effectiveness by reengineering them totally. The old paradigm of isolated auditors operating in local teams can now be replaced using today's technology with analytical specialists providing support to internal audit functions on a global basis. The sources and forms of audit evidence available to today's auditor are radically different from the paper audit trails available to the previous generation of auditors. This is already being seen in the increasing development of data mining technology and data visualization tools in audit practice in order to derive a greater depth of insights. Combine this with the increasing pressure on internal audits to reduce the cost of the audit process while handling increasingly more complex business operations, and it can be seen that the pressure is on to achieve more using less resources and focusing more intently on areas of high corporate risk.

Tomorrow's auditors will utilize the Internet and cloud technology to take audit processes and spread them to where they can be performed most effectively and efficiently. The audit processes themselves will soon include techniques such as pattern recognition, correlations, data visualization, Big Data analytics, and text and process mining. This will, in all probability, be matched by a change in the auditing standards to put an increased emphasis on the role of data analysis within audit practice.

This means that by making more effective use of audit technology, higher levels of assurance can be achieved on a lower cost basis, reducing both audit risk and audit liability. Audit risk will also be reduced with the provision of the tools directly to the auditors, thus increasing the independence of the audit function and reducing the degree to which audit must rely on analyses performed by the IT department.

This independence removes the need for predefining the audit program based on what is expected to be found and then carrying out the audit to a preset time scale. Any unexpected occurrences during the audit will then force a re-scoping of the audit with the concomitant changes to the resource requirement and timing. When the audit is based on the analysis of raw data, a more flexible approach can be taken, allowing scopes to vary with changes to the data analysis itself but with a minimal requirement to change the data downloaded. This form of auditing may be *exploratory* in the sense that the audit approach is continually variable based on what the data analysis indicates may be happening within business and control processes. The more traditional form of audit analysis follows a confirmatory model in which the standard audit objectives drive the analysis in order to confirm that all known controls are functioning as intended and no material misstatements are occurring within the corporate records.

The analysis of Big Data has yet to crystallize as an essential component of the internal audit process but must inevitably become part and parcel of both internal and external auditing in large, data-based organizations.

Improvements in identifying operational business risks as well as the need for early fraud identification in high-volume systems are driving the recognition that data analytics of Big Data will be both essential and impossible without effective use of appropriate analytical technology.

Another dramatic change in internal audit practice will involve the timing of audits. The ability to automatically conduct continuous auditing with minimal auditor intervention means that audits can take place at a frequency appropriate to the level of risk rather than based primarily on the availability of audit resources. Audit assignments can be scheduled on an *as required* rather than an *it's March, so we do the audit of payroll section* basis.

What Stays the Same?

The data analysis stage is still a judgmental process. Judgment is involved in the audit decisions regarding the following:

- *What is the audit objective?* Typically, to determine whether control and business objectives have been achieved, are being achieved, and will continue to be achieved.
- *What are the control objectives of the area under review*, and do they map appropriately onto the overall business objectives?
- *What degree of assurance will the auditor require?* Here a judgment will be required in deciding do we seek a higher level of assurance for the same cost, or do we seek the same level of assurance and reduce the cost of the audit?
- *What degree of skills will the auditor have to have to conduct the analysis and interpret the outputs?*

Skilling-Up for the Job

One of the fundamental roles of internal audit management is to ensure staff have the appropriate levels of competence to carry out internal audit functions. Generically, this can be seen as operating within three categories:

- *Interpersonal skills*, which are essential in allowing the auditor to effectively interact with general management, auditees, coworkers, and audit management.

- *Problem-solving skills*, which may be seen as the ability of an individual to handle non-routine tasks and solve problems as they arise. This is particularly critical in carrying out data analysis because the next stage of the process is always dependent on the results of the preceding stage.
- *Technical skills*, which, in general, involve the auditors' ability to carry out whichever tasks have been assigned. In terms of data analysis, this involves the appropriate skills and understanding of the analytical techniques we have already covered in this book. In addition, technical skills will be required in general IT architectures and controls as well as specific skills in the use of the software tools selected for analysis.

Internal audit competencies are normally developed or enhanced through appropriate training. This can include formal training in the form of workshops and webinars, but it may take the form of on-the-job training or mentoring from a more experienced auditor. It is important that auditors realize that the internal auditor's competence is to their benefit, and keeping themselves up to date through research on state-of-the-art techniques and technology is ultimately their own responsibility.

Specialists or Generalists

Because of the high skill levels required to implement effective data analysis, the inclination for many audit sections is to establish a dedicated analytical function within internal audit. This facilitates the provision of a specialist level of knowledge as a resource for the whole audit function while simultaneously it can be used to bring up the overall skill level of the non-specialist auditors. This can include the following:

- Expanding the analytical knowledge base of each and every auditor
- Improving the use of IT-based analytical tools
- Providing technical supervision of non-specialist analytical usage

This can be a highly effective and cost-effective option when audit first starts to introduce data analysis as an occasional additional source of audit evidence. Ultimately, the objective is to integrate the analysis into the overall audit program such that it becomes a tool for any auditor and, in many cases, first choice for an evidence source.

In this event, data analysis must ultimately become a standard tool of generalist auditors in the same way that other tools, such as word processors and voice recognition, are automating the audit process.

Centralized or Decentralized

Although a certain amount of data analysis must become the norm, there will always be a requirement for specialists with a higher level of knowledge to carry out tasks classified as being beyond the scope of the conventional auditor. Such tasks may include technical analysis of computerized architectures, security, or telecommunications. In each of these areas, a more advanced knowledge of IT itself as well as database architectures and communication protocols is required. Because audits in these areas, although technically advanced, do not occur at the same frequency as normal data analysis, it may be cost-prohibitive to attempt to bring all auditors to the required standard of expertise and to keep it up-to-date and relevant. Should the organization opt to go this route, audit management must be aware of the dangers inherent. Career progression may be problematic because an auditor with the high level of skills required may be

- Apt to become bored if not constantly employed on advanced projects
- Head-hunted by other organizations specifically because of their high levels of knowledge, resulting in losses of special skills and the need to invest even more in bringing the next technical specialist up to speed

Today's IT environment does enable the general audit team in a large organization to be centrally supported, thus allowing the technical skills to be leveraged even on a global basis so that a technical analytical auditor, even one based in South Africa, can support the internal audit function in New York or London either by reviewing the analytical work done by the overall audit team or actually conducting the analysis on the remote data. By deconstructing the audit program, analysis can be carried out wherever it is most cost effective while maintaining security and confidentiality of information by making use of appropriate encryption technology.

With the proliferation of cloud-based technology for the actual corporate data processing itself, the need to have all analysis carried out in one central location has diminished.

In a small internal audit department where this type of auditing is infrequent, outsourcing of this form of technical analysis to an external specialist may be a viable alternative. This has the advantages of knowing that the technical specialist is current with the technology in use on a contractual basis as well as the removal of the cost element involved in training at this level with minimal utilization of the skills. Once again, this outsourcing need not necessarily be local and can allow corporate access to the world's best analyzers and audit resources.

Analytical Problems Now and in the Future

There are two major stumbling blocks that present themselves to today's auditor: skill levels as discussed above and managerial acceptance of analytical evidence.

Many of today's managers recognize the need for analytical review and the value that can be added to bottom-line profitability by understanding information flow within the organization and the impact on business processes. Unfortunately, there is still a generation of management who see the results of audit data analytics as being derived by some mystical means wherein they are being asked to accept the results blindly.

This is a carry forward from the suspicion over results produced by statistical analysis and, in some cases, because of erroneous audit conclusions drawn from statistical analysis as discussed in Chapter 2. In order to overcome the mistrust, audits must initially focus on areas in which the analytical results can be empirically proven in a non-analytic manner. Once audit data analysis has built a reputation for delivering meaningful results in an understandable way, the barriers to communication can be broken down and audit credibility and cost-effectiveness enhanced. Management today is already familiar with both the jargon and techniques of information processing, including the structuring of data and the use of data mining to derive useful patterns from within data. If care is taken, it becomes a straight-forward step to gaining management acceptance of audit results generated by the same techniques. The use of technology to enable continuous monitoring is becoming commonplace, and the concept of continuous auditing is gaining increased acceptance. It is, of course, a potential danger area in that when continuous auditing is being effectively implemented, management may step back from the continuous monitoring role and pass the whole control perspective across to the internal auditor.

Getting Hold of the Data

As previously discussed, the purpose of an internal audit using data analysis is to seek evidence in order to determine that the control objectives of the area under review have been met, are being met, and will continue to be met.

Gaining access to the data where the evidence may reside has always been problematic, but as cloud technology increases and the distribution of data proliferates on a global basis, access to the data and confirmation of the validity of the data examined become increasingly difficult. When cloud computing first came on the scene, the emphasis was on cost savings using techniques such as software as a service (SaaS). Today, organizations are looking to cloud computing to help them achieve business agility through innovation. As a result, business users are arriving at the benefits by mixing and matching data from a variety of sources, including the cloud, but the analytical value comes from its merger with their own on-site data. Corporate data analytical software is now commonly available and facilitates the acquisition of cloud data for analytical purposes as well as for data visualization and the generation of business intelligence by allowing managers to explore and visualize data. At present, most audit analysis involves file sizes of under 1 GB. Larger analyses are possible in a client–server environment, but high-volume data analysis allowing predictive analytics may require the implementation of data-streaming technology such as Google's Cloud Dataflow combined with its BigQuery data analysis tool.

This is merely one example of technology that provides the auditor with the ability to analyze data directly from the data stream of live updates as well as the ability to manage both current and historical data analysis.

The future of internal audit data analysis can be predicted only to the extent that we can confidently say now that in the future, things will change, and not as we currently expect them to.

Appendix 1: ACL Usage

This appendix is intended to cover all aspects of the use of ACL Version 9 in a hands-on environment. It is aimed primarily at auditors, both internal and external, who already have a working knowledge of generalized audit software and particularly in the use of ACL. It assumes that readers have access to the ACL software.

This appendix covers the use of the software in executing some of the analysis techniques already covered in this book and includes the following:

Analytic Techniques
- Statistical samples
- Seeking duplicates and missing items
- Use of pivot tables
- Correlation and regression
- Trend analysis
- Time series analysis
- Continuous monitoring

Compliance
- Analysis of sales by rep
- Unauthorized Internet access
- Pricing rules not followed

Fraud
* Identifying duplicate employees in the employee master table
* Excessive sole vendor contracts
* Ghost employees
* Duplicate payments
* Benford analysis

Start the ACL software, and on the opening screen, the auditor will be given the choice of creating a new project or opening an existing project. In this case, we will start a new project called *Book*.

Starting a New Project

Starting a new project takes the auditors straight to the *Data Definition Wizard*, which allows the auditor to import data into ACL from a variety of sources as detailed in Chapter 19.

For the purposes of this case study and to illustrate the functionality, I am using tables downloadable on the table *ACL Data.zip* available at http://www.rcascarino.com/Book%20Data%20Files.zip.

As such, we will not use the Data Definition wizard. Instead, we will start with opening Book.Project in the zip file you have just downloaded.

Analytic Techniques

Statistical Samples

We shall start by opening the Inventory table. As can be seen, this table contains Product Number, Product Class, Location, Product Description, Product Status, Unit Cost, Cost Date, Sale Price, Price Date, Quantity On Hand, Re-Order Point, Quantity On Order, Inventory Value at Cost, and Market Value.

We will start off our exercise by doing some basic analytical review for these fields. ACL offers the choice under the *Analyze* tab of choosing between two types of basic statistical analysis:

* Statistics—In which the auditor can choose numeric and date fields to analyze statistically and combine it with a conditional statement if required. Field-by-field information will

be provided on number totals and averages for positive, negative, and zero values within the fields as well as the highest and lowest values. The number of values defaults to five but can be increased at the auditor's discretion.

Statistical results can be saved, printed, or simply observed on the screen, for example, in the profile shown in Diagram A1.1.

- Profile—Which allows the auditor to profile, again combined with a conditional statement, requires numerical fields only in order to gain such basic information as Total Value, Absolute, Minimum, and Maximum as in Diagram A1.2.

In this table, the auditor can see that, for example, in the Market Value field there are two negative values. This fact is shown in blue on the screen. By clicking on the blue Negative heading, a filter will be applied to the Inventory table and the two records that have negative Market Values will be shown. The filter can be removed to return to the full view of the Inventory table.

In the same way, the negative Unit Costs can be identified and examined, and the auditor will find three inventory items that have a negative Unit Cost. This type of data anomaly will typically create a need to follow up to determine how such a thing occurred, why it occurred, who authorized it, and who actually caused the event.

As of: 02/29/2016 11:05:08

Command: PROFILE FIELDS MINQTY MKTVAL QTYOH QTYOO SALEPR UNCST
      VALUE
Table: inventory

Field name	Total value	Absolute value	Minimum	Maximum
Re-order point	58,805	58,805	0	4600
Market value	1,029,061.61	1,031,588.81	−839.76	143,880.00
Quantity on hand	169,285	169,325	−12	71,000
Quantity on order	117,145	117,145	0	40,000
Sale price	3748.66	3748.66	0.04	499.98
Unit cost	2625.47	2659.23	−6.87	381.20
Inventory value at cost	680,479.94	708,243.94	−10,167.60	100,800.00

Diagram A1.1   Statistical results.

As of: 02/29/2016 11:12:50

Command: STATISTICS ON MKTVAL TO SCREEN
NUMBER 5
Table: inventory

Market value

	Number	Total	Average
Range	–	144,719.76	–
Positive	148	1,030,325.21	6961.66
Negative	2	–1263.60	–631.80
Zeros	2	–	–
Totals	152	1,029,061.61	6770.14
Abs value	–	1,031,588.81	–

Highest	Lowest
143,880.00	–839.76
47,647.00	–423.84
44,098.53	0.00
42,163.20	0.00
32,970.00	90.00

Diagram A1.2   Profile results.

Should there have been a pattern of such negative values, the auditor may have had cause to consider the possibility of intentional cost manipulation and fraud.

The auditor may also note that for pure numeric fields the absolute value is also calculated for future use in sampling should the auditor so desire.

Once the general statistics have been reviewed, the auditor can return to the data by clicking the Inventory tab.

As has been previously stated, it is critical that, before data analysis is commenced, the auditor have a clear idea of what information will be sought and why. In the case of our examination of Inventory records, the auditor may be interested in determining the following:

- No negative quantities, costs, or prices exist
- No excessive quantities are ordered
- No slow moving stock is being reordered unnecessarily

Testing these may involve the auditor extracting a sample of Inventory records to compare to purchase transactions on the Trans file by joining the two files based on a match on product number, and should a fraud be suspected, using the product number on the inventory table to link to the accounts payable table (ap-trans) and then connecting to the Vendor table via the Vendor Number.

In examining the accounts receivable (ar) table, the auditor may wish to select a sample of transactions for verification. Once again, the starting point would be to analyze the table to determine the general statistics on the numeric fields and to obtain the absolute values for them.

Sampling the data involves first calculating the appropriate sample size. From within the Sampling window, the auditor would select Calculate Sample Size and must then select between Record Sampling or Monetary Unit Sampling.

Record Sampling—In order to select a sample for testing from the 772 in the population (number of records in the bottom left hand of the screen), the auditor will typically agree with management and the auditees in advance on the following:

- The degree of confidence required that the sample will be representative
- The maximum tolerable error beyond which all invoices will need to be reviewed (Materiality)
- The expected total error rate

Working on the assumption that these numbers would be a 95% confidence level with a maximum error rate of 5% and expected error rate of 1%, the auditor would move to the Analysis Window on the Menu bar and select Attribute from the Sampling area. The auditor would then enter the following:

- Confidence Level—95
- Population Size—772
- Upper Error Limit (%)—5.00
- Expected Error Rate (%)—1.0

Clicking on Calculate gives the auditor a sample size of 95, a sampling interval of 8.12, and number of tolerable errors of 1, as can be seen in Diagram A1.3.

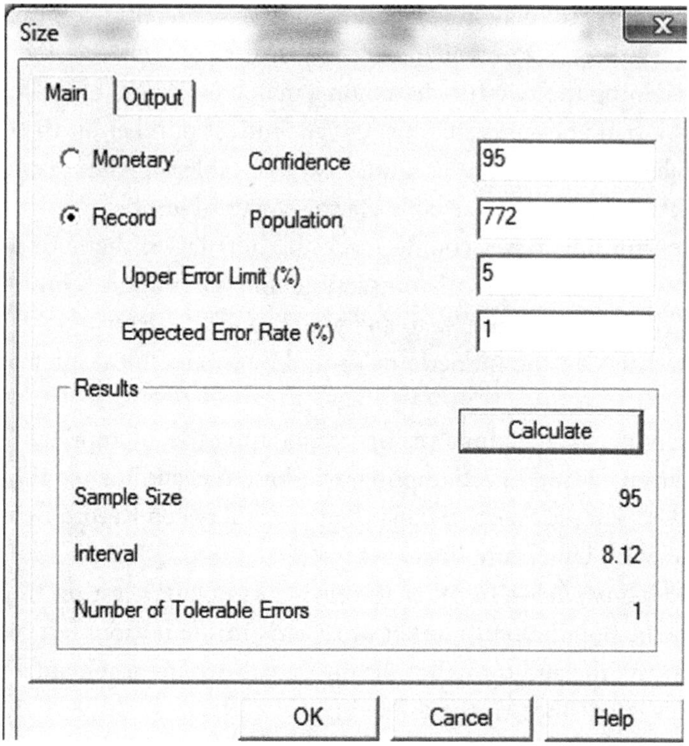

Diagram A1.3 Calculate results.

This means that if, in examining the sample, only one error is found, the auditor can state that, at a 95% confidence level, the probability is that the error rate is, indeed, 5% or less (i.e., within the tolerable deviation rate). The Interval is used when a sample is to be drawn from the population using a random starting point between one and eight in choosing every eighth item of the population to make up the sample of 95.

Using the Sample Records option within the Sampling window, the auditor can first calculate the size and then move directly into the extraction of the sample from the population within the table.

After the sample has been selected and the audit tests undertaken, the auditor can evaluate the results of the sample testing by clicking on Evaluate, selecting Record sampling, and entering the following:

- The desired conference level (95%)
- The sample size (95)
- The number of deviations found in the sample (for example, one)

The auditor may then note that, at a 95% confidence level, the population deviation will be no more than 5%. In fact, at that confidence level, the deviation rate in the population has an upper error limit frequency of 5%. Should the number of errors in the sample be two, the upper error limit frequency could be as high as 6.63%, which would exceed the tolerance level.

Credit Note extraction—When the auditor wishes to extract all records containing only credit notes or even a table containing those records to be sampled at a later date, the auditor will typically use an Extract Data from within the Data window.

The auditor may choose to use a table name such as Credit Notes and, by clicking on the *If* button, may enter the equation Type = "CN." The fields may be selected by double-clicking on the field name at the bottom of the editor, and the = may be selected by single clicking the = above the equation window. The CN must be in quotation marks because it can be seen to be a character field. When the OK is clicked on, the table called Credit Notes will be created containing the 108 records identified as credit notes. Should the resulting table size be too large for audit purposes, sampling may be done on this table. To return to the full accounts receivable table, a simple tap on the *ar* table in the Project Navigator window will return the auditor to the full table.

Monetary unit sampling—This sampling technique is designed to automatically bias the sample toward selected items containing the highest cumulative value (see Chapter 3). Once again, within the sampling portion of the Sampling window, the auditor may now select Calculate Sample Size and leave the radio button on Monetary. Because this sample technique uses cumulative values, the auditor must tell it what the value of the appropriate field is. The auditor may decide to use only positive values, only negative values, or absolute values (all the numbers are totaled regardless of whether they're positive or negative). If the auditor reaches this position via the Sample Records selection and choosing Size, the Absolute Value will already have been calculated by the Analyze Statistics route. The confidence level may again be entered (in this case, we will again choose 95%) and the tolerable error and expected error may also be entered. It will be noted that, in this kind of sampling, this will be the maximum value of error acceptable to the auditor. In this case, we will use a Materiality of 25,000 and an Expected Total Errors of 1,000. By clicking on Calculate, we

Size	X

Main	

⊙ Monetary	Confidence	95
○ Record	Population	585674.41
	Materiality	25000
	Expected Total Errors	1000

Results

	Calculate
Sample Size	75
Interval	7,750.00
Maximum Tolerable Taintings (%)	12.90

OK	Cancel	Help

Diagram A1.4   Sample size calculation.

can now see the Sample Size has been calculated as 75, the Sampling Interval is 7,750, and the Maximum Tolerable Taintings percentage permitted in the sample is 12.9% to express the auditor's 95% confident opinion regarding the population as in Diagram A1.4.

Once again, a new table is created. Once again, these items can then be tested by the auditor with resultant deviations being entered using the money to unit options to evaluate a single sample or multiple samples.

Seeking Duplicates and Missing Items

Finding duplicates and missing items are perhaps two of the more common audit inquiries facilitated by CAATs. Whenever there are requirements for uniqueness of information, check numbers, purchase order numbers, identity numbers, and the like, the ability to search easily and quickly across a large database for evidence of duplicates may be critical. In this case, we shall take the *trans* table. In order to check for duplicates, it is useful to be able to have the table sorted into the appropriate order. In ACL, this is achieved by right-clicking the field name and choosing Quick Sort Ascending order or Descending order. In this case, we sort by Invoice Number in ascending order.

We can now analyze for duplicates by going to the Analyze menu and choosing *Look for Duplicates*. The auditor may then select which fields are to be included in the duplicates search. In this case, we will choose Invoice Number. The fields to be included will be selected using *List Fields*, and we will select *Add All*. If the auditor clicks on *OK* at this point, approach will be given for the output file name. Should the auditor wish only to view the duplicates, a selection can be made to output to *Screen* instead as in Diagram A1.5.

Invoice number	Invoice amount	Invoice date	Product class	Product number	Quantity
12857	3552.00	01/05/1997	04	040240664	120
12857	−141.24	01/06/1997	01	010803760	44
12872	31.80	01/22/1997	02	024130572	6
12872	184.80	01/22/1997	03	034255003	22
12897	2208.96	02/12/1997	01	010134420	708
12897	1973.60	02/16/1997	03	034255003	229
12940	0.73	04/02/1997	03	030321663	1
12940	42.36	06/02/1997	03	030305603	3
12970	−27.20	03/09/1997	09	090506331	4
12970	644.80	05/02/1997	03	030364163	13
12971	1.83	03/11/1997	09	090501551	1
12971	953.60	05/04/1997	09	090069591	40
12972	36.15	03/12/1997	08	080126008	15
12972	1.24	05/05/1997	05	052770015	4
12974	24.24	03/12/1997	09	090507811	3
12974	14.12	05/06/1997	04	040270354	1
12975	319.16	03/13/1997	02	024128712	316
12975	1706.28	05/07/1997	08	080126008	708
12975	4.82	05/07/1997	08	080126008	2
12976	277.15	03/15/1997	08	080126008	115
12976	20.76	05/08/1997	05	052530155	697
12977	6.00	03/17/1997	06	060100356	1

Diagram A1.5 Duplicate invoice analysis.

As can be seen at invoice 12975, not only duplicates, but any multiple of an Invoice Number has been detected.

Returning to our *trans* table, we may choose to seek unused invoice numbers by clicking on *Analyze* and carrying out a *Look for Gap*. This immediately highlights the missing invoice numbers either individually or in groups. ACL will default to producing the output on the screen but, once again, the auditor can select to have the output as a table. In this case, gaps in invoices may not be critical but, if the key value had been check numbers, this could have identified checks that had been issued but not yet cleared through the bank.

Seeking duplicate records within, for example, an employee file could include searching for the following:

- Duplicate bank account numbers into which direct payments may be entered
- Duplicate addresses to which checks should be sent

It would now be up to the auditor to determine whether these were members of the same family, whether some other valid reason existed for the duplication, or if this was part of some internal fraudulent scheme.

Use of Cross-Tabulate (Pivot Table)

Occasionally, the auditor will find a list of data more complex to analyze than if it was in tabular form. To convert a data list into tabular form involves the use of Cross-Tabulate creation within the Analyze menu. Using the *inventory* file, the auditor has decided to examine values by *Product Class* using both the cost value and the market value and breaking it down by *Location*. To create the Crosstab, the auditor will click on the Cross-Tabulate selection within the Cross-Tabulate creation within the Analyze menu. The rows will be selected for PRODCLS, the columns by LOC, and the subtotal fields will be MKTVAL and Value. The results are shown as in Diagram A1.6.

Aging

Again, a common audit requirement is to examine how long transactions have existed in suspense accounts, how long the invoices have

As of: 02/29/2016 15:14:26

Command: CROSSTAB ON PRODCLS COLUMNS LOC SUBTOTAL VALUE MKTVAL TO SCREEN
Table: inventory

Product class	VALUE LOC 01	MKTVAL LOC 01	VALUE LOC 02	MKTVAL LOC 02	VALUE LOC 03	MKTVAL LOC 03	VALUE LOC 04	MKTVAL LOC 04	VALUE LOC 05	MKTVAL LOC 05	VALUE LOC 06	MKTVAL LOC 06	VALUE LOC 22	MKTVAL LOC 22
01	34,954.68	54,581.76	0.00	0.00	0.00	0.00	0.00	0.00	0.00	0.00	0.00	0.00	0.00	0.00
02	707.30	874.50	19,836.90	25,075.35	0.00	0.00	0.00	0.00	0.00	0.00	0.00	0.00	0.00	0.00
03	0.00	0.00	0.00	0.00	99,595.24	144,478.44	3107.52	4860.96	0.00	0.00	0.00	0.00	0.00	0.00
04	0.00	0.00	0.00	0.00	89,018.95	123,112.50	0.00	0.00	0.00	0.00	0.00	0.00	0.00	0.00
05	0.00	0.00	0.00	0.00	0.00	0.00	0.00	0.00	42,479.36	52,752.62	0.00	0.00	0.00	0.00
06	0.00	0.00	56,458.40	84,686.38	0.00	0.00	0.00	0.00	0.00	0.00	0.00	0.00	2021.20	2767.74
07	0.00	0.00	0.00	0.00	0.00	0.00	0.00	0.00	0.00	0.00	47,609.10	98,801.10	0.00	0.00
08	0.00	0.00	188,230.86	252,609.64	0.00	0.00	0.00	0.00	0.00	0.00	0.00	0.00	0.00	0.00
09	0.00	0.00	0.00	0.00	0.00	0.00	80,646.05	158,909.60	0.00	0.00	0.00	0.00	0.00	0.00
13	0.00	0.00	0.00	0.00	11,352.48	18,475.92	0.00	0.00	0.00	0.00	0.00	0.00	0.00	0.00
18	0.00	0.00	4461.90	7075.10	0.00	0.00	0.00	0.00	0.00	0.00	0.00	0.00	0.00	0.00
Totals	35,661.98	55,456.26	268,988.06	369,446.47	199,966.67	286,066.86	83,753.57	163,770.56	42,479.36	52,752.62	47,609.10	98,801.10	2021.20	2767.74

Diagram A1.6 Cross-tabulate (pivot table) result.

As of: 02/29/2016 11:38:12

Command: AGE ON date CUTOFF 19970901 INTERVAL 0,30,60,90,120,10000
          SUBTOTAL amount IF type="IN" TO SCREEN
Table: ar

If Condition: type="IN" (588 records matched)

Minimum encountered was −100
Maximum encountered was 687

Days	Count	Percent of count	Percent of field	Trans amount
<0	576	97.96%	97.51%	512,163.73
0–29	6	1.02%	1.68%	8807.24
30–59	1	0.17%	0%	8.85
60–89	1	0.17%	0.29%	1524.32
90–119	1	0.17%	0.14%	737.36
120–10,000	3	0.51%	0.38%	2017.66
Totals	588	100%	100%	525,259.16

Diagram A1.7   Invoice aging result.

remained unpaid, and other inquiries involving the use of aging of information. As an example, we will examine our accounts receivable table (ar), in this case seeking to establish how long invoices have remained unpaid.

From within the *Analyze* menu, the auditor would pick *Age*. In this case, there are two date fields, Invoice Date (date) and Due Date (due). We will select the field *date* and subtotal the field *amount*. The cutoff date defaults to the system date, but in this case, we wish to choose the date of September 1, 1997, for the cutoff period in our analysis. Because our only concern is examining invoices, we will create an *If* statement for which the *type* = *"IN."*

Running this inquiry will show us the aging of the invoices, including showing the percentage of the number of invoices in each strata as well as the value and percentage of total value in each as in Diagram A1.7.

Stratification

When there is a need to produce an analysis based on something other than dates, the auditor may use the *Stratify* command to explicitly defined intervals of numeric fields or expression values and create multiple subtotals per strata. In this case, the auditor wishes to determine from the accounts receivable file (ar) how many low-, medium-, and high-value accounts receivable records there are. Once again, the auditor is interested only in invoices (IN). The auditor has the choice of using a fixed number of equal-sized intervals or of defining multiple ranges by selecting the *Free* radio button. In this case, we choose a minimum value of zero and a maximum of 10,000 with 10 equal-sized intervals, resulting in the analysis in Diagram A1.8.

The output default is to the screen, but the auditor may choose to output to Print, File or Graph, and the graph type selected or tailored as in Diagram A1.9.

As of: 02/29/2016 11:43:20

Command: STRATIFY ON amount SUBTOTAL amount MINIMUM 0 MAXIMUM
        10000 INTERVALS 10 TO SCREEN
Table: ar

Minimum encountered was −3582.98
Maximum encountered was 5549.19

Trans amount	Count	Percent of count	Percent of field	Trans amount
<0.00	161	20.85%	−12.45%	−58,396.86
0.00–999.99	421	54.53%	44.55%	208,898.46
1000.00–1999.99	151	19.56%	43.96%	206,110.67
2000.00–2999.99	24	3.11%	12.15%	56,980.77
3000.00–3999.99	12	1.55%	8.61%	40,357.68
4000.00–4999.99	2	0.26%	2%	9380.78
5000.00–5999.99	1	0.13%	1.18%	5549.19
6000.00–6999.99	0	0%	0%	0.00
7000.00–7999.99	0	0%	0%	0.00
8000.00–8999.99	0	0%	0%	0.00
9000.00–10,000.00	0	0%	0%	0.00
Totals	772	100%	100%	468,880.69

Diagram A1.8   Stratification result.

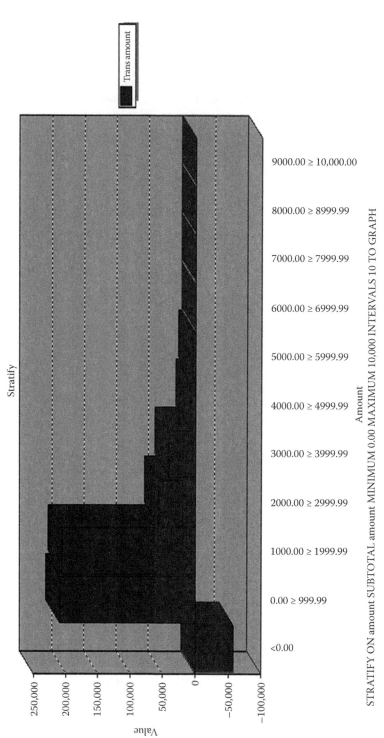

Diagram A1.9 Graphical result.

Analysis of Sales by Product Class

When a straightforward analysis is required, for example, using our *trans* table to get an analysis of sales by product class, the auditor may simply open the table, and by clicking on the Analyze menu, may select *Classify*. The auditor may then choose which fields to summarize by, for example, PRODCLS and choose the fields to subtotal such as AMOUNT and again outputting to Screen, Printer, File or Graph. As always in ACL, key fields are highlighted in blue and by clicking on any of the blue numbers, in this case to Product Class, the auditor may see the detailed transactions that made up the summarization as in Diagram A1.10.

By returning to the Sample-Detailed Sales table, the auditor may repeat the exercise for Sales by Customer and create a table of that name.

Rules Not Followed

Whenever rules are supposed to be applied to data, the auditor can seek exceptions by creating a virtual field and appending it to the record definition such that the virtual field is calculated using the

As of: 02/29/2016 12:06:56

Command: CLASSIFY ON PRODCLS SUBTOTAL AMOUNT TO SCREEN
Table: trans

Product class	Count	Percent of count	Percent of field	Invoice amount
01	39	11.5%	13.22%	39,762.63
02	52	15.34%	9.91%	29,804.48
03	34	10.03%	5.65%	16,985.59
04	25	7.37%	12.36%	37,156.30
05	51	15.04%	10.18%	30,610.77
06	12	3.54%	6.28%	18,887.60
07	8	2.36%	−0.59%	−1779.33
08	56	16.52%	12.06%	36,260.56
09	62	18.29%	30.93%	92,993.44
Totals	339	100%	100%	300,682.04

Diagram A1.10   Classification result.

predetermined rules. The auditor can then seek discrepancies where the virtual field and the actual field contained within the data do not correspond. For example, the organization may have chosen a standard mark-up on sales such that

- In general, all sales prices must have at least a 20% profit margin *but*
- If the Product Class is 01, the profit margin must be >25% *and*
- If the Product Class is 02, the profit margin must be >30%

Within the table *inventory*, it may be seen that the field Profit Margin does not currently exist.

From the *Edit* menu, the auditor can select *Table Layout*. This gives the auditor the option of adding new fields or expressions. In this case, the auditor wishes to add a new expression defining the Percentage Profit Margin. The field will be named Margin and will be defined (*f(x)*) as the sale price minus the unit cost) divided by the unit cost times 100 (((SALEPR-UNCST)/UNCST)*100). Once the expression has been created and accepted using the green tick sign, it may be added to the current view of the file using the Add Column button. Fields that are added will always appear on the right-hand side of the view but may be moved to any position the auditor desires. In this case, we will move Margin next to Product Class. We will also move the Unit Cost and Sale Price next to the Margin. The auditor can now create an expression for filtering called Margin-Too-Low using the classifications laid down by the organization. In this case, via the *Edit* menu and the *table layout* option, the auditor can create an expression with the name Margin Too Low and a Default Value of Margin <20 (i.e., the profit margin of all goods must be 20% or more). This only satisfies the first corporate requirement, however. The auditor now needs to add in the other requirements by using the *Insert a Condition* icon on the left-hand side. The condition will be that the PRODCLS = "01." The Value for Margin-Too-Low will then be Margin ≤ 25. The final requirement can then be inserted in the same way such that the Value for Margin-Too-Low will then be Margin ≤ 30 if the PRODCLS = "01" as seen in Diagram A1.11.

From there, the auditor can then select Margin-Too-Low as a filter in the expression editor to see only those items that do not fall within the rules laid down by management.

| Table Layout Options | Edit Fields/Expressions | Add a New Data Filter |

Name	Default Value
Margin_Too_Low	**f(x)** Margin < 20

Format	▼	☐ Suppress Totals
Width	1	☐ Static
Alternate Column Title	Margin Too Low	☐ Date
		☐ Control Total
	◄ ►	☐ Default Filter
If...		

Condition	Value
PRODCLS = "01"	Margin <= 25
PRODCLS = "02"	Margin <= 30

Diagram A1.11   Data filter definition.

This form of filter-building may be used for any management crite-ria when compliance is sought and audited for.

Fraud

As noted in Chapter 22, it is only once fraud risks are understood that an appropriate system of internal controls can be designed and implemented to address those risks. Even then, fraud can never be fully eliminated, and early detection becomes a critical backstop in minimizing the impact of corporate fraud. As such, it is critical that the appropriate audit trails be maintained and analyzed to seek pat-terns pointing to potential fraud events.

Identify Duplicate Employees in the Employee Master Table

Many frauds involve the introduction of duplicate transactions as well as duplicate entries on master tables. By selecting the *empmast* table and conducting a simple Look for Duplicates analysis and choosing a *Duplicates On* of Last Name and First Name, the auditor can cre-ate a table containing only duplicates. The same test can be done for addresses or any other significant field, such as postal addresses or banking details.

Finding Excessive Sole Vendor Contracts

Another common form of fraud is the excessive use of specific vendors within the supply chain. This may, in fact, be good business practice when a specific vendor has a track record of providing requisite supplies and services at a cost-effective price at an appropriate quality level. Nevertheless, it may also be an indicator of fraudulent practices when a vendor who is not optimal is chosen because of bribery, kickbacks, and the like, resulting in the potential supply of inferior goods and services at an inflated price.

Analysis of purchasing records may give an indication in this area that a specific vendor is being chosen excessively. As stated, this may not indicate fraud but should be worthy of the auditor's follow-up. When tendering processes exist, analysis of tender documents may indicate preference given to specific vendors, excessive use of sole vendor contracts, or common bidding patterns in which the failing bids are always submitted by the same companies who may have some relationship to the winning bidder. An analysis of purchases from vendors or payments made to vendors may disclose a relationship between vendors and individual buyers.

Ghost Employees

"Ghost employees" is a term used to define payments made via payroll systems to individuals who are not actually employees. These may be ex-employees who, having left the organization, may be resurrected on the payroll with banking details changed to those of a payroll clerk. Alternatively, they may be brand new fictitious employees with, again, payment made into an individual's bank account. When payment is made by checks, the postal address for delivery may tie into an individual's address. Ghost employees may be difficult to spot under normal circumstances; however, they may show up in examining the payroll records seeking duplicate bank numbers, addresses, or even names.

In this case, we shall take the table Sample-Employees and look for duplicate addresses. From our Analysis tab, we will select Duplicate

Key and choose Detection. The Key field is the ADDRESS field in ascending order output to a table called Duplicates. From the output, we can see that we have four sets of duplicates. Once again, these are not necessarily fraudulent or ghost employees; they may simply be members of the same family employed by the organization. Nevertheless, the auditor would once again seek confirmation that this is the case.

Seeking Duplicate Payments

Using a similar technique, duplicate payments can be seen from a Payments Perform table seeking payments made to the same vendor for the same amount or, alternatively, payments made to the same vendor on the same date. Once again, the danger lies in the auditor assuming that any duplicate found is an automatic proof of fraud. The transactions may be genuine, and any repeating patterns should be followed up.

As of: 02/29/2016 14:43:42

Command: BENFORD ON amount LEADING 1 IF type="IN"
            TO SCREEN
Table: ar

If condition: type="IN" (588 records matched)

Leading digits	Actual count	Expected count	Zstat ratio
1	173	177	0.315
2	51	104	5.634
3	68	73	0.619
4	53	57	0.486
5	64	47	2.587
6	74	39	5.632
7	31	34	0.459
8	38	30	1.389
9	36	27	1.696

Diagram A1.12 Benford analysis.

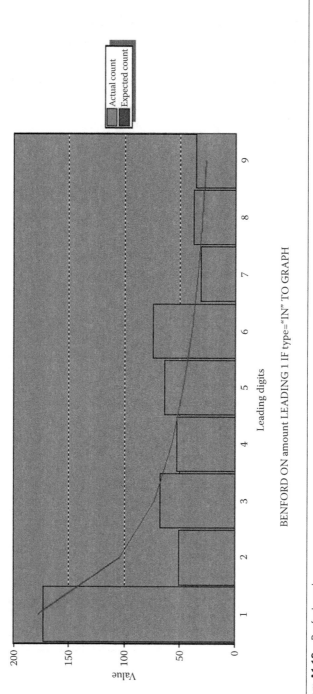

Diagram A1.13 Benford graph.

Benford Analysis

As noted in Chapter 13, Benford analysis is a form of pattern analysis used in the analysis of high volumes of data looking for evidence of fraudulent transactions. Taking our *ar* table as an example, from our Analyze tab we can select Perform Benford Analysis. In this particular table, there is only one field that we could be interested in and that is the AMOUNT. We know that there are a mixture of transaction types, so again, we will filter for type = "IN." The result will be shown as in Diagram A1.12.

Again, as discussed in Chapter 23 on data visualization and presentation, the table showing the counts and the ZStat Ratio may not be particularly informative. Presenting the results in a graphical form as shown in Diagram A1.13 makes it more obvious where the numbers are not performing as expected.

Appendix 2: IDEA Usage

This appendix is intended to cover all aspects of the use of IDEA Version 10 in a hands-on environment. It is aimed primarily at auditors, both internal and external, who already have a working knowledge of generalized audit software and particularly the use of IDEA. It assumes that readers have downloaded the software and data files of the demo version at http://ideasupport.caseware.com/public/downloadidea/.

This is the latest version and is a fully functional version but is limited to 1,000 records. Once installed, the applicable files will be found in a Project called *Samples*. Other files used may be found in a Project called *Tutorial*.

This appendix covers the use of the software in executing some of the analysis techniques already covered in this book and includes the following:

Analytic Techniques
- Statistical samples
- Seeking duplicates and missing items
- Use of pivot tables
- Correlation and regression
- Trend analysis
- Time series analysis
- Continuous monitoring

Compliance
- Analysis of sales by rep
- Unauthorized Internet access
- Pricing rules not followed

Fraud
- Identifying duplicate employees in the employee master file
- Excessive sole supplier contracts
- Ghost employees
- Duplicate payments
- Benford analysis

Start the IDEA software and, on the opening screen, observe that the basic screen consists of eight main areas as indicated in Diagram A2.1:

1. The Menu Bar
2. Operations Toolbar
3. File Explorer Toolbar
4. File Explorer Window
5. Database Window
6. Flyout Windows
7. Status Bar
8. Properties Window

On the right-hand side, the Properties window includes the ability to view or edit the properties of the active file including the following:

- Data
- History
- Field Statistics
- Control Total
- Criteria
- Results
- Indices
- Comments

In order to start a new project or open an existing one, the auditor will click on *SELECT*—the third button from the left in the menu bar. This allows the auditor to select the *Samples* project. Once selected,

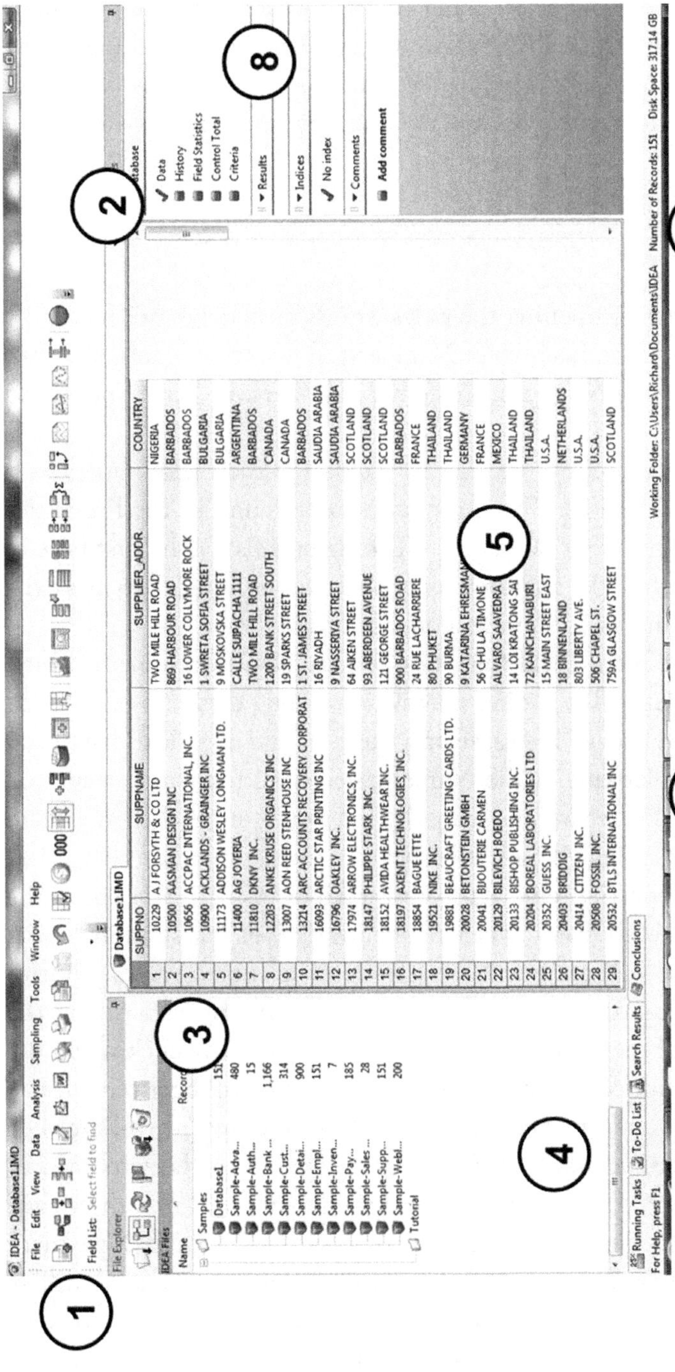

Diagram A2.1   Basic screen.

the File Explorer will be populated by the databases already defined to the project. By double-clicking on one of these, the database will be opened in the Database Window. It may be closed by clicking on the X by the name in this window. We shall use the Samples files to try out some of the techniques described earlier in this book.

Analytic Techniques

Statistical Samples

We shall start by opening the Sales Transaction database. As can be seen, this file contains Invoice Numbers, Transaction Dates, Payment Types, Salesman Numbers, Customer Numbers, Product Codes, and Amounts.

We will start off our exercise by looking at the Field Statistics for these fields. The Field Statistics tab is to be found in the Properties Window on the right-hand side. Clicking on this for the first time in examining a file, the auditor may be told that no Field Statistics exist for the file, and the system will offer to create them.

As can be seen, Field Statistics are available for Numeric, Date, and Time Fields. The auditor may switch among these alternatives. In this file, there are no Times, so only numeric and date fields have been analyzed. In looking at the Numeric fields, all four have been analyzed. In this case, we are primarily interested in the Amount field. By double-clicking the selection boxes against the other fields, they may be temporarily removed from the view. As can be seen on the Amount fields, IDEA has calculated a variety of statistics, including such items as the number of records, number of zero values, positive totals and negative totals, minimum and maximum values, and the like. Some of these values are highlighted in blue. By clicking on the value, for example Negative Values, the auditor will be given a list of the records with negative Amounts on the invoice record. These can be saved, printed, or simply observed. In the same way, the zero invoices can be identified and examined, and the auditor will find three cash payments for invoices with zero values as well as an AMEX payment for a zero invoice. All of these are for different customers, on different days, and by different salesmen. Should there have been a pattern of such zero invoices, the auditor may have had cause to consider the possibility of intentional manipulation and fraud.

Similar examination of the Date field indicates that the most popular sales day is a Saturday with July sales almost doubling any other month.

Once the general statistics have been reviewed, the auditor can return to the data by clicking the Data button in the Properties Window.

As has been previously stated, it is critical that, before data analysis is commenced, the auditor have a clear idea of what information will be sought and why. In the case of our examination of Sales, the auditor may be interested to ensure the following:

- Invoice values are materially correct compared to orders
- All cash sales reconcile to bank deposits
- High-value invoices are calculated correctly

Testing these may involve the auditor extracting a sample of invoices to compare to Orders while checking cash totals to Bank Deposit totals and recalculating values of invoices sampling to include specifically high-value transactions.

Attribute Sampling—In order to select a sample for testing from the 900 in the population (number of records in the bottom right hand of the screen), the auditor will typically agree with management and the auditees in advance about the following:

- The degree of confidence required that the sample will be representative
- The maximum tolerable error beyond which all invoiced will need to be reviewed
- The expected error rate on invoices

Working on the assumption that these numbers would be a 95% confidence level, maximum error rate of 5%, and expected error rate of 1%, the auditor would move to the Analysis Window on the Menu bar and select Attribute from the Sampling area. The auditor would then enter the following:

- Population size—900
- % Expected Deviation Rate—1.00
- % Tolerable Deviation Rate—5.00
- Confidence Level—95

Clicking on Compute gives the auditor a sample size of 88 and a table showing where errors occur in the sample and the percentage error rates in the sample as well as the probability percentage that the error rate is, indeed, 5% or less (i.e., within the tolerable deviation rate). As can be seen from the calculation, in this case, the auditor could find one error in the sample (a 1.14% error rate in the sample) and still be 95.15% sure that the error rate of the population would not exceed 5%.

After the sample has been selected and the audit tests undertaken, the auditor can evaluate the results of the sample testing by clicking on Evaluate and entering the following:

- The population size (900)
- The number of deviations in the sample (for example, one)
- The sample size (88)
- The desired confidence level (95%)

The auditor may then note that, at a 95% confidence level, the population deviation will be no more than 5%. In fact, at that confidence level, that deviation rate in the population will fall somewhere between 0.11% and 5.89%.

Cash sales extraction—When the auditor wishes to extract all records containing only cash sales or even a file containing those records to be sampled at a later date, the auditor will typically use a Direct Extract from within the Analysis Window.

The auditor may choose to use a file name such as Cash Items and, by clicking on the representation of a calculator next to the file name, may enter the equation Pay_Type = "CASH." The fields may be selected by double-clicking on the field name at the bottom of the editor, and the = may be selected by single clicking the = above the equation window. The word CASH must be in quotation marks because it can be seen to be a character field. When the large green tick is clicked on, your file called Cash_Items will be created containing the 91 records identified as cash payments as can be seen in the file explorer (left-hand side). Should the resulting file size be too large for audit purposes, attribute sampling may be done on this file. To return to the full sales transaction file, a simple tap on the sales transactions IMD tab will return the auditor to the full file.

Monetary unit sampling—This sampling technique is designed to automatically bias a sample selected toward items containing the highest cumulative value (see Chapter 3). Once again, within the sampling portion of the Analysis Window, the auditor may now select Monetary Unit and click on Plan. Because this sample technique uses cumulative values, the auditor must tell it which field to accumulate. In this case, we're happy to use AMOUNT. The auditor may decide to use only positive values, only negative values, or absolute values (all the numbers are totaled regardless of whether they're positive or negative). The confidence level may again be entered (in this case, we will again choose 95%), and enter the tolerable error and expected error. It will be noted that, in this kind of sampling, this can be expressed either as an amount or a percentage. For ease of comparison, we will choose the same percentage as we used for attribute sampling. By clicking on Estimate, we can now see the approximate sample size, sampling interval, and the sum of tolerable sample taintings permitted in the sample to express our 95% confident opinion regarding the population. If these figures are accepted, the auditor is taken directly to an option to extract the appropriate records. Once again, a new file is created, but this time, in addition to the original fields in the master file, additional fields indicate the record number selected, the cumulative monetary within which the selected value occurred, the unit which resulted in the item being selected, etc. Once again, these items can then be tested by the auditor with resultant deviations being entered using the money to unit options to evaluate a single sample or multiple samples.

Seeking Duplicates and Missing Items

Finding duplicates and missing items are perhaps two of the more common audit inquiries facilitated by CAATs. Whenever there are requirements for uniqueness of information, check numbers, purchase order numbers, identity numbers, and the like, the ability to search easily and quickly across a large database for evidence of duplicates may be critical. In this case, we shall take the Sample-Customer file. In order to check for duplicates, it is useful to be able to have the file sorted into the appropriate order. In IDEA, this is achieved by double-clicking the field name to create an index in ascending order or double-clicking again to create another index in descending order. In this case, we will create indexes for Company, Last Name, and Credit

Limit. We can now analyze for duplicates by going to the Analysis menu on Duplicate Key, Detection. For this exercise, we will use the Last Name and build a file called DuplicateNames. As can be seen, not only duplicates but any multiple of a last name has been selected. By returning to Sample-Customer, the exercise may be repeated looking for duplicate Credit Limits. Obviously, there will be multiples of these.

Returning to our Sample-Customer file, we may choose to seek unused customer numbers by clicking on Gap Detection. This immediately highlights the missing customer numbers either individually or in groups. In this case, it is not critical, but if the key value had been check numbers, this could have identified checks that had been issued but not yet cleared through the bank.

Seeking duplicate deposits into the bank account can be achieved by selecting the Sample-Bank Transactions file and, under the Analysis tab, selecting *Duplicate Key* and choosing *Detection*. Key fields to be selected would include Type, Date, and Amount with the output file named as *Duplicate*. This extraction will produce a file containing six deposits with duplicate dates and amounts. As can be seen, the transactions in all of these cases have sequential transaction IDs. It would now be up to the auditor to determine whether these were accidental, part of a fraudulent scheme, or genuine sequential transactions.

Use of Pivot Tables

Occasionally, the auditor will find a list of data more complex to analyze than if it was in tabular form. To convert a data list into tabular form involves the use of Pivot Table creation within the Analysis tab. Using the Sample-Detailed Sales file, the auditor has decided to examine sales by product class using the sales value before tax. To create the pivot table, the auditor will click on the Pivot Table selection within the Categorize box of the Analysis tab. The result name will be left as Pivot Table. Clicking on OK gives the auditor a table in which to drag the appropriate data items. Thus, the Salesrep_No can be dragged to the area marked *Drop Row Fields Here*. The Sales representative numbers will now appear in that column in ascending number order. The Prod_Code field may now be dragged to the area marked *Drop Column Fields Here*. Because the auditor wished to examine sales using the sales value before tax, that field, Sales_Bef_Tax will now be dragged to the area marked *Drop Data Items Here*, and the table may be closed, resulting in a pivot table ready for analysis. As can be seen from the Properties list on the right-hand side of the screen, the auditor is now looking at the results for the pivot table. To return to the full data, the auditor will simply click on the Data box within the Database Properties. To return to the pivot table, the auditor can click on the Pivot Table box within the Results Properties.

Correlation and Regression

As previously mentioned, two variables are said to be correlated when they move together in a detectable pattern. In this case, the auditor wishes to determine that tax charged on sales remains at a constant rate when compared to movements in sales themselves. If these fields are fully correlated the answer should be 1 (a result of −1 would indicate a perfect inverse relationship).

We can start by closing down the files currently open in the Database Window.

In this case, the auditor has been tasked to determine whether a particular country is performing better than others in terms of carbon emissions. To do this, the auditor will seek to determine the extent of correlation that exists between the amount of carbon emissions produced by a country and the overall worldwide carbon production. The figures are available for the carbon emissions between 1985 and 2004.

The auditor will begin by importing into the project files containing information on the emission of carbon by individual countries as well as for the world as a whole. The files are called *CountryEmissions. XLS* and *WorldTotalEmissions.xls* and may be found in a directory called *tutorial*.

These files must now be joined together. From within the CountryEmissions file, the auditor will move to the Analysis menu and the Relate box and click on Join. The primary database will show as CountryEmissions database. The secondary database will be selected as the WorldTotalEmissions database matching the two on the key of Year by clicking on Match and selecting primary key and secondary key both as Year. In this case, the wish is to see *All records in the primary file*. The result will be a joined database. This will be sorted through the Data menu in the Order box into Country order in Ascending sequence creating a file called Emissions. Once the file has been created and sorted, the auditor can proceed again to the Analysis menu and, within the Explore box, may choose Statistics and select Correlation. To answer the audit objectives, the fields to be correlated are Carbon and Total. The auditor will select the audit unit field as Country with all the units selected and a database to be created called Correlation. In some versions of IDEA, the author has experienced some difficulty in selecting the audit units. If this should happen, change the audit unit field to Year and immediately back to Country. All countries should now be selectable. The Carbon scores indicated a range from −0.80, which is a high level of negative correlation to 0.94, which is a high level of positive correlation. Those countries showing a negative correlation indicate that the carbon emissions trends have been decreasing over time. The auditor may note that some countries have near-zero correlations, indicating a static trend, neither increasing or decreasing, and some bear a highly positive correlation to the world average. This correlation may be graphed from within the results window.

Trend Analysis

Having completed his or her correlation, the auditor has now been asked to determine the reliability of using historical data to forecast future trends based upon the previous years' results. This form of trend analysis will involve taking the data from the CountryEmissions database and extrapolating it into the succeeding years. Before the future forecasts are created, however, the auditor would create a forecast for 2004 based upon the existing history and compare it to the actual carbon emissions for 2004. This would be carried out by taking the database file and doing a direct extraction from the Analysis menu and creating a file called Pre2004 and using the Equation Editor (the calculator in the middle) to create the equation *Year <> 2004*. Using this new file, the auditor can again proceed to the Analysis menu and select Statistics, Trend Analysis. The trend that the auditors are interested in is Carbon, the audit units are once again All Countries, and the auditor wishes to Generate Forecasts. The output will involve the creation of three separate databases: The Trend Analysis database, the Forecast database, and the MAPE database.

In conducting a Trend Analysis, IDEA attempts to fit a straight line, called the *Trend Line*, which represents the linear relationship that is applied to the actual data, in order to predict future values. The trend line calculates the slope of the line and a measure of how good the fit of the straight line is to the actual data. The Mean Absolute Percentage Error (MAPE) is a measure of the fit between the fitted values and the set of actual values, or expressed another way, it indicates the "goodness of fit" or reliability of the forecast.

Having produced this analysis for pre-2004, the auditor would then repeat the extraction exercise from the CountryEmissions database selecting only those years equal to 2004 to create a 2004Emissions. These two extracted files may now be joined using the 2004Emissions file as the primary file and the TrendAnalysisForecast file as the secondary file. The matching key will be Country. Once again, *All Records In The Primary File* will be selected, but *Fields* from the secondary file will only include the *CarbonForecast*. The file name will be *Joined*. Using *Joined* as the primary file, it may now be joined to the TrendAnalysis MAPE file including the fields Carbon_Slope and Carbon_MAPE from the secondary database. Again, matching will be based upon Country and include all records in the primary file, creating a file called 2004Trend.

This file can now go on to be analyzed by extracting only those countries whose forecasts seem to be reliable.

The higher the MAPE score, the greater the difference between the actual values and forecast values. A MAPE score higher than 50 may indicate erratic trends where, for example, some element has changed, and the historical trend has not continued.

The extract would therefore be a direct extract with the criteria that the CarbonForecast would be greater than 10, the carbon slope would be greater than zero, and the carbon MAPE would be less than 50.

Time Series Analysis

Time series analysis is a common technique in auditing in order to identify the characteristics of the data as indicated over a period of time. In this case, the auditor wishes to extract information from a file called Unemployed.XLS, which is an Excel file to be found in the Tutorial directory.

For auditors who are not experienced in the importing files process, in this case, it would involve the following:

From the Home menu, click on Desktop within the Import box. This will open the Import Assistant, allowing the auditor to choose the format of the data to be imported and its location. The format in this case is Microsoft Excel, and the location is in the Tutorial/Source_Files.ILB subdirectory of Projects. One at a time, these files must be imported, taking care to indicate on the import menu that the first row is field names.

From the Analysis menu in the Explore box, the auditor will click on Statistics, Time Series.

The Time Series Field for the analysis will be *People*, and the audit units to be selected will be State and will include all states. In terms of the Model Information required, we will use the following:

- Seasonal length—13
- Forecasts—13
- Calendar month (4 weeks)
- All three databases will be created

The auditor may then examine the results state by state. Each of the databases created may also be examined with the MAPE being sorted into descending order.

Continuous Monitoring

From time to time, the auditor may wish to take a standard test and incorporate it within the normal production run processing. This will involve taking a test that has been carried out and creating an executable program from it. Let us take, for example, the pivot table that we created from our Sample-Detailed Sales. This is the kind of analysis that may be required to be executed on a monthly basis without direct auditor intervention every time. To create the executable program, the auditor will return to the Sample-Detailed Sales file. Once again, clicking on the Pivot Table within the Properties Results will take us back to the pivot table previously created. On this occasion, the auditor wishes to examine the program that created the pivot table. This is achieved by clicking on *History* within the *Database Properties*. As can be seen, the history includes the importation of the file from Excel as well as the creation of the pivot table. By right-clicking on the first line, the auditor will have a choice of Copy or Copy all IDEAscript. Copy all IDEAscript will be selected. This has had the effect of creating an interactively executable script (which may also be edited at the auditor's discretion). By clicking on the File tab, the auditor may select *Build New Script.Exe* and save the program as Create Pivot Table. This has created the job as an executable program that may now be incorporated into any production run. It should be noted that this program will import the file and create a pivot table. It will not create a printout of this pivot table.

Compliance

Analysis of Sales by Rep

When a straightforward analysis is required, for example, using our Sample-Detailed Sales file to get an analysis of sales by representative or sales by customer, the auditor may simply open the file, and by clicking on the Analysis tab, may select Summarization within the Categorize box. The auditor may then choose which fields to summarize by, for example, Salesrep_No and choose the fields to total, such as Sales_Plus_Tax, creating a file named Sales by Rep. As can be seen, in this file, the number of records is highlighted in blue. By clicking on any of the blue numbers, the auditor may see the detailed transactions that made up the summarization. By returning to the Sample-Detailed Sales file, the auditor may repeat the exercise for Sales by Customer and create a file of that name.

Unauthorized Internet Access

Using the weblog file we created in Chapter 20, the auditor has the option to search the file seeking specific partial website names within the Site field. For example, by performing a Direct Extract under the Analysis tab, the auditor could perform an extract seeking the upper or lower case of the name *lotto* within the site field by doing an extract to a file called Lotto and using the Equation Editor to define an expression using the Character @function *Isini*. This is not case sensitive, and it searches for the occurrence of a specified string or piece of text in a Character field, Date field, or string. The equation desired will then read @Isini("lotto," SITE). This will create a file containing all of the records that have the word lotto in any case anywhere within the field SITE. Obviously, this can be used to check access to any unauthorized or improper sites. In the same way, user access at unauthorized times may be analyzed by doing extractions comparing the TIME to authorize login times or the DATE to logins on unauthorized dates.

To a great extent, the auditor is limited only by his or her own definition of what is unauthorized.

Pricing Rules Not Followed

Whenever rules are supposed to be applied to data, the auditor can seek exceptions by creating a virtual field and appending it to the record definition such that the virtual field is calculated using the predetermined rules. The auditor can then seek discrepancies where the virtual field and the actual field contained within the data do not correspond.

For example, within the file Sample-Detailed Sales, it may be seen that the field SALES_BEF_TAX should equal the Quantity times the Unit Price. There are several ways of determining whether this rule has been applied but to illustrate this example, under the menu item Data, the auditor can Append a virtual field to the database. Using a field name of TEST_SALES, with two decimal places, and using the equation editor to define the field as QTY times UNIT_PRICE, it will be seen that the field TEST_SALES has been appended to the right-hand side of the database. It is now simple to do a Direct Extraction where SALES_BEF_TAX does not equal (<>) TEST_SALES. Obviously, this could have been achieved without the creation of the virtual field by doing the extract directly from the file and using the equation editor to define the temporary inequality equation. As can be seen in this example, four records exist in which the SALES_BEF_TAX amount is suspect and will require a follow-up by the auditor to determine the reason.

Fraud

As noted in Chapter 22, it is only once fraud risks are understood that an appropriate system of internal controls can be designed and implemented to address those risks. Even then, fraud can never be fully eliminated, and early detection becomes a critical backstop in minimizing the impact of corporate fraud. As such, it is critical that the appropriate audit trails be maintained and analyzed to seek patterns pointing to potential fraud events.

Identify Duplicate Employees in the Employee Master File

Many frauds involve the introduction of duplicate transactions as well as duplicate entries on master files. By selecting the Sample-Employees file and conducting a simple Duplicate Key analysis and choosing a Key of Name, the auditor can create a file containing only duplicates. The same test can be done for addresses or any other significant field, such as postal addresses or banking details.

Finding Excessive Sole Supplier Contracts

Another common form of fraud is the excessive use of specific suppliers within the supply chain. This may, in fact, be good business practice when a specific supplier has a track record of providing requisite supplies and services at a cost-effective price at an appropriate quality level. Nevertheless, it may also be an indicator of fraudulent practices when a supplier who is not optimal is chosen because of bribery, kickbacks, and the like, resulting in a potential supply of inferior goods and services at an inflated price.

Analysis of purchasing records may give an indication in this area that a specific supplier is being chosen excessively. As stated, this may not indicate fraud but should be worth the auditor's follow-up. When tendering processes exist, analysis of tender documents may indicate preference given to specific suppliers, excessive use of sole-supplier contracts, or common bidding patterns in which the failing bids are always submitted by the same companies who may have some relationship to the winning bidder. An analysis of purchases from suppliers or payments made to suppliers may disclose a relationship between suppliers and individual buyers.

For example, in the file Sample-Payments, the auditor may choose to do a cross-evaluation by creating a pivot table showing payments made to suppliers categorized by the authorizer. Under the tab Analysis, the auditor can choose Pivot Table. The auditor is then given the choice of moving fields into row fields, column fields, and page fields. In this case, we shall take the supplier name field SUPPNAME and drag it into the row field column, following this by taking the authorizer field AUTH and dragging it to Drop Column Fields Here. The Amount can then be moved to Drop Data Items Here. The resulting table can then be examined seeking suppliers who are used frequently by multiple authorizers, such as BURKHARDT, or unusual patterns in authorizers, such as H.M., H.M.V., H.V., HMV, and HV who, on examination, may prove to be the same person operating using multiple authorizing IDs.

Ghost Employees

"Ghost employees" is a term used to define payments made via payroll systems to individuals who are not actually employees. These may be ex-employees who, having left the organization, may be resurrected on the payroll with banking details changed to those of a payroll clerk. Alternatively, they may be brand new fictitious employees with, again, payment made into an individual's bank account. When payment is made by checks, the postal address for delivery may tie in to an individual's address. Ghost employees may be difficult to spot under normal circumstances; however, they may show up in examining the payroll records seeking duplicate bank numbers, addresses, or even names.

In this case, we shall take the file Sample-Employees and look for duplicate addresses. From our Analysis tab, we will select Duplicate Key and choose Detection. The Key field is the ADDRESS field in ascending order output to a file called Duplicates. From the output, we can see that we have four sets of duplicates. Once again, these are not necessarily fraudulent or ghost employees; they may simply be members of the same family employed by the organization. Nevertheless, the auditor would once again seek confirmation that this is the case.

Seeking Duplicate Payments

Using a similar technique, duplicate payments can be seen from our Sample-Payments file seeking payments made to the same supplier for the same amount or, alternatively, payments made to the same supplier on the same date. Once again, the danger lies in the auditor assuming that any duplicate found is an automatic proof of fraud. The transactions may be genuine, but any repeating patterns should be followed up.

Benford Analysis

As noted in Chapter 13, Benford analysis is a form of pattern analysis used in the analysis of high volumes of data looking for evidence of fraudulent transactions. Taking our Sample-Bank-Transactions file as an example, from our Analysis tab we can select Benford's Law. In this particular file, there is only one field that we could be interested in, and that is the AMOUNT. From our field statistics, we know that there are negative entries; therefore, we may wish to exclude the negatives and only include positive values.

For the purposes of this example, we will select only an analysis test of the first two digits. As will be seen and as shown Diagram A2.2, certain of the transaction distributions are labeled as *suspicious* with others as *highly suspicious*. As always in such analysis, even those more highly suspicious cannot automatically be assumed to be fraudulent. By clicking on the distributions marked as highly suspicious, the auditor may display the suspicious records for follow-up and further investigation.

Continuous Monitoring

Continuous monitoring and continuous auditing have both been covered in depth in Chapters 15 and 16. In order to implement these within the IDEA context, the auditor will typically carry out the analysis desired and then copy the script and convert it into an executable program for incorporation into the ongoing daily, weekly, or as required schedule.

Copying the script with IDEA is extremely easy. Taking as an example our Benford analysis we conducted on the Sample-Bank

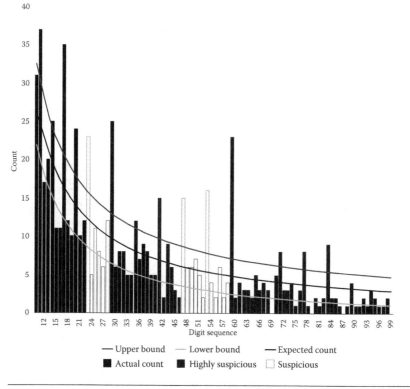

Diagram A2.2   Benford analysis example.

Transaction file, by moving to the field properties, we can look at the History of our activities. As can be seen, we imported the file from Excel, Indexed it, and conducted a Benford's Law analysis. By right-clicking on any of these activities, we are given the choice of copying, copying the IDEAScript for the selected task, or copying all IDEAScript. In this case, we will copy all IDEAScript. It will be seen that the IDEAScript editor is now displaying the whole of the computer source code required to carry out the tasks previously undertaken by the auditor. This script can be saved and may be executed in the future by going to the Macros tab, selecting Open, retrieving the macro and clicking on Run. Within the IDEAScript window, the auditor may alternatively open the File tab and click on Build New Script.Exe. When this is clicked and an appropriate name for the script given, it will be saved as an executable program that may then be incorporated into any conventional processing run without requiring the presence of IDEA itself.

Basic Script Writing in IDEA

As shown above, the basic concepts of script writing and benefits of automating your data projects within IDEA are enabled by a development tool known as IDEAScript for creating macros to extend the functionality of IDEA. IDEAScript can be recorded, written from scratch, or a combination of both.

Developing scripts and implementing best practices will show the auditor how to increase the efficiency of data analytics projects by analyzing transaction sets on a regular basis as well as facilitating the running of preprepared scripts by less experienced auditors.

As previously noted, IDEAScript can be copied from tasks already undertaken. Alternatively, they may be written from scratch or recorded as instructions are executed. IDEAScript itself is an object-oriented programming language consistent with Microsoft's Visual Basic for Applications™ (VBA). The language itself consists of *objects*, their *public methods*, and *properties*. Most objects are tasks that can analyze and manipulate a database.

This book is not intended as a course on using IDEA Script. For those with a particular interest in this area, John Paul Mueller has written an excellent book, *Mastering IDEA Script*.* For those with a passing interest to discover whether it would be useful or not to be able to program in IDEA Script, the HELP function will prove helpful and easy to use.

Using Advanced @Functions

As noted above, IDEA provides @Functions to enable the performance of more complex calculations and exception testing, such as

---

* Mueller, John Paul. (2011). *Mastering IDEA Script—the Definitive Guide*. Hoboken, NJ: John Wiley & Sons.

date arithmetic and financial and statistical calculations as well as text searches. In addition, the auditor can also create custom functions. Once again, these are designed to appear similar in style and operation to function capability contained in packages, such as Excel or Lotus.

Appendix 3: Risk Assessment: A Working Example

The Cascarino Cube

The following discussion is a generic approach to risk identification and prioritization. Its use requires tailoring to the requirements of an individual organization. It is referred to here as a "cube" although it is, in actuality, a cuboid with the numbers of layers dependent on the individual functions, threat sources, and risks to which the organization is exposed.

Using a methodology similar to the five-layer process mentioned in Chapter 8, the participants from each functional area meet in an open workshop in order to identify the principle risks and major sources of threats in their particular business function. In the example here, the primary risk is fraud. This process is open-ended and can operate as a modified Delphi group in which each participant identifies one single fraud opportunity in the business area assuming there were no controls or that none of the controls worked. The process then moves on to the next participant seeking another single fraud opportunity. This process is repeated, participant by participant, until none can think of any fraud opportunities other than those identified. At this point, the workshop facilitator will seek common themes within the fraud opportunities in order to summarize into generic fraud risk categories with each one spelled out as understood by the group. These risk categories are then prioritized by the group by combining likelihood and damage potential in order to arrive at an overall risk ranking.

The process is then repeated in order to identify the sources of fraud threats and risk-rank them.

When placed on a spreadsheet, it can be seen that the top left-hand corner consists of the greatest threats coming from the most likely sources.

This workshop is repeated for each of the functional areas in order to draw up a three-dimensional cuboid representing the prioritized fraud threats ranked against the sources of those threats for each functional area of the organization (Diagram A3.1).

When prioritized and structured, the organization's fraud risk profile may be represented by *higher* ranked threats from the most significant threat sources forming the upper left-hand corner of each functional slice.

Each functional slice may then be evaluated separately, and the preventative, detective, and corrective controls identified and allocated to

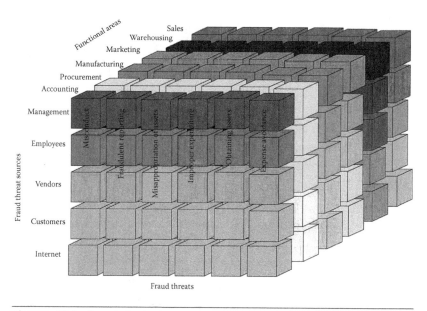

Diagram A3.1   Example fraud cube.

the specific cell representing a fraud threat (such as misconduct) from a given fraud threat source.

At this stage, no attempt is made to determine whether the controls believed to exist actually do exist and function as intended.

The objective of the assessment is to determine whether the accumulation of controls intended to mitigate a particular fraud risk from a particular fraud threat source would be adequate to reduce the risk to acceptable levels assuming the controls function as intended. Inadequacy of controls indicates a level of fraud risk at too high a level even if all of the controls work as intended, and such a vulnerability must then be addressed, usually by the introduction of additional controls.

Once all mitigating controls have been identified, they can be evaluated in order to determine which controls can give management the most assurance (whether it be from a preventative, detective, or corrective perspective). These are designated the key controls and form management's most critical defenses against those specific fraud risks. From management's perspective, these controls would be subject to the most stringent monitoring in normal operations. From an audit perspective, these would typically be the controls selected to be tested for effectiveness.

If these controls, after testing, function as intended, management may gain the assurance that fraud risk is being controlled to the desired level in an adequate and effective manner and that the likelihood of a successful fraud occurring in that area from that source, although not eliminated, has been reduced to a level within a band of tolerance specified in advance.

Where such testing of controls determines that the key controls are not functioning as intended, the cause of failure must be determined and rectified. In the meantime, the other controls in that particular mini-cube can be evaluated to determine whether they have sufficient cumulative impact to maintain the overall control at the desired level. If so, then the effectiveness of these controls must also be tested.

If the controls do not function as intended, the response plan should be to address the reasons why the controls are not functioning. Given that those controls were deemed acceptable, the objective is not to introduce additional controls but to make the "acceptable" but nonfunctioning controls function as intended. This has the benefit of not introducing extra controls for the sake of them but focusing on the achievement of the risk control objectives instead.

This approach has an additional benefit in that it becomes easier to see which procedures consume excessive resources without significant contribution to the overall fraud risk control objectives. When such a procedure exists but is not a key control in any area within the cube, its appropriateness can be called into question, and the impact should that procedure be eliminated can be evaluated. In this way, progress management can demonstrably be not only effective, but also efficient.

Once key controls have been identified within each of the individual mini-cubes, they may be traced three-dimensionally into other mini-cubes within other functional areas and threat sources. This then permits a three-dimensional map of the impact the failure of the key control could have across all functional areas facing the same sources of risk.

Additionally, the three-dimensional nature of the cuboid enables management and auditors to examine control adequacy and effectiveness in vertical slices of functional areas indicating all fraud risks and threat sources affecting them, horizontal slices of threat sources indicating the functional area and fraud risk affected, or sliced by fraud risk showing all threat sources and functional areas affected.

By maintaining the cube and associated controls as risk levels change with the business and by keeping the control list current and tested, the overall fraud risk and control architecture can be monitored in order to ensure that the overall residual fraud risk to the organization is maintained at acceptable levels.

Index